IT Strategy for Non-IT Managers

IT Strategy for Non-IT Managers

Becoming an Engaged Contributor
to Corporate IT Decisions

Amrit Tiwana

The MIT Press
Cambridge, Massachusetts
London, England

This book was entirely handwritten in Athens, Georgia, on Tops legal pads made in St. Charles, Illinois, using Hi-Tec-C 0.4mm pens made in Tokyo, Japan. The illustrations were created using SmartDraw.

This book was set in Sabon LT Std by Scribe Inc. Printed and bound in the United States of America.

Author royalties will be donated to charity.

Library of Congress Cataloging-in-Publication Data

Names: Tiwana, Amrit, 1974– author.
Title: IT strategy for non-IT managers : becoming an engaged contributor to corporate IT decisions / Amrit Tiwana.
Description: Cambridge, MA : MIT Press, [2017] | Includes bibliographical references and index.
Identifiers: LCCN 2017000439 | ISBN 9780262534154 (pbk. : alk. paper)
Subjects: LCSH: Information technology–Management. | Strategic planning. | Information technology–Decision making.
Classification: LCC HD30.2 .T57 2017 | DDC 004.068/4–dc23 LC record available at https://lccn.loc.gov/2017000439

10 9 8 7 6 5 4 3 2 1

To my mom, her Mac, and the memory of my dad

Contents

Introduction

This is a short book on a vast theme. Its sole purpose: helping non-IT managers become engaged contributors in formulating their firms' corporate IT strategy. I believe that their contributions can infuse the competitive oomph into their *strategy* that their IT colleagues alone cannot.

I base this book on one premise: cheap yet strategic IT is a unicorn only until IT strategy meets non-IT managers. Corporate IT is a *business* tool; how your firm *uses* it alone differentiates whether it is a competitive weapon or the costly obstacle that it usually is. IT can make or break businesses. Firms spend more on IT than all other capital assets *combined*, yet few grasp how it is reshaping their industries and what they can do about it. Within this asymmetry lies the opportunity. Without non-IT managers' business acumen in corporate IT decisions, IT lacks purpose. The true quality of corporate IT is how well it advances your firm's strategy, not how well it is constructed.

Lack of business involvement is *the* primary reason that IT is often uneconomical and strategically feeble. It's rare that non-IT managers don't want to be involved; they often don't know *how*. I'll equip you to be sufficiently conversant to create business value with your IT colleagues and help you grasp when, where, and how you can contribute. My goal is to help you ask the right questions. I hope to provide you an enduring foundation and analytical skills to envision IT opportunities invisible to an untrained eye. An engaging conversation needs effort from both sides of the business-IT divide; I'll give you the language to make that effort.

Who This Book Is For

This book is for midlevel *functional* managers—in line functions such as marketing, sales, finance, operations, or accounting—with no IT backgrounds or IT career aspirations. I assume that you have spent three to four years' time in the trenches, none

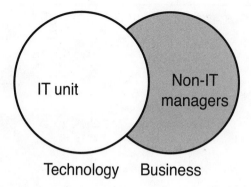

Technology   Business

Figure 0.1
This book focuses on the contributions of the shaded part to corporate IT decisions.

of which was in IT. IT matters far beyond just large or legal businesses. This book covers small business, nonprofits, and government agencies. (The United States has 28 million small businesses and 1.5 million nonprofits but only 4,000 publicly traded corporations.[1]) Even drug dealers,[2] prostitutes,[3] and food carts rely on IT to compete—and differentiate themselves—in their markets. My examples are global, spanning Asia, Africa, Europe, North America, and South America.

What This Book Is Not

This is a textbook, not a scholarly book, an airplane read, or an IT strategy-in-a-box book. I'll give you the tools, but you'll have to do the thinking. This book is *not* intended for IT managers and IT professionals, nor is it intended to make you one. It does not survey the IT field, provide a condensed version of an IT manager's training, educate a potential CIO, or create a competent IT manager (figure 0.1). My ideal reader is an executive MBA student who has taken *some* introductory MBA courses. I assume neither an undergraduate business degree nor prior IT knowledge.

Why This Book

This book was born out of exasperation. Imagine buying a shiny new car, only to find its user guide chock-full of explanations of how it works, engineering diagrams, and fuel compression ratios. It might be a mechanical engineer's idea of fun, but not an owner's. Most existing MBA IT strategy textbooks are like that car manual, attempting to create an IT manager lite. Instead, I focus on what non-IT managers need to know to intuitively grasp how IT fits in your total business. It is jargon-free, acronym-light, and industry-agnostic and focuses on enduring fundamentals. However, it is research-based, building on more than 250 studies by more than 350 researchers cited. I connect IT strategy to your other MBA core courses on strategy, corporate finance, accounting, marketing, operations, and statistics.

A Roadmap of the Book

I have structured this book as four modules shown in figure 0.2, each of which builds on the ones before it. Each chapter opens with a *jargon decoder*—nontechnical explanations of its five to seven key ideas digestible by a random colleague at your office water cooler. To converse with your IT colleagues, you need to know what they mean by the words that they use. The jargon decoder that you'll need to get started appears in table 0.1. Each chapter covers why, where, and how non-IT managers can contribute to their firms' IT decisions and the business penalties of leaving them to your IT unit. Each chapter ends with a checklist summarizing how you can contribute to your firm's corporate IT decisions. Table 0.2 previews the takeaways from each chapter.

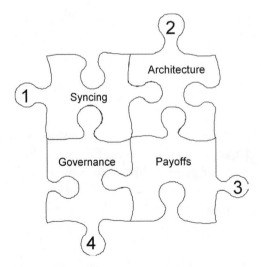

Figure 0.2
This book is organized as four modules, which correspond to its four parts.

Table 0.1
Every Chapter Opens with Such a *Jargon Decoder*—
a Table of Lay Explanations of Its Main Conceptual Ideas

Jargon decoder terms	The five to seven central concepts in lay language that precede every chapter in this book.
Firm	A generic reference to a for-profit corporation, small business, nonprofit organization, or government agency.
Archrivals	Your firm's top three industry competitors today.
A rose by any other name	Corporate IT in this book has different labels in different parts of the world: information systems (IS), business information management (BIM; used in the Netherlands), information and communication technology (ICT; used in Europe and Africa), and management information systems (MIS; used in North America). I simply call it IT to avoid all this pedantic obfuscation.
Information technology (IT)	The *business technology*—including hardware, software, and data—used to run your business. Throughout this book, people and business processes are *not* IT but an integral part of IT strategy.
IT unit	Your in-house department responsible for your firm's business technology; historically called the corporate IT unit or the MIS department.
Line functions	Specialized functional departments such as accounting or marketing that constitute your firm; a synonym for departments, business functions, business units, or functional areas.
Non-IT manager	A midlevel manager in a line function *other than IT*; this book's sole audience.
Market offering	A revenue-generating product or service.

An Index-Card Preview of This Book's Message

An index-card summary of this book's message—in figure 0.3—spans five ideas (→) as follows:

1. A "trifecta"—digitization, infusion of software, and connectivity—is disruptively transforming nontechnology industries (chapter 1).

2. You grasp your firm's place in the new order using a three-lens framework to analyze how IT is changing your industry, how your firm can use IT to deliver more value than its archrivals, and whether an IT asset is a sustainable edge (chapter 2).

3. IT inches your firm toward its strategic aspiration (chapter 1) only when it is *sync*hronized with its tactical strategy.

4. Syncing demands obsessively focusing your portfolio of IT assets—infrastructure, software applications, and data (chapters 1 and 3)—on its fundamental corporate goals and governing them well (chapter 5).

Table 0.2
A Preview of Each Chapter's Takeaways for Non-IT Managers

	What you will learn
Part 1: Syncing	
Chapter 1	How corporate IT—often a costly liability—can become both strategic and economical; a "trifecta" of IT trends disrupting nontechnology industries; and how non-IT managers infuse competitive firepower into their firm's IT strategy
Chapter 2	How IT alters an industry's balance of power; how you can spot opportunities to leverage IT to beat your archrivals; and how the amalgamation of software and data can create a hard-to-copy competitive advantage
Part 2: Architecture	
Chapter 3	Ensuring that irreversible choices about IT assets fulfill today's business needs without handicapping future strategy
Part 3: Payoffs	
Chapter 4	Ensuring that your IT investments deliver operational and financial impact; and investing under uncertainty
Part 4: Governance	
Chapter 5	How establishing *who decides what* about IT simultaneously gives it strategic oomph and economy
Chapter 6	Why IT projects fail to deliver business benefits; and three antidotes from non-IT managers
Chapter 7	Choices, challenges, and solutions in sourcing corporate IT
Chapter 8	Protecting your IT assets against malice and disaster in ways that your IT unit cannot
Chapter 9	Recognizing the business potential of emerging technologies

5. Firms that do this well thrive in a "Red Queen" competitive race; others fumble and die. Over the course of all this, you've got to keep your IT projects from sinking (as most do; chapter 6), avoid sourcing decisions you'll regret (chapter 7), keep your IT assets safe (chapter 8), and credibly measure what you're getting for your money (chapter 4).

Archrivals

Identify your top three competitors in your industry *today*: your firm's nemeses. I'll call them your *archrivals* throughout this book. This is important: Think of just these

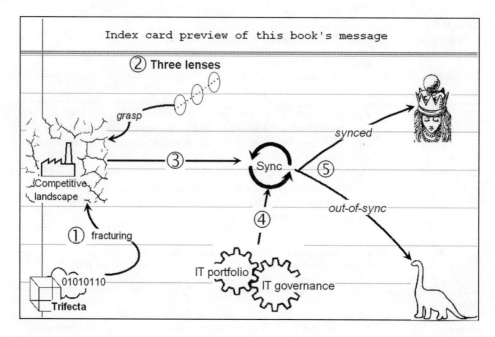

Figure 0.3
An index-card preview of this book's message.

three every time you see the word "archrivals." Everything in IT strategy is relative to them. Before you continue reading, pencil in the names of your three archrivals below and then again on the first page of this book:

1. _____

2. _____

3. _____

Think of this book as a conversation between you and me. Whether you are a student or a professor, I'd love to hear your reactions, suggestions, and quibbles at tiwana@uga.edu.

Part 1

Syncing

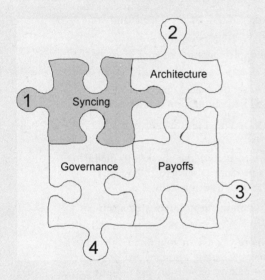

Jargon Decoder

Trifecta	The three IT-based drivers—digitization, software infusion, and ubiquity—that are fracturing industries.
Red Queen race	One firm's IT investments trigger matching spending by its archrivals, creating a vicious cycle of ever-increasing IT investments needed just to keep up with your archrivals.
Strategic aspiration	A combination of *who* your firm aspires to target (a mass market or a market segment) and *how* (being cheap or unique).
Operational strategy	The tactical implementation of your firm's business strategy.
IT strategy	An integrated set of choices that define how your firm will use IT to outperform its archrivals.
Software infusion	Baking software into a product, service, or business activity.
Digitization cube	A framework to analyze the physical-to-digital shift in (a) a product or service, (b) how it is purchased, and (c) how it is delivered.
Ubiquity	The proliferation of cheap Internet connectivity everywhere.
Competitive advantage	Delivering more value than your archrivals to your customers. *Creating* a competitive advantage is widening—relative to your archrivals—the gap between your costs and what your customers pay; *sustaining* it is to keep it that way.
IT portfolio	Your firm's collection of IT apps, infrastructure, and data assets.
IT epochs	The four big waves of corporate IT since the 1970s, each with a different thrust; the Internet epoch in the mid-1990s marked a switch from information scarcity to abundance.
IT app	A business software program used to perform a business activity; it can be operational or strategic and purchased or custom built.

1

Syncing IT and Strategy

Competition as a Red Queen Race

There is a little snippet in the 1867 edition of Lewis Carroll's *Through the Looking Glass* where Alice is racing the Red Queen (figure 1.1).[1] Huffing and panting, Alice asks the Red Queen why she is constantly running yet remaining in the same spot. "Now, here, you see, it takes all the running you can do to keep in the same place . . . to get somewhere, you must run twice as fast!" This competitive dynamic—dubbed Red Queen competition—means that you must run faster *just to keep up* with your competitors. Running faster does not get you ahead. It simply keeps you from dropping out of the race altogether.[2]

Figure 1.1
This 150-year-old sketch with Alice racing the Red Queen inspired the idea of Red Queen competition. (Illustration by John Tenniel in the 1871 edition of Lewis Carroll's *Through the Looking Glass*.)

The more firms invest in IT—50 percent[3] of all capital investments today—the more they appear to be stuck in a Red Queen race.[4] You introduce a clever IT innovation; your archrivals replicate it the next morning. Slip once and it becomes a vicious liability. Slow down and you irrecoverably fall behind. Rival firms have become spectators in a blood sport of corporate IT spending, each hoping for the others to first call it quits. This tit-for-tat cycle keeps raising the table stakes to survive in your industry.

How then can your firm break out of this vicious cycle to make IT *strategically* forceful without bankrupting itself? This is the question the following pages intend to help you answer. We begin with the premise that IT does *not* strategically matter because it lacks scarcity that gives any asset its competitive value. We then dissect corporate IT into three classes of assets, *some* of which can be used strategically. We then chronicle the four eras of corporate IT that led us to a trifecta—digitization, infusion of software into everything nontechnology firms make and do, and ubiquitous connectivity. We then explore why IT often handicaps firms and how non-IT managers can add the sort of firepower to their firms' IT strategy that their IT colleagues cannot.

Does IT Matter?

A *Harvard Business Review* article provocatively titled "IT Doesn't Matter" argued that IT has become so pervasive that its strategic importance has diminished.[5] Even though firms spent $4 trillion on IT in 2016, scarcity—not pervasiveness—makes any asset valuable. IT is easy to replicate because it is a commodity that any firm can buy from the same IT suppliers. It drew parallels to the railroads, telegraphs, and electricity to urge firms to spend less, to follow rather than lead, and to manage risks rather than obsess over opportunities. (The article was rarely read but widely bandied about in corporate boardrooms.)

Would you agree? Let us do a little thought exercise. Now replace the word "IT" with, say, "electricity." Electricity cannot be a competitive advantage because everyone has it. Spend less and manage risks. Do not try being a hero. Now replace IT with Post-it notes. Boiled to its essence, if everyone has X, X will never provide a competitive advantage. Replace X with any commodity; the logic is incontestable. It is bulletproof. Ancient Greek philosopher Aristophanes (figure 1.2[6]) called this sort of argument a *false premise*: the argument is correct, but its premise is incorrect.

The IT-equals-commodity premise is based on a common misunderstanding of what corporate IT *is*. IT is the costliest yet least understood corporate asset.[7] Before declaring something a commodity, we must know what that "something" is. The computers,

Figure 1.2
Ancient Greek philosopher Aristophanes (circa 500 BC) would call Carr's argument a false premise.

iPads, Microsoft Office, Apple Pay–like systems, and Internet connections that Mr. Carr is thinking of are a fraction of corporate IT. Such things are indeed commodities. Like commodities, 100 percent of their strategic value comes from *how they are used* together with your firm's other assets. The same IT system can deliver completely different results in two different firms. Given the same hammer, you might create a masterpiece and I might hurt my pinky finger. Like a calculator, a hacksaw, a steam engine, and a factory, IT is just a tool. *How* it is used matters. The firm that best uses it wins.

Corporate IT does not exist in a vacuum; 100 percent of its strategic value comes from its connections to *your* firm's business strategy. Insight into using IT to rethink what is possible comes from deep business knowledge, not technical knowledge.[8, 9] There is only one way of making this happen: you—a non-IT manager—becoming an engaged contributor to corporate IT decisions.

Two classes of IT assets besides IT infrastructure are IT applications (business software programs used by a firm's various line functions) and data. IT's strategic potential lies primarily in how they are meshed with your firm's strategy. Commodity IT infrastructure plays only a support role. Cutting off innovative IT investments sure cuts down risk, but it also deprives firms from future opportunities and their eventual survival. IT-equals-commodity is a self-defeating mind-set that misses the point of IT strategy.

Repeat after me: IT is just a tool. How it is used matters.

Yet as IT spending dwarfs all other corporate investments combined, firms increasingly expect IT to be economical yet strategically forceful.[10] This might strike you as an unreasonable demand; how can something be cheap yet unique? Once you appreciate the distinction between different classes of IT assets—especially IT apps versus IT infrastructure—the dichotomy dissolves away.[11] One is the enabler of business innovation and the other a target for fiscal stinginess. Separating them allows you to economize on IT that does not strategically matter to invest in more that does.

An IT Portfolio Is a Collection of Three Classes of IT Assets

A firm's *IT portfolio* is its entire collection of IT assets spanning three broad classes: IT infrastructure, IT apps, and the data that flows through them (figure 1.3). Business processes and the people responsible for them and using them are not part of IT but an integral part of IT strategy.

If you metaphorically envision a firm's IT portfolio as a pizza (figure 1.4), IT infrastructure is the crust and apps its toppings.[12] Just as a combination of toppings can differentiate one pizza from another, apps can *sometimes* competitively differentiate one firm's IT portfolio from its archrivals'. IT infrastructure—like a pizza's crust—is never a source of competitive advantage. Yet a good enough IT infrastructure is a necessary foundation to run apps, just as a good enough crust is needed to bake a decent pizza.[13]

Although your IT portfolio changes one project at a time, you must not lose sight of the whole. Thinking of the whole portfolio is how you rally data and apps to serve a distinctive business purpose. It is how you build the parts but plan the whole. Table 1.1 summarizes the forthcoming differences between IT infrastructure and apps.

IT Infrastructure

IT infrastructure is a firm-wide technology foundation—the pizza crust—shared by the various apps that line functions use.[14, 15] It is the substrate that knits them

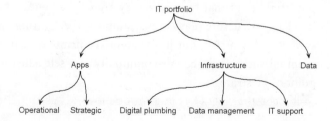

Figure 1.3
The three classes of IT assets in a firm's IT portfolio.

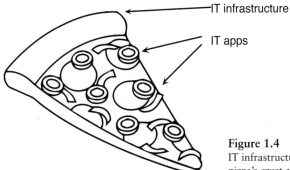

IT infrastructure

IT apps

Figure 1.4
IT infrastructure and IT apps are analogous to a pizza's crust and toppings.

together.[16] IT infrastructure serves the entire firm and is not unique to individual line functions. IT infrastructure includes a firm's digital plumbing that moves data (e.g., network connectivity) and stores data and a firm's IT support (e.g., IT operations, maintenance, and support). Hardware and networks—the most visible parts of IT infrastructure—are commodities that your rivals can also buy. *Hardware* is anything you can kick: laptops, smartphones, cash registers, scanners, and servers. Although hardware is the most visible part of IT, it is a miniscule 10 percent of corporate IT budgets. *Networks* connect hardware to the Internet.

IT infrastructure demands deep technical skills and a holistic understanding of firm-wide IT assets but not a deep knowledge of line functions' work. IT infrastructure must be (a) *economical* because it rarely competitively differentiates firms and (b) *reliable* because apps cannot function without it. Economies of scale, bullet-proof reliability, and security are therefore critical in provisioning IT infrastructure. Carr's argument focuses almost entirely on such commodity IT, which he—like many non-IT managers—thinks is the entirety of corporate IT. That is like thinking of biology as being only about microscopes.

Table 1.1
Properties of the Two Classes of IT Assets besides Data

	IT infrastructure	IT apps
Pizza analogy	Crust	Toppings
What they are	Foundation shared by all apps	Programs used by line functions
Imperative	Cheap and reliable	Enabling line functions
Demands	Technical know-how	Business know-how
Strategic role	Competitive necessity	Potential advantage

IT Apps

IT apps are software programs that individuals in a firm's various line functions use for their core activities. Apps is short for enterprise-grade software application programs, either purchased or custom developed by your firm. Anytime you interact with any software anywhere, you are using an app.

Apps consume only about 20 percent of corporate IT budgets[17] but generate almost all the competitive differentiation from IT investments. When they are interwoven with your business strategy, they can punch above their weight to create a competitive advantage. For this, apps must be uniquely tailored to individual line functions' needs and priorities. Apps draw primarily on business know-how of line functions' activities, business processes, and problems. There is only one way to ensure the inflow of business know-how on which apps' business value depends: direct involvement of non-IT managers. Hiring business-savvy IT staff cannot make up for its absence.[18]

Operational versus Strategic Apps

Apps in a firm's IT portfolio can be either operational or strategic. *Operational* apps support a firm's core business processes and transactions and can crosscut line functions. They either automate mundane, repetitive transactional activities to reduce time-consuming, error-prone manual tasks or facilitate collaboration. Operational apps can be (a) inward-facing (e.g., for inventory, warehousing, point-of-sale, payroll, production support, human resources, or accounting) or (b) outward-facing ones that customers use (e.g., mobile tools, websites, or Internet-connected devices) or that your retailers and suppliers use to interact with your firm (e.g., supply chain management, logistics, or procurement).[19] (Apps also include mundane commodity packaged software such as word processors and spreadsheets that are strategically irrelevant.)

Operational apps are the foundation for executing your firm's core business processes that you must perform efficiently and reliably just to remain in business (e.g., invoicing, order-taking, accounts payable, payroll, human resources, inventory management, and shipping).[20] The more you can automate such mundane, repetitive activities, the more attention you can devote to the novel business activities that can create a competitive advantage over your archrivals. Although operational apps often are commodities, some can be expensive. (A typical enterprise resource planning [ERP] system, for example, can cost several million dollars.)

Operational apps are competitive necessities.[21] They often embody an industry's "best practices," which by definition means that they quickly become widespread among your rivals. Having them will never give your firm a *sustainable* competitive advantage, but not having them is a liability if they let your archrivals do any value-creating activity better, faster, or cheaper. Having them creates competitive parity with your archrivals, not differentiation.

The second type of app is a *strategic* app. A strategic app attempts to create a competitive advantage by doing something valuable that your archrivals cannot do. They might introduce new ways for outsiders to interact with your firm, expand into new lines of business, or exploit proprietary data in new ways to help your firm, customers, or business partners make better decisions. Most of the data that strategic apps use comes from operational apps. Once (and if) your rivals replicate a strategic app, it eventually becomes an operational app—a competitive necessity rather than a differentiator in your industry. A big part of IT strategy is about making your value-producing IT apps harder to copy.

Data

The third component of a firm's IT portfolio is data. Data is the most valuable asset at the heart of modern firms. Fundamentally, IT is all about data. *Everything* else in a firm's IT portfolio exists solely to serve it—its raison d'être. Infrastructure is the conduit through which it flows; apps are what scrub, organize, and structure data into business insight. But their lifeblood is data.

Most data in firms is collected either by *transaction processing systems* that are used to transact with customers (such as cash registers or self-checkouts to complete a sale, process an order, or check a price) or firm-wide *"enterprise" systems* that execute business processes that crosscut line functions (e.g., recording customer interactions with your firm and managing your supply chain).

If we extrapolate the analogy of a human body to your firm's IT portfolio, hardware infrastructure mirrors your skeleton, networks your blood vessels, business apps your major organs (e.g., brain, liver, and heart), and data the blood that flows through them.

Proliferation of data being generated not just by humans but also by machines and transactional systems of all stripes is exponentially exploding opportunities to strategically exploit data. In a foreseeable future, most data will be collected and consumed by Internet-connected machines. Of all data, proprietary data—that you collect yourself—is the most potent for constructing competitive barriers for your archrivals. There are no shortcuts and no easy substitutes for it. IT apps and data—the least visible parts of corporate IT—together can potentially help create a competitive advantage. Their *combination* is harder for your archrivals to replicate, as we explore in the next chapter. If proprietary apps are like a competitive barbed-wire fence, proprietary data is a moat, and their combination is Kevlar.

Box 1.1
A Billion Biometrics: How Leapfrogging with IT Is Fighting Corruption in Rural India

A thousand years ago, India accounted for almost one-third of the entire world's GDP (28 percent in 1000 AD; China was 22 percent). It was a flourishing hub of commerce, mathematics, science, and philosophy. And then its fortunes reversed, invaders pillaged it, and it devolved from the world's largest economy to a dirt-poor third-world nation that barely contributed 7 percent to the world economy in 2016 (US: 16 percent; China: 16 percent).

India is home to one out of every six humans, yet a massive problem worsening the plight of its illiterate poor has been that too few of them could prove who they were. They had no passport, no driver's license, no proof of address, and no evidence of their identity. Their inability to prove who they were excluded them from bank loans as well as their rightful share of government welfare benefits. Corrupt officials—in the guise of fictional workers invented by them—stole more than 80 percent of the billions of dollars in generously subsidized food grain.

To solve this problem, India created the world's largest biometric database with retina scans and fingerprints of more than a billion Indians (see uidai.gov.in). The Indian federal government issued a biometric equivalent of the US social security number to a billion—mostly illiterate—Indians in 2016, using digitized fingerprints and retina scans. Unlike the US social security number issued to all Americans since 1935 that is ironically now the basis of identity theft, the Indian system's biometric data cannot be faked. The project *Aadhaar*—that translates to foundation—links directly to more than two hundred million bank accounts that provide complete transparency into the disbursement of government money.

To confirm receipt of any government benefit, the recipient must scan their retina and fingerprints. The system has literally wiped out corruption and bribery in this part of the public sector. An unintended benefit of being able to verify the identity of an individual is that it has brought hundreds of millions of poor Indians into the formal economy. Banks are more comfortable giving them loans, online stores selling them goods, insurance companies willing to cover them, and phone companies letting them open accounts on credit. The cost of enrolling one person was about $1.50. India recovered most of the cost of the project within the first year with savings from the money that did not fall into the wrong hands.

Developing countries can sometimes leapfrog developed countries in innovative uses of IT because they have fewer legacy technologies to displace.[22] India became the cheapest place to have a smartphone plan because it barely had landlines to displace; it leapfrogged straight from telegrams to smartphones. African countries—especially Kenya—became the largest users of mobile payments because it is often the only functioning currency and there were hardly any banks to displace. Hungary and China similarly leapfrogged straight from cash to ATM machines, and the concept of writing a check familiar to most Americans is unknown to most Hungarians and Chinese.

The Four Epochs of Information Technology

Figure 1.5 chronicles the evolution of corporate IT through four epochs, each with a different thrust. The data-processing epoch that began in the 1970s yielded *efficiency* improvements in large organizations that could afford expensive mainframe computers.[23] The personal computing epoch started by affordable PCs in the 1980s yielded *productivity* improvements in organizations of all sizes. The Internet epoch that began in the mid-1990s marked a shift from an era of information scarcity to information abundance. It fostered *collaboration* among organizations and individuals as affordable global connectivity gave us e-mail, Internet commerce, social media, and global supply chains.

The current *cyborg epoch* began around 2010 with the advent of ubiquitously connected personal smart devices. The term *cyborg* refers to a blurring boundary between man and machine; the machines become tools for amplifying human abilities. Think of how much of your own knowledge resides in Wikipedia than in your modest brain and how your smartphone makes *you* a constant part of a network exactly like a laptop might have been ten years ago. This obfuscation of where you end and the Internet begins is expanding. For example, Wi-Fi-enabled pacemakers, smart watches strapped to your wrist, fingerprint readers, augmented-reality glasses, and chip implants make *you* increasingly indistinguishable from the Internet. In organizations such as Amazon and Zappos warehouses, thousands of robots work alongside humans, allowing one human to do a job that once required twenty people.[24]

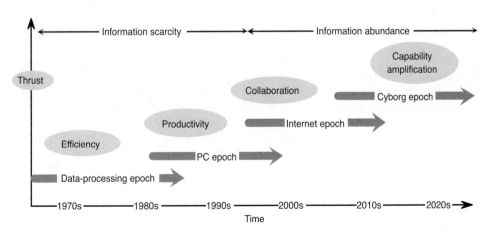

Figure 1.5
The four epochs of IT in business.

The Internet increasingly resembles several billion brains and several billion devices wired into one large circuit.[25] It is a gigantic masterpiece composed of a trillion loosely connected pieces, organic and silicon. The seven billion humans make it more alive than machine. (Humans connected to the Internet outnumbered humans with electricity and water by 2016.[26]) Such connectivity comes close to directly connecting human brains to approximate a global superorganism right out of H. G. Wells's fictional *world brain* in his 1938 novel.[27] Their oneness is easy to miss.

The value of IT in this epoch is not as a conduit of information but as a tool to amplify human ability by enabling better decisions and greater productivity, both within and outside firms. This epoch compensates for our cognitive and physical limitations but is also deepening the need for skills that allow us to race with—rather than against—our machines. The bar for how we add meaningful value in our professional work is rising. As this epoch unfolds, the growing bounty will be unevenly distributed. The winners will be individuals and organizations that develop the skills to work alongside these machines.[28] If IT does not prop you up, it will smother you. If IT does not prop up your firm, it will smother your firm too.

When a new epoch begins, technologies from previous epochs often persist as *legacy technologies* that we cannot simply wish away. Computer systems of different vintages and different degrees of incompatibility exist concurrently. Leveraging organizational investments from preceding epochs—and the data stuck in them—is an integral part of IT strategy.

Box 1.2
The Legacy of Floppy Disks and Nuclear Missiles

Although IT constantly evolves, the safety of the human race is tied to a half-century-old technology: the eight-inch floppy disk. The US nuclear weapons force uses them to run its missile control systems that were built in the 1970s.[29, 30] This IT system coordinates American intercontinental ballistic missiles, nuclear bombers, and support aircraft. In many industries, floppies are still being used in too-valuable-to-scrap machines that run production lines—precision cutting and milling machines, knitting machines, and metal molding machines. Even though their capacity is more than 250,000 times smaller than a disposable sixty-four-gigabyte thumb drive, the reason they have persisted is their longevity. The US military routinely reads data from floppy disks more than half a century old, which far exceeds the usable life of a CD, hard drive, or magnetic tape. A proven legacy technology that is reliable is not worth discarding just because it is old. Spending money updating it will be risky, will not strategically advance your firm, and might cause your firm to miss out on an opportunity to innovate elsewhere where it competitively counts.

The Trifecta of Digitization, Infusion, and Ubiquity Fracturing Industries

A fracture is a crack that heals into an altered industry structure (figure 1.6). Three IT-centric drivers are fracturing existing industries: (1) digitization, (2) infusion of software in non-IT offerings, and (3) ubiquity (table 1.2). The rest of this book refers to them collectively as the *trifecta*.

Digitization

Digitization is conversion into electronic form of a product, service, or activity that was historically physical.[31] The earliest industries steamrolled by digitization were music,[32, 33] books, and movies. It is now the turn of manufacturing, services, finance,[34] engineering, medicine, insurance, advertising, education, and retail.

To grasp its consequences, we must appreciate *what* can be digitized. Delivering any market offering (e.g., a product or service) has three dimensions (figure 1.7): (①) the offering itself, (②) how it is purchased, and (③) how it is delivered. A shift from physical to digital for any one dimension can disrupt your industry.[35]

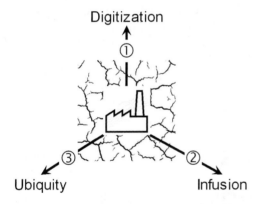

Figure 1.6
The trifecta of IT-centric drivers fracturing industries.

Table 1.2
The Trifecta's Consequences

Driver	What it means	Consequence
Digitization	Digitization of a product, service, or activity that was previously physical	Geographical constraints are erased
Infusion	Baking software into a product, service, or business activity	Products become services
Ubiquity	Omnipresence of cheap Internet connectivity	Costless communication occurs at the speed of light

1. *Offering* digitization—for example, with books, music, software, movies, and services—not only lets them reach a broader market than previously possible but also changes how and where they are produced. For example, the invention of physical check cashing using smartphone cameras digitized a service that previously required a trip to an ATM or a bank.

2. *Purchase process* digitization—for example, with "site-to-store" services that allow you to pick up in-store an item purchased online—removes geographic constraints on where a market offering is bought. Similarly, Starbucks enabled purchasing of a customized drink using a smartphone before a customer arrives at a physical store; it accounted for a quarter ($4 billion in 2016) of its annual sales.

3. *Delivery* digitization—for example, with video streaming—erases geographic constraints on where a market offering can be delivered. The advent of 3-D printing could foreseeably even make it possible to deliver physical goods digitally. The shift can also work in reverse, as Redbox did when it tapped into a latent need in the market by switching to physical delivery of movie rentals that had largely been digitized.

Whatever is digitized becomes information, governed then by the peculiar economics of information: near-zero reproduction and transportation costs.[36] Digitization

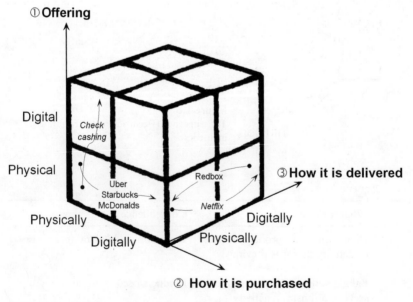

Figure 1.7
The digitization cube.

dematerializes atoms into bits.[37] Bits—the zeroes and ones into which they have been rendered—can costlessly be transported over the Internet. Digitization, by crossing over the boundary between the physical world and the digital world, simply erases geographical constraints in where work is produced and where it can be delivered.[38]

It takes one-eighth of a second for an Internet signal to travel between the two ends of the globe; that is how far a digitized activity will ever be from your markets. A digitized activity can be completed anywhere an Internet "packet" can be sent. Digitization—even in one cell—tilts the playing field by enabling distribution of the activities that go into producing a market offering; disassembled activities can be completed by specialists who might be thousands of miles apart and then instantaneously be reaggregated. This opens up new possibilities for division of labor among humans and even between humans and machines. Such vanquishing of coordination costs is making tiny multinational firms possible.[39] Digitization is therefore enabling new business models that were the realm of science fiction a few years ago. It is silently creating an invisible parallel economy on a trajectory to dwarf the visible economy in most industries.[40]

Digitization raises an entire industry's bar for operational efficiency; if your rivals use it to become more efficient, you only have a limited window before you fall into a vicious Red Queen trap. Digitization can even make a firm's offering outright irrelevant, as Timex watches, Sony's CD players, Western Union's telegram service, and Polaroid's cameras illustrate. Digitization makes non-IT managers' inputs to corporate IT decisions even more vital. If technological advances that enable digitization of any one of the cube's three dimensions blindside your firm but not your archrivals, you will quickly find yourself unable to keep up with your customers' ratcheting expectations.

Think of your own industry. Are advances in technology making digitization possible in any one of these three facets? You must think of digitization not just in products but also in every facet of your firm's operations.

Infusion

Infusion means baking software into products and services. As Netscape's founder put it, software is eating the world.[41] There is growing software content in products and in how they are produced and delivered. Infusion can make IT an integral part of a product, even allowing some of its functions to exist outside the product itself.[42] Watches, door locks, toilets, thermostats, sneakers, refrigerators, coffeemakers, and even lightbulbs have software content.[43] A car today can have the processing power of up to one hundred laptops and one hundred million of lines of code; it is more like a giant iPad with software complexity exceeding Facebook that also transports you (see figure 1.8 for a comparison[44]). Automakers entrenched in a Henry Ford mind-set fail to realize that they are as much in the software business as Google. (Software and electronics were up to 40 percent of the cost of a new car by 2016.[45]) No wonder that an astounding number of cars are recalled each year due to *software* glitches. In 2015 alone, Chrysler recalled 1.4 million, Toyota 625,000, Ford 433,000, GM 250,000, Range Rover 65,000, and Jaguar 17,500 cars. In the low-margin auto business, such recalls wipe out a chunk of firms' profits.

The emerging Internet of Things (IoT)—where everyday objects are gaining the ability to talk through the Internet—is accelerating this driver. ("Things" that connect to the Internet all speak TCP/IP, the language of the Internet.) Firms are even attempting to make legacy things part of the Internet by augmenting them with IoT capabilities (e.g., Amazon's Dash Buttons in figure 1.9). This trend is unconstrained by economics or technology. IoT sensors are becoming tiny and cheap enough to embed in everything, and the Internet protocol has one hundred unique "addresses" for every atom on our planet. By 2020, expect two hundred billion "things" to be connected to the Internet, including three hundred million electric meters and one

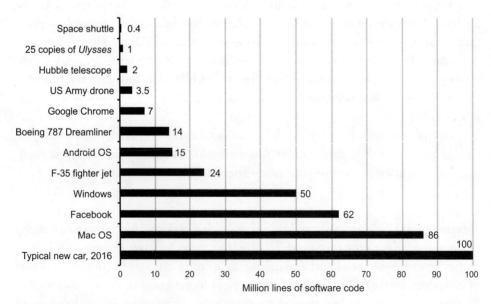

Figure 1.8
A new car has almost twice the software content as Facebook.

Figure 1.9
Amazon's Dash Buttons add IoT capabilities to existing appliances.

hundred million lightbulbs.[46] Two hundred billion connected things open up a lot more possibilities than two hundred billion things. These objects can provide data streams full of *context* (e.g., location and temperature); firms must figure out how to competitively leverage what they are saying.

The business consequences of software infusion are twofold. First, all industries are increasingly acquiring characteristics historically unique to the software business. Tesla's cars, for example, receive new features via software updates just as your smartphone does. Second, IT is gradually morphing products into services, which require different business models. For example, Rolls-Royce—one of the largest producers of aircraft engines—no longer sells jet engines; it sells a service metered in hours that an engine is actually propelling a plane.[47] In theory, service businesses have greater long-term revenue potential. Services create an ongoing revenue stream (unlike products' one-time sale), their value drives pricing (unlike products that are priced by adding a markup to costs), and they can lock in customers.

Cars, for example, offer services like live traffic monitoring, congestion-driven navigation and rerouting, and wear-based maintenance scheduling. Berina generates as much revenue from selling digital sewing patterns as it does selling its embroidery machines. Similarly, Kraft's Internet-connected Tassimo coffee machines report flavors of coffee being consumed, and Coke's fountain drink dispensers track what beverages customers are mixing. However, this product-to-service transformation demands making a service progressively so much more valuable to your customers so they would not *want* to ditch you for an archrival. Netflix and Amazon exemplify how firms can use IT to create such noncoercive lock-ins.

The questions for non-IT managers to ask: Can we infuse software in our products? To what end?

Ubiquity

Ubiquity refers to the proliferation of cheap and fast Internet connectivity any-where and everywhere. People, computers, smartphones, and a growing variety of unexpected objects can increasingly communicate literally at the speed of light at near-zero cost across large distances. Growth in ubiquity has neither economic nor technical constraints. Competition guarantees plummeting costs. The cost of Inter-net connectivity is *asymptotic*, which means that the cost progressively gets closer and closer to zero but never quite reaches it. By 2016, a typical Internet connection was able to transmit the entire Bible twice every second.[48] Reuse of the retired analog TV spectrum for mobile broadband promises blazing speeds (more than ten gigabits per second) and coverage of ten times the area of existing cell towers. (Ubiquity is indispensable enough today that Finland made broadband access a constitutional right in 2010.)

When Intel was founded in 1971, the fastest Ferrari drove at 174 mph and the tallest skyscrapers were the 1400-foot Twin Towers. If cars and skyscrapers had pro-gressed at the speed of computing power, the Ferrari would drive at one-tenth the speed of light and the tallest skyscraper would reach halfway to the moon.[49] Little wonder then that an entry-level iPad in 2017 had the computing power that would have cost $100 million in 1980.[50] Couple ubiquity with the computing power that a dollar buys—growing tenfold every 3.5 years—and you can throw impressive com-puting horsepower at anything that is digitized.[51] Ubiquity is a powerful tool at our disposal, but it must be *used* to create business value.

Confluence of the Trifecta

The *confluence* of digitization, software infusion, and ubiquity is creating terrify-ing and exhilarating possibilities in many industries. It is precipitating radically new business models, entirely new classes of competitors, and a reimagination of firms. Rookies are not beating industry incumbents; they are simply changing the game. Activities can be disaggregated into pieces that can be completed in different places—even by machines—and then be instantly reaggregated. This instantaneous task mobility is creating unprecedented scale and specialization in services, education, even menial jobs. The digitization-infusion-ubiquity trifecta can cause one industry to bleed into another, creating unanticipated rivals from previously unrelated busi-nesses. It is demoting some industry heavyweights to middleweight journeymen and obliterating others. Turning a blind eye to these shifts is a fast track to oblivion.

Consider an entry-level, minimum-wage job at McDonald's. Ten years ago, if you ordered a meal at a McDonald's drive-through, you would talk to an employee

inside through a speakerphone. Order-taking wa[...]
tion. Then McDonald's had an epiphany: the in[...]
Skype call.[52] Today, the employee you talk to migh[...]
in Santa Maria, California, or in rural North Dakota w[...]
into a computer that shows up in your store's kitchen in Gu[...]
back-and-forth trip of four thousand miles occurs in less than[...]
takes you to pull up to the pickup window. A few seconds shaved off[...]
of orders everyday add up. *Digitization* allowed McDonald's to disper[...]
chase process, *ubiquitous* Internet connectivity made it economically feasib[...]
infusion of software into the meal preparation process made coordination seamle[...]
It is the confluence of the trifecta.

McDonald's gains: professionalization of blue-collar work (software-scrutinized order-takers specialize only in taking orders), fewer errors, and speeding throughput at the drive-through. This tweak in a single dimension of the digitization cube bolstered McDonald's fast and cheap value proposition, raising the bar for its archrivals. This gain in productivity has a social cost: fewer generalist jobs.[53] Machines did more than simply substituting costlier human labor. The blending of humans and machines increased its employees' productivity. McDonald's employees fortunate enough to survive are now racing with the machine, not against it.

Why IT Is Often a Strategic Handicap

IT increasingly underpins individual line functions' work and glues together their contributions into firm-wide business processes. Tweaking any of this work requires tweaking the IT in which they are embedded.

IT Is Line Functions' Operational Backbone

Firms are organized as line functions (departments) that specialize in *different* things (figure 1.10): marketing, sales, finance, accounting, and operations. (Non-IT managers throughout this book are midlevel managers in these line functions.) IT is the backbone that increasingly unpins these line functions' work, as the examples in table 1.3 illustrate. Their ability to do their job is increasingly dependent on the IT apps that they use, irrespective of industry. The IT unit is an oddball in figure 1.10 because it historically was a backstage support function like human resources, just helping the other "real" functions do their job.

If your firm's IT systems help your function do its job better than your archrivals, it can translate into a competitive advantage over them. Otherwise, IT

Figure 1.10
A firm's line functions specialize in different things, which IT increasingly glues together.

becomes a handicap. It often does because even the most conscientious IT colleagues do not have *your* knowledge of your own line function. It is just not what they were trained to do. If your line function's needs and priorities do not come from you, your IT unit can only assume what it *thinks* your function needs.

Table 1.3
IT Permeates Every Functional Activity

Functional activity	How it relies on IT
Strategy	Strategy execution, value chain design, decision making
Operations	Supply chain management, production management, product mix, and inventory optimization
Finance	Managing capital assets and investments (the largest of which today is IT)
Accounting	Connecting operational transactions to managerial accounting metrics, bookkeeping
Human resources	Optimizing employee assignments, payroll, recruitment
Marketing	Pricing, analytics, marketing planning, customer segmentation, channels management, and metrics for judging marketing effectiveness
Sales	Customer relationship management, social media, tracking leads, prospecting, ordering, and salesforce monitoring
Product development	Design and delivery of products and services; crowdsourced innovation
Customer service	After-sales support, remote diagnostics, self-service portals, and online customer communities

Box 1.3
IT Strategy for Drug Dealers

IT's impact on competition is even more pronounced in the drug trade than it is in legitimate industries.[54, 55, 56] The evolution of this industry offers unique insights into how IT will impact other industries that share its attributes: commodity products, international competition, powerful and literally deadly incumbents, Red Queen competition, and quality variance.

As the drug trade moves from the street to online "cryptomarkets," drug dealers are forced to compete on price and quality since drugs are a commodity. Yet unlike the quality of, say, a commodity book or toilet paper, the quality of drugs is more unpredictable (e.g., mixing of impurities to increase weight). Online drug markets have all the features of eBay including escrow services to ensure delivery, feedback and star-based seller rating systems, formal trading policies, discussion boards with support staff, and paid moderators to resolve customer complaints. The marketplaces—with names such as Silk Road, Alphabay, Evolution, Utopia, and Agora—are frequently shut down by law enforcement, but new ones sprout up to replace them.

The Economist estimated the fast-growing online drug market in 2015 at about $180 million worldwide, which was a small fraction of the whole $300 billion market. Such markets operate on the dark web, which is an underground part of the Internet visible only through specialized browsers such as Tor. The dark web routes communication through several random computers and uses multiple layers of encryption that make it nearly impossible for law enforcement agencies to track users. Money changes hands using Bitcoin, an untraceable digital currency that can be swapped for dollars at that day's exchange rate. The trading sites get a 5–10 percent commission for each sale. Dark net search engines such as Ahmia and price comparison engines such as Grams increase the transparency of prices in such markets just as their counterparts do elsewhere for airfares and consumer products.

Once a purchase is made, the payment waits in an escrow account. Drug dealers pack the drugs in vacuum-sealed bags packed using rubber gloves to avoid leaving DNA traces or fingerprints. They then dip the sealed bag in bleach to minimize the risk of being traced or detected by drug-sniffing dogs. They then attach printed mailing labels because handwritten labels on international mail packages raise red flags at customs. (Shipping and handling add up to about a third of the total price.) Some sellers offer extra services such as sending an empty package to new customers to check for signs of customs inspection. *The Economist* estimated that 90 percent of the shipments make it through without detection.

Drug dealers try all of the gimmicks of legitimate businesses in an attempt to differentiate themselves (e.g., drugs that are guaranteed to be "conflict-free," "fair-trade," or "ethically sourced"). Even mission statements, money-back guarantees, loyalty discounts, and help desks are common among online drug dealers. Unlike most commodities where IT lowers prices, it has increased prices in the drug trade. *The Economist* found that the same drugs carried as much as a 40 percent premium online relative to street prices and were of higher quality. An explanation for the price premium is that online ratings enforce quality and discourage dilution. A good reputation matters

Box 1.3 (*continued*)

more in this trade than in legal markets. (They are also safer than the violence-prone street markets.) No wonder that drug dealers care far more about their online reputation; it translates into a price premium. This pattern illustrates how competing sellers can differentiate themselves using IT even in a commodity market. Drug dealers are also early adopters of security technologies. Ninety percent of the dealers analyzed by the *Economist* correspondents used encryption, a far higher rate than in legitimate businesses.

Another noteworthy pattern is the incumbents' reactions to the rise of online drug trade. The powerful drug cartels have shown almost no interest in online drug markets for two possible reasons. First, their business is high volume, measured in tons, not ounces. Second, their well-honed competencies such as smuggling, intimidation, and violence are worthless on the dark net.

The broad insight for managers in legitimate firms from online drug dealers is twofold. First, they show how it is possible to differentiate using IT even in a commodity industry when one dimension—here the purchase process—of the digitization cube changes. Second, the cartels illustrate that incumbents often dismiss signs of a brewing IT-driven disruption until it becomes too late.

That might not be what you need or want. When a line function wants to tweak how it does any of its own activities, the rigidity of the IT in which they are embedded is often a roadblock to change. This rigidity is often a consequence of their irreversible "architecture" (chapter 3). Only by actively engaging in IT decisions that affect your line function can you ensure that its IT tools match its evolving priorities.

IT Glues Line Functions

Most business processes—activities that deliver products and services to customers—crosscut line functions, even though firms are organized as line functions. IT is what glues together the contributions of collaborating line functions to execute business processes. Therefore, instead of thinking of IT as a functional department, think of it as the glue that binds modern firms. It is also the glue that connects your firm to its business partners (e.g., suppliers and retail channels). This glue should be good enough to create operational efficiency that matches your archrivals yet flexible enough to foster business agility.

Reliance on IT as a foundation for *executing* your firm's business processes means that it often becomes a source of rigidity and a barrier to change.[57, 58, 59] No matter how brilliant your market offerings, it is increasingly impossible to execute your firm's strategy without synchronizing your IT strategy to it. Without solid execution, strategy is hollow intent. Synchronization flounders when non-IT managers who set business priorities and those who manage IT are disconnected.

Yet mismatches between firms' business processes and the IT apps into which they are baked are common. Ideally, business processes and IT apps must be designed *concurrently*.[60] This however requires firms to custom build their own apps instead of buying them. That is singly the costliest, riskiest, and most time consuming way to acquire an IT app. One in three such projects succeeds, they are buggy,[61] and a moderate-sized app with one hundred thousand lines of software code costs $1.5–$4 million.[62] They are also costly to maintain because you need employees who understand them. So add another 700 percent in maintenance costs, and a $1.5 million app could cost $12 million over its lifetime. Non-IT managers can help discern whether an IT app project has enough strategic potential to justify custom development. If its strategic potency is not sustainable, it is by definition a cost driver.

IT Strategy as a Conversation

Formulating IT strategy is primarily a human activity, not a technical one.[64, 65, 66] For IT to help your firm accomplish its goals, your IT unit needs to first understand them. This is easier said than done because IT and non-IT managers speak different languages. Inventory turns, ROIC, financial leverage, marketable securities, gross margin on inventory investment, bounce rates, and close rates sound as Greek to your IT colleagues as SOAP, RESTful, NAT, virtualization, APIs, and 802.11c are to you. This language chasm prevents IT investments from becoming strategically meaningful.

You must think of IT strategy as a conversation between you and your IT colleagues. Conversation requires empathy—seeing things from the others' perspective. Even if your IT colleagues earnestly tried, it would be harder for them to learn the languages of the five different line functions in your firm. Knowing how to speak *just enough* of their language opens the door to conversation.[67] Only then can you and your IT colleagues develop a shared understanding of your line function's priorities, threats, and opportunities.

Assume positive intent. Assume that your IT colleagues care about wanting to make a difference to your firm's well-being. You have to help them help you. Even small contributions by non-IT managers can make an outsized impact—like adding

Box 1.4
Getting Edgy: When Obvious IT Opportunities Trump Disruptive Ones

Media obsession with firms that use IT disruptively can lead firms to overlook IT-enabled growth opportunities in existing operations right under their nose. For most firms, IT strategy is more about pragmatic, incremental ways to extract more value from the edges of their business—underexploited spaces where a firm meets its customers.[63] Three such edges are (a) complements, (b) services, and (c) underproductive assets. Complements are products or services that your customers need to use what they purchase from your firm. Apple, for example, generates a healthy part of its margins from selling cases and for-fee services (e.g., iCloud), which customers invariably need to use its products. A second edge is using IT to create services tied to products to help customers create an end result for which they buy your firm's offerings. For example, IKEA customers buy a flat-packed desk because they need a work environment, not because they like assembling furniture. IKEA therefore offers online how-to assembly videos for its popular products. Ford customers buy a car because they want to get from point A to point B, not because they like depleting ozone. An edge strategy is for Ford to sell them additional in-car services beyond just emergency telematics and navigation, such as self-driving capabilities, helping find cheaper fuel, or whatever else it takes to better get them from point A to point B. If Ford does not, someone else will. Similarly, Caterpillar allows users of its bulldozers and diggers to monitor their performance as a monthly paid service. The third edge—also often enabled by IT—is to extract new value out of underutilized assets that your firm already owns. Cargill, an American agricultural firm, combines the data collected as a byproduct of its commercial activities with proprietary software as a for-fee service to help farmers decide how to optimize crop sowing using more than 250 variables, such as soil type, seeds, and weather patterns. Uber's business model also occupies this edge.

yeast to bread—on the business value that your firm's IT investments deliver. Even little contributions add up because they are outside the comfort zone of your peers in rival firms.

The number-one reason most firms are unprepared for disruption is their lack of technology-savvy non-IT managers.[68] There is no substitute for what you as a non-IT manager can bring to the IT strategy table. Without non-IT managers' engagement, firms cannot comprehend the opportunities nor imagine the trifecta's disruptive possibilities. The world will still go on without your contribution, but your firm will be worse off.

Your firm's IT strategy needs both vision and capability (figure 1.11); one without the other is a dead end. Non-IT managers contribute the business vision for what IT should accomplish, and the IT unit contributes the capabilities to execute it. Together, they transform IT from a handicap into a weapon.

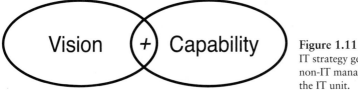

Figure 1.11
IT strategy gets its vision from
non-IT managers and capability from
the IT unit.

Strategic Aspiration Is Market Positioning

A journey of a thousand steps begins with a destination. Your firm must know where it wants to go before IT can help get it there. All strategy begins with two questions: Who will you target and how?[69] Your firm's strategic aspiration is the combination of their answers, which puts your firm in one of the four cells in figure 1.12. You can pursue either a mass market or a smaller segment within it.[70] You can compete by either being cheaper (a low-cost strategy) or being different enough from your archrivals to command a price premium (a differentiation strategy).

The chosen cell is your firm's *strategic aspiration*. It is your firm's jargon-free positioning as either a low-cost player or a purveyor of a unique offering in your target market. It singularly defines its *actual* mission of how it intends to deliver value. This should not be confused with the sorts of mission statements that are the stuff of *Dilbert* comics or lofty, ambiguous statements about being best of breed, the dominant player, or appeasing shareholders. To get to the heart of it, try fitting into a tweet what your firm is really about. Clarity about this is imperative because it defines competitive advantage, which is often loosely used to the point of meaninglessness.

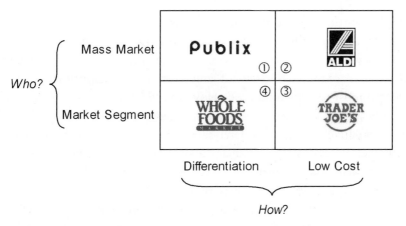

Figure 1.12
A firm's strategic aspiration is a combination of who it pursues and how.

Competitive advantage means delivering more value than your archrivals to your customers. Your cell defines who your archrivals are. It is in this cell alone that your firm must deliver comparable value either more efficiently or differently in ways that your customers will happily pay more for.

The 2 × 2 in figure 1.12 illustrates this for firms in the American grocery store industry. Publix and Aldi both pursue the mass market, but Aldi follows a low-cost strategy, and Publix follows a differentiation strategy focused on service quality. In contrast, neither Whole Foods nor Trader Joe's pursues the mass market targeted by these grocery store chains. Instead, they pursue a smaller segment of that market. While Trader Joe's follows a low-cost strategy, Whole Foods follows a differentiation strategy by offering more unique products that you would not find elsewhere. Similarly, in the clothing industry, Target, Walmart, Costco, and J.Crew might populate cells 1 through 4.[71] Try placing your own firm and your archrivals in this 2 × 2.

Strategic Aspiration Is Sticky

A firm must be clear-minded about what it aspires to become by committing to one cell in figure 1.12. You cannot be indecisive. The low-cost strategy is like going south and differentiation is like going north. Trying to straddle both panders to incompatible objectives, like trying to go south and north at the same time, getting you nowhere. You will fail to be as efficient or as effective as a more focused archrival.

Each strategic aspiration in figure 1.12 requires a different approach to IT strategy and different types of IT investments. What is right for Target might be terrible for Walmart. One size does not fit all. Mismatches between a firm's strategic aspiration and its IT strategy exact competitive penalties.

Your firm's IT portfolio must obsessively focus on how it has *chosen* to compete—being cheaper *or* different. IT for a low-cost strategy focuses on operational effectiveness, which means doing the same things as your archrivals but doing them better. It emphasizes the productivity of your existing assets, prioritizing those that contribute the most to your total costs. However, the low-cost strategy is not for the faint of heart; there will always be a rival willing to go out of business faster than you. The alternative strategy is differentiation. However, inducing your customers to pay higher prices demands a value proposition that is substantively more compelling *to them* than your cheaper rivals'. Value in their eyes is the true arbiter. The focus of IT for a differentiation strategy should be doing activities differently from your archrivals to deliver something that your customers are willing to pay more for. The trifecta can create unprecedented insight into how a product or service is being used, opening opportunities for differentiating and tailoring them to specific market segments. However, differentiation works only as long as your archrivals cannot copy you.[72]

You cannot waver about your chosen cell either. It takes time to nurture the whole raft of IT assets tailored to one strategic aspiration and years to reconfigure entire systems of activities to shift focus. It also takes time to optimize linkages in your value chain for one strategic aspiration and for IT and line functions to come to a shared understanding around it. You also cannot change customer perceptions of your firm's value proposition overnight.

Even if your strategic aspiration is steadfast, the cells themselves might be unstable because technology can redefine what a mass market is. Proliferation of the Internet has made the once niche market of online shoppers a new mass market. Similarly,

Box 1.5
How Wavering Almost Killed Banana Republic

American clothing chain Banana Republic was once the prized jewel of the Gap Group. Banana Republic had successfully operated in a high-quality differentiated cell of the mass-market clothing industry (cell 1 in figure 1.12), honing a reputation for good-quality classic clothing at a fair price that appealed to working professionals. It had intensely loyal customers. By 2013, its sales dropped as an aftermath of a multiyear recession in the economy. By 2014, it felt squeezed between online discounters such as Amazon and an evolved postrecession American consumer unwilling to pay sticker price. As the market evolved, it attempted to resuscitate flagging sales, resorting to perpetually offering 40 percent discounts throughout 2014 through 2016. (This put it in head-on competition with firms in cell 2.) This resulted in conditioning its customers to never pay full price, worsening its plight. It then attempted to compete with fast-fashion retailers such as the lower-priced Zara (cell 3) by offering teenager-oriented clothing, who could not afford its professional-oriented prices. As a result, it lost its core customer base and a new one never materialized. Its error: it wavered from its strategic aspiration in figure 1.12, unable to realign its value chain and brand around its vacillating positioning. Banana Republic was trying to operate in all four cells of figure 1.12, sending a confused message about its strategic aspiration. Instead of wavering, it should have realized that the new landscape has upped the ante for being a mass-market, differentiated-clothing retailer. Customers' unwillingness to pay asking prices was a market signal that they did not believe what it peddled was now worthy of its price premium. The cells in figure 1.12 were being redefined by online retail and shifting customer mind-sets, but Banana Republic did not recognize this. Increasing quality and differentiation, not trying to compete with misperceived competitors outside of its strategic aspiration cell, was needed. It misjudged who its new archrivals were. It needed to increase the value delivered for the money in the eyes of its core customers, not waver around the 2 × 2. Its more focused archrival, J.Crew, which did not waver from its chosen cell, navigated the same industry shifts much more successfully.

new niche markets can also emerge out of mass markets (e.g., Netflix customers wanting movies that do not yet stream created a market for Redbox).

Syncing, Not Alignment

Your firm's strategic aspiration—where it seeks to go—should drive both your firm's operational strategy and its IT strategy (figure 1.13). *Operational strategy* is the tactical implementation of its business strategy. It includes the organizational structure, control mechanisms, and incentives intended to move your firm toward its strategic aspiration. It is about *how* your firm will deliver—always relative to its archrivals—more value to its customers.[73] IT is the foundation for *executing* this operational strategy.[74] *IT strategy* is an integrated set of choices that define how your firm will use IT to outperform its archrivals in its chosen cell.[75, 76, 77]

You often hear about "alignment" of IT and business. Alignment is a self-defeating mind-set. It dangerously assumes that operational strategy and IT strategy are static.[78, 79] Neither is static, which makes unwavering alignment unachievable. Operational strategy rarely is static because the trifecta is making stable markets extinct in most industries. Instead, firms require an adaptive operational strategy to find out what variant works best as markets evolve. IT can also be used to envision new operational strategies, entirely new ways of competing, and novel business models. Therefore, operational strategy and IT strategy can influence each other.[80, 81, 82]

Synchronizing—syncing for short—captures better than alignment this two-way, dynamic relationship between IT strategy and operational strategy. *IT synchronization* refers to the extent to which a firm's IT portfolio enables the execution of its

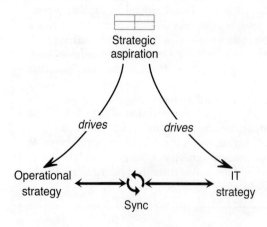

Figure 1.13
IT strategy must be synchronized with operational strategy.

operational strategy. Above all else, the deeper purpose of corporate IT is inching your firm toward its strategic aspiration.[83] Syncing means forging together your firm's IT and operational strategy with that singular purpose. Far from a one-shot activity, it is a continuous process of repairing misalignments as either evolves. Syncing can create breakthrough business value out of ordinary IT assets. The two being out of sync is like driving a nice car with a flat tire; it will not get you far.

Syncing—not the IT itself—can create a hard-to-copy competitive advantage over your archrivals. Syncing indistinguishably fuses IT strategy and operational strategy, creating a constant harmony of purpose between IT and line functions. A historical analogy is why the Germans easily defeated the French in the Second World War even though both had comparable tanks and aircraft: their use was better synchronized.[84] Today, Spanish retailer Zara's IT syncing allows it to introduce new clothing collections four times as often as the rest of its industry. Rivals such as Banana Republic and Aeropostale unsuccessfully tried to copy Zara; they could copy everything else except the unobservable linkages between Zara's IT strategy and operational strategy.

Syncing matters because operational strategy and IT strategy are interdependent. Your statistics coursework called this joint probability. You must get both right because the likelihood that you will be able to execute your firm's operational strategy is a *product* of their individual probabilities. If you are 90 percent likely to be able to pull off your operational strategy, as the likelihood of getting the IT part right drops to 90 percent, 70 percent, and 50 percent, your prospects for progressing toward your strategic aspiration drop to 81 percent, a depressing 63 percent, and a guaranteed-to-fail 45 percent (products of the two percentages).[85]

Syncing increases the overlap among the three things in figure 1.14: what your line functions want from IT, what the IT unit thinks they need, and what is economically and technologically feasible. The less they overlap, the more you risk throwing money at the wrong problems.

Determining what's right for *your* firm depends entirely on non-IT managers' contributions to IT strategy. Only their engagement as equal contributors gives IT strategy its substance.

How Non-IT Managers Contribute Firepower to IT Strategy

Non-IT managers abdicate control over IT decisions to their IT unit because of their discomfort with making IT decisions.[86] IT strategy is the tradecraft of modern business, strategically too important to be left just to your IT unit. Non-IT managers

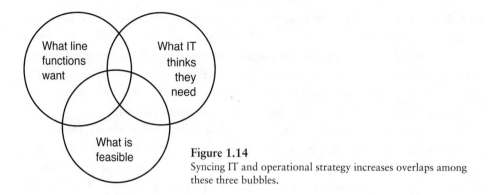

Figure 1.14
Syncing IT and operational strategy increases overlaps among these three bubbles.

ought to be their firms' curators of business technology, the professionals between the firm's business users and the IT creators. Non-IT managers can contribute competitive firepower to their firm's IT strategy in ways that your IT unit simply cannot for three reasons:

1. *Spending smarter, not more.* Most common problems with corporate IT stem from doing the wrong things, not doing things wrong.[87] It does not matter how right your IT unit is doing things if it is not doing the things right *for your firm*. It is not IT itself that differentiates but the new business processes it enables. Many firms mistakenly assume that their IT unit will drive their strategic use of IT, but IT units rarely have the skills to do it. Letting them alone drive IT delegates your firm's business strategy to its IT department. It leads to missed opportunities and wasted investments. Non-IT managers can contribute a clear view of business priorities to ensure that their firms' IT decisions reflect the operational strategy that it intends to execute. This fosters a capacity for your firm to envision and act on opportunities spawned by the trifecta before your archrivals. Firms cannot afford non-IT managers watching from the sidelines as their tech-savvy rivals exploit business opportunities and threats.

2. *Syncing breaks out of the Red Queen race.* Non-IT managers' contributions to IT strategy can help their firms break out of a vicious trap of Red Queen competition. Imitation perpetuates it: your archrivals copy every IT-based innovation your firm comes up with, pressuring your firm to reciprocate. Non-IT managers' involvement breaks this arms race in two ways. First, to imitate your firm, your archrivals must replicate not only your operational and IT strategy but also their linkages that outsiders cannot observe. Second, syncing IT chooses which IT initiatives to *not* pursue. This prevents overspending on IT and instead focuses on a *just right* level that delivers more business value. You do not need a Cadillac when a Chevy will do. This

laser-focuses IT investments on your firm's strategic aspirations rather than mimicry or a mindless pursuit of industry trends.

3. *Preventing today's IT decisions from becoming tomorrow's strategic handicaps.* IT architectures (chapter 3) are irreversible but have inescapable strategic consequences. Facebook's gargantuan monthly Internet connectivity bills, Netflix's scalability, iOS's phenomenal profitability, and Skype's competitive durability are rooted in early architectural choices made long before anyone had heard of them. Even though IT architectures determine your firm's technological DNA, firms often treat them as technical decisions best left to the IT unit. Non-IT managers' input into these choices ensures that today's architectural choices do not become tomorrow's strategic handicaps.

Where Non-IT Managers Can Contribute

The key areas where non-IT managers can contribute to IT strategy—corresponding to the next eight chapters of this book—include

- competitively exploiting your data assets using analytics (chapter 2);
- strategically choosing your IT architecture (chapter 3);
- avoiding the Goldilocks trap, ensuring payoffs, and investing under uncertainty (chapter 4);
- governing IT to simultaneously be strategic and frugal (chapter 5);
- ensuring that IT projects deliver tangible business benefits (chapter 6) and are appropriately sourced (chapter 7);
- securing IT assets and ensuring resilience (chapter 8); and
- monitoring emerging technologies to spot business opportunities (chapter 9).

Key Takeaways

1. *Red Queen competition.* IT spending by one firm triggers retaliatory investments by archrivals, creating a vicious cycle where ever-increasing IT spending gets no firm ahead.

2. *The trifecta fracturing industries.* Three IT drivers upending industries—collectively the *trifecta*—are digitization of physical products, services, and activities; infusion of software into them; and omnipresent Internet connectivity. The trifecta can usher in unexpected rivals from outside your own industry.

3. *The four epochs of IT.* Corporate IT has progressed in four major waves, each with a different thrust. The mainframe epoch boosted efficiency, the PC epoch boosted productivity, the Internet epoch fostered collaboration, and the ongoing

cyborg epoch is interweaving humans with machines. The Internet epoch replaced information scarcity with information abundance.

4. *The three big pieces of an IT portfolio.* A corporate IT portfolio is a firm's collection of its (1) IT infrastructure, (2) IT apps, and (3) data assets. IT infrastructure is a competitive necessity incapable of competitive advantage; it must be good enough but economical. IT apps and data—especially together—can potentially create at least a *temporary* competitive advantage.

5. *IT often handicaps strategy.* IT underpins line functions' work and glues together business processes. Executing business strategy, therefore, increasingly relies on a firm's IT assets, yet non-IT managers' hands-off approach to corporate IT makes IT an unexpected roadblock. Non-IT managers can contribute what IT managers alone are ill equipped to. They can help firms spend IT dollars smarter, break out of the destructive Red Queen rat race, and prevent today's IT decisions from handicapping tomorrow's strategy.

6. *Strategic aspiration as your firm's positioning in the 2 × 2.* It is a combination of *who* your firm targets (a mass market or a segment within it) and *how* (being cheap or unique). Your firm must beat its archrivals in the chosen cell alone. Your firm's strategic aspiration should drive both your firm's IT strategy and its operational strategy.

7. *IT syncing as a competitive edge.* The strategic value of IT is in *how* it is interwoven with your firm's tactical strategy. Synchronizing IT strategy and operational strategy can edge your firm past its archrivals. They fall out of sync because operational strategy is not static, and IT can make possible novel ways of reimagining it.

The Non-IT Managers' Checklist

☐ Are technical advances making it possible to digitize your firm's offerings (or the activities that produce them), how customers purchase them, and how they are delivered (the digitization cube)? How does a change in *any one* of these dimensions of the digitization cube alter taken-for-granted assumptions in your industry's dominant business models?

☐ How is the digitization-infusion-ubiquity trifecta affecting your industry? Can your firm infuse software into its products or business processes? To what end? How will this make your firm's revenue sources more service-like?

☐ What is your firm's strategic aspiration? This is a combination of *who* it targets (a mass market or a segment within it) and *how* (being a cost leader or a purveyor of a differentiated offering that commands a price premium).

☐ List the key legacy IT assets that your firm owns that are not commodities available to your archrivals. Why do they have competitive value today? How do they fall short today in executing your firm's operational strategy?

☐ Is your firm's IT infrastructure both reliable *and* as low-cost as your archrivals'? If not, what part of it (a) costs the most or (b) is less reliable than it ought to be?

☐ Which major *operational* apps used (a) within line functions or (b) across them prevent your firm from being at least as efficient as your archrivals? Which ones are constant roadblocks to improving your core revenue-generating business processes?

Jargon Decoder

Data, information, and insight	Data is a raw fact that becomes information when contextualized and aggregated; actionable information is insight.
Small versus big data	Small data is a data *point*; big data is a fleeting *stream* of data points almost too large to store.
Analytics	The process of using data to predict what will happen; it requires good data and good models.
Margins	The difference between what your customers pay for a product or service and what it costs you to produce it.
Three-lens framework	A collection of three lenses to analyze how IT affects your firm's competitive landscape. They help analyze how it is affecting your *industry*, how your *firm* creates value, and whether an IT *asset* can create a sustainable competitive advantage.
Disintermediation	Using IT to bypass other firms.
Five-forces model	The fierceness of competition in your *industry* is driven by the negotiating clout of your customers and suppliers, new firms entering it, and the threat that some substitute can meet your customers' needs. IT intensifies each of them.
Value chains and streams	A series of bread-and-butter activities through which your firm creates a product or service; its value stream includes upstream firms that it buys inputs from and downstream firms through which it reaches its customers.
Litmus test	Whether an IT asset can (a) create and (b) sustain a competitive advantage. It creates one if it is valuable and rare; it sustains one if your rivals cannot copy or substitute it.

2

In·for·ma·tion

In the 1987 movie *Wall Street*, Gordon Gekko says that the most valuable commodity he knows of is information. Fast-forward thirty years from Gekko's era of information scarcity, and information abundance has now stricken firms with a poverty of attention.[1] The epicenter of strategy—not just IT strategy—is information, the stepping-stone between raw data and actionable insight. The quest all along has been for foresight that your rivals do not have. When you act on something your rivals do not know, information is power. Understanding how IT can be strategic must then begin with how information alters—unintentionally and intentionally—how firms compete. That is this chapter's focus.

We first trace prediction over the past millennia, the evolving role of information in strategy, and how information extracted from data—small and big—can edge out archrivals. We introduce a three-lens framework to help grasp how information alters (a) the balance of power in your industry, (b) how your firm creates value vis-à-vis its archrivals, and (c) competitive advantage. Most disruptive effects of IT on your entire industry are beyond managers' control. Grasping them helps you extract antidotes from the same disruptive forces. However, any competitive advantage gained through IT is short-lived if your archrivals replicate it. We therefore explore how strategy-driven combinations of IT assets can thwart imitation.

A Brief History of Prediction

Humans have obsessed over predicting the future since early civilization. For a thousand years, around 8 BC, the ancient Greeks thronged the Oracle of Delphi to hear her predictions. Since then, prediction has bounced around among common sense, nonsense, and wishful thinking.[2] Prediction turned scientific only about three hundred years ago with the emergence of statistics in England, progressing more around World War II (1939–1945) than in the preceding two hundred years combined.[3]

The bread and butter of analytics is predictive models. You feed them data, and they can predict something you care about: a future baseball superstar, rain, a box-office hit, insurance pricing, spam, or which book you would like. They have always relied on historical data—a baseball player's slugging percentage, atmospheric pressure changes, analyzing scripts of previous hit movies, demographics, matching e-mail patterns to known spam, and analyzing customers' online behavior. The assumption was reasonable: humans are creatures of habit, so how they will behave will resemble how they have behaved.

Using data to predict the future worked well enough that firms began collecting more of it. Data that firms had was historically scattered across departmental silos, so firms created firm-wide IT systems to consolidate it. Such "enterprise" systems gave firms—for the first time—a coherent glimpse of their operations and their customers. Spreadsheets gave way to data warehouses, and predictive models increasingly became a reality check for managerial intuition. This led to a flurry of innovative practices in all functional areas. Firms could segment markets more finely, tier customers on their lifetime value, and forecast demand for a particular product on a particular day well enough to ensure enough stock. The moniker "business analytics" refers to this whole business of using data to predict what will happen. We define it as coupling data with statistical approaches to predict outcomes that your firm cares about.

Two Ingredients of Business Analytics: Data and Models

Business analytics needs two things: (a) sound data and (b) sound reasoning.

Sound Data

Data is the raw material of analytics. It is raw facts, which become *information* when they are sorted, condensed, and contextualized. *Insight*, or knowledge, is simply actionable information. For example, 24, 32, and 28 are data. Knowing that they are the low, high, and mean temperatures in Fahrenheit for your zip code tomorrow makes them information. Deciding then that you will need to wear a warm coat to work tomorrow is insight that you can act on.[4] The essence of analytics is doing this data→information→knowledge conversion to guide business decisions. If your firm can do this better than its archrivals, it has some insight that they do not. Your firm can gain an advantage over them. It is like being the Gordon Gekko of your industry without breaking laws.

Unreliable data produces untrustworthy insight—garbage in, garbage out. (A case in point is Donald Trump's unexpected election to the American presidency in 2016.)

Collecting, cleaning, organizing, and making data flow are largely the IT unit's job. However, not all data is worth managing better because not all information that it produces is competitively valuable. The market does not give out gold medals for collecting data. This is where you—the non-IT manager—must help your IT colleagues figure out what types of information are competitively valuable to your line function and how fast you need it. Without business input, IT units get better at collecting more data but without a clear business purpose. This makes a bad problem worse; troves of irrelevant data bog down business decisions. You will never find the proverbial needle in a haystack if you are searching in the wrong haystack.

Sound Reasoning

Insight does not emerge spontaneously from data without a lot of energy deliberately directed to transform it.[5] Software apps transform data into business insight. They are models translated into software code, so their predictions are only as good as the managerial insight in the underlying models. Their underlying reasoning is based on functional domain knowledge, which can come only from non-IT managers. For example, classifying a customer in a high-maintenance group requires a marketing manager's insight into what predicts membership in that group (e.g., purchase frequency, average order size, and returns history). Similarly, models in other functional areas require that line function's insight (e.g., fulfillment timeliness from operations, account delinquencies from accounting, demand-and-supply models from operations staff, and product pricing from senior management).

Turning raw data into actionable insight must begin with questions from you, without which your data will never progress beyond information. As a non-IT manager, you can help identify what business outcomes are competitively important to predict, within what time constraints, and which model you would use to predict

Box 2.1
Metadata: Data about Data

With the deluge of distributed data, the problem increasingly is knowing where to look for it. We need data about data: metadata. Your library's catalogs are metadata about the books on its shelves. The library catalog idea is a reincarnation of the clay tablets that the Assyrians used three thousand years ago. Each tablet had a little clay tablet attached to tell whether it was available on a shelf or in a basket. Tagging electronic information today is a form of metadata (think posts on Facebook or pictures on Pinterest).

them. Begin with just one business outcome that you believe could differentiate you from your archrivals (e.g., share of wallet).

Arrival of "Big" Data

The "big" in big data is not simply a magnification of volume but rather one qualitative difference: ephemeral data *streams* are supplanting data points.[6, 7] *Ephemeral* means that the data lasts for a very short time because its volume far exceeds our capacity to store it. If you do not use it within a brief moment, you lose it. *Streams* means that the data is continuously flowing as a series of data points. An instructive analogy is to think of data points as a lake and data streams as Niagara Falls. IT has historically been built to manage ever-growing data points (e.g., bigger data warehouses replaced databases) but not to cope with a continuous stream of data. Boat-rowing skills in a serene lake will not help you navigate Niagara Falls.

The digitization-infusion-ubiquity trifecta perpetuates these data streams. Firms now have data streams coming from instrumented, interconnected supply chains; mobile devices; Internet-connected things; and social media. The million transactions that Walmart handles every hour produce more than two hundred times the entire content of the Library of the Congress.[8] A Boeing 787 jet generates forty terabytes of data every hour in flight; it would take 2,500 iPhones to store it. Data exceeding the entire Library of Congress zips across international borders *every second*, contributing more to global growth than the trade of physical goods.[9] Most firms have more data than they know what to do with. They often fail to capitalize on the data that they already have. It is like having a hefty bank balance but no ATM card to access the money. Strategy—historically built around the assumption of information scarcity—must now be built around information abundance.[10] Abundance can be disorienting to managers who grew up with scarcity because it removes familiar trade-offs.[11]

Big data raises the bar for what constitutes a valuable insight. If your archrivals can extract and act on a valuable insight faster than you can, it is worth far less to rediscover it.

Unless you analyze data streams in near real time, the Red Queen effect will viciously victimize your firm.

Dusting Off Opportunities

Lumber companies historically treated sawdust as waste until someone figured out how to turn it into particleboard, synthetic wood, and snow traction material. This spawned entire new industries, with IKEA's $40 billion-a-year business at the helm. The sawdust of our era is data. Every time a piece of software runs, it generates data as a byproduct. The trail of clicks you leave behind is no longer a worthless byproduct but can be mined for insights to shape products and services, optimize operations, and develop new business models. Analytics is a baby step in repurposing historically wasted data to create business value. Big data is creating two types of opportunities for firms: (a) replacing prediction with foresight and (b) offering insight into what causes what.

a. *Foresight instead of prediction.* An entry-level iPhone in 2017 had the computing power of one hundred Cray supercomputers in the 1980s. Cheap computing power is shortening the lag between the arrival of data streams and their analysis. As this lag approaches zero, analytics is becoming so real-time that prediction appears to become foresight.[12]

Data streams from all sorts of connected devices—such as your phone or your car—also provide contextual data about where you are, where you have been, what you did a moment ago, and where you are going (called location analytics). This opens up unprecedented opportunities for real-time foresight into how your firm can create more market value. For example, it enables finer-grained microsegmentation of markets, dynamic pricing, and instantaneous price discrimination (i.e., changing the asking price to what you predict a particular customer will pay). The business challenge is imagining how to *consume* such foresight to deliver more value.

b. *Understanding causation.* Traditional analytics use correlation, which you know from your statistics coursework: two things move together beyond reasonable doubt. (Statistical significance indicates this.) You do not know what causes what and often do not care why. Walmart, for example, stocks up on diapers on Fridays because it knows that their sales correlate with beer sales on Friday nights. To exploit that insight, it need not know why.

The time-series nature of big data is advancing analytics from mere correlation toward the Holy Grail of prediction: causation. That is finding out what causes what. This makes insights gleaned from data more actionable because knowing what drives the outcomes that your firm cares about (e.g., sales, returns, customer loyalty, or increased spending) allows you to tweak things that cause them. It allows you to test business hypotheses by running little experiments to make your offering resonate better with your customers.

Born-digital firms such as Facebook, Amazon, and Google have used such experiments to refine the customer experience for decades. The digitization-infusion-ubiquity trifecta is opening up similar opportunities in other industries. Such opportunities most abound in information-intensive activities such as financial management, operations, supply chain management, marketing, customer service, and new product development.

Textbook strategy views managers as chess masters executing a master plan to sustain competitive advantage. In contrast, the analytics-driven strategy views competitive advantage as temporary and instead relies on baby steps driven by constant experimentation to keep one step ahead of rivals.[13]

Three Lenses for IT Strategy

To envision how IT can be used strategically, you must discern how information is affecting your entire industry and your own firm's place in it. This helps you judge what information is worth managing better. The three lenses in figure 2.1 *together* produce a sharp insight for formulating IT strategy. Each lens provides a different level of zoom (see table 2.1), so it clarifies a different aspect of the competitive landscape.

1. The *five-forces* lens—your telescope—zooms out to the level of your *industry*, helping you understand how IT is altering the rules of competition for every firm in your industry, including your archrivals.[14]

2. The *value-chain* lens—your magnifying glass—zooms in to compare your firm to its archrivals in how it creates value. It helps you recognize where your firm can use IT to reimagine how it earns its keep.

3. The *litmus-test* lens—your microscope—zooms in on an individual IT asset for whether it can offer a *sustainable* competitive advantage over your archrivals.

Lens #1: The Five-Forces Model

The crux of the five-forces model is that the fierceness of competition in your *industry* is driven by the bargaining power of your customers and suppliers, the threat of new entrants, and the threat that a substitute offering can meet your customers' needs.

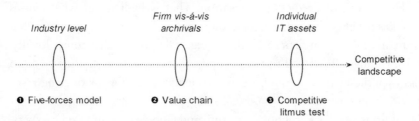

Figure 2.1
Three lenses for understanding how IT affects your firm's competitive landscape.

Table 2.1
The Three Lenses

	Lens	Level	Zoom level	What it clarifies
1	Five forces	Industry	Telescope	How IT alters your entire industry
2	Value chain	Your firm vis-à-vis archrivals	Magnifying glass	How your firm creates value vis-à-vis its archrivals
3	Litmus test	Individual IT assets	Microscope	How an IT asset creates and sustains a competitive advantage

(These forces appear as ↞ in figure 2.2.) You have likely used this model in your strategy course to analyze what makes *an industry* attractive or unattractive—defined as profit potential—to firms. Fiercer competition—by squeezing margins—can make even a high-growth industry unattractive to firms. The more powerful these forces become, the more firms will either pass on more value to customers or spend more on competing (e.g., on advertising, incentives, R&D, or customer service).[15]

Four Nuances
Keep in mind four nuances about the five-forces model before using it for analyzing IT strategy.

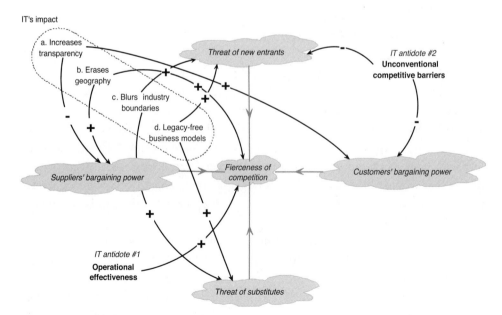

Figure 2.2
How IT affects the five forces (↞).

• It analyzes an *industry*, not an individual firm.
• *Bargaining power is about who has negotiating clout to force prices down.* The model captures the bargaining power of suppliers from which firms buy inputs and customers to which they sell. An increase in either suppliers' or customers' bargaining power erodes the margins of all firms in an industry.[16]
• *Substitutes rarely come from your own industry.* A substitute is an offering that meets the same customer need as your industry but in a different way. For example, Redbox is a substitute for Netflix; Uber for car ownership; and Pandora for FM radio. The mere *threat* of a substitute caps prices that firms in an industry can dare to charge, especially when buyers incur low costs to switch to it. The trifecta makes IT a breeding ground for hard-to-anticipate substitutes.
• *All it takes is the* threat *of new entrants.* Low entry barriers—hurdles that an industry newcomer must surmount—lower an industry's profitability. The *threat* alone caps the prices you can charge and raises costs. (Raising prices would make the industry more attractive to new entrants, and firms must spend more on existing customers to discourage entry.) Traditional strategy texts emphasize brute-force entry barriers such as initial capital outlays (e.g., $10 billion "fabs" in the microchip business) or unique intellectual property (e.g., patents). IT instead allows erecting of unconventional competitive barriers.

Before you continue, pencil the names of your industry's major suppliers, substitutes, and archrivals into figure 2.2.

The Five Forces Matter Because They Drive an Industry's Margins
The five forces matter because they shape an *industry's* margins. A successful business delivers something valued by its customers at a price they are willing to pay.[17] To survive, its costs must be less than this price. The essence of competition then is a tug-of-war over who keeps the value that your industry creates.[18] This tussle is not just with your rivals but also with your customers, suppliers, and substitutes' producers that would all be happy to get a larger share. Competitive advantage, boiled to its essence, is then widening—*more than your archrivals*—the gap between your costs and what your customers pay.[19]

Margins—the difference between a dollar earned and the costs to earn it—are an objective indicator of value created by an industry.[20] (I call it "margins" throughout this book simply because the word "profit" carries tremendous cultural baggage.) Competition guarantees that firms will *eventually* pass on any increase in their margins to consumers as lower prices or better products and services. Historical data confirms that the price of commoditized goods overall has been decreasing about 1 percent a year for the past 140 years running.[21] This means that goods that Thomas Jefferson paid one hundred dollars for in the 1780s now cost you sixteen dollars. Until competition forces you to pass along these margins, you can reinvest them in your business as R&D funding and employee benefits, bonuses, and raises.

Margins are your firm's oxygen supply; it cannot survive without them.[22] Being competitive then is having *enough* margins to keep going. The goal is sustainability, not profiteering and not painful-sounding "rent extraction" that economists love. Being the best, customer loyalty, or revenue growth are merely pathways to acceptable margins, not an end in themselves.[23] What is considered a healthy margin depends on your industry and on your firm's revenues (higher revenues make lower margins sustainable). Even a nonprofit needs a surplus to invest in its future. For nonprofits, better margins mean achieving more of their social goals per dollar spent. For government agencies, better margins mean delivering more for its citizens' tax dollars. The real test for whether you have a competitive advantage is if your margins are consistently better than your archrivals.[24] Ignore your margins and you are postponing your day of reckoning.

Margins are simply what your customers pay minus what you spend producing a market offering (figure 2.3). This means that there are only two ways to improve margins, increasing what your customers are willing to pay or reducing your costs. As figure 2.3 shows, the more powerful any of the five forces become, the more they increase your costs or lower what you can charge.[25] More customer power, new entrants, and substitutes put downward pressure on prices by capping what you can

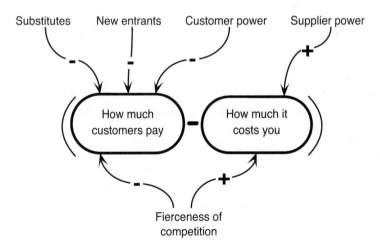

Figure 2.3
Every competitive force affects your costs or how much you can charge.

Box 2.2
How Will Self-Driving Cars Remake the Insurance Industry?

Human mistakes cause 90 percent of all auto accidents. As software-controlled self-driving cars go mainstream, analysts expect accidents to drop by 80 percent and the insurance industry to shrink by 60 percent.[26] The shrunk industry will become less profitable because lower risks means lower premiums. It might even make car ownership less widespread, shifting the insurance market from individuals to fleet operators and automakers. Yet new threats such as car hacking open new opportunities for IT-savvy insurance firms even as the old doors close.

charge. Supplier power increases your costs, and fierceness of competition in your industry hurts both.

How IT Impacts the Five Forces

Let us take a step further by asking how IT can alter each of the five forces. Overall, IT weakens *industry* margins but benefits consumers by intensifying competition. Many once-flourishing firms have floundered because they failed to grasp how IT was reconfiguring their entire industry. IT can make an attractive industry unattractive or an unattractive one attractive. The antidote also comes from cleverly using IT—like a vaccine extracted from an illness-causing microbe—to counteract IT's influence on each force.

This lens's analytical value for IT strategy is helping discern how IT affects your entire industry and the IT portfolio you need to remain viable in it.[27]

Figure 2.4 summarizes the six ways in which IT impacts the fierceness of competition within an industry, only the last two of which are under the direct control of managers.

a. *IT increases transparency.* The Internet has increased the transparency of suppliers' costs for firms and of market prices for customers. For example, firms can more readily compare prices offered by rival suppliers just as you can compare prices charged by rival firms for a car or airfares. Similarly, price comparison tools on smartphones (e.g., Amazon Price Check) can allow consumers to instantaneously scan barcodes of products in a store to check rivals' and online prices.[28] Such transparency reduces suppliers' bargaining power over firms that buy from them but simultaneously increases customers' bargaining power over firms in an industry. If the product exposed to such transparency is a commodity, it can turn a retailer's physical store into a showroom for its online rivals. Physical retailers can also strike

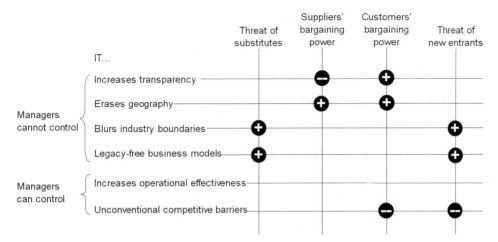

Figure 2.4
How IT alters an industry.

back by turning online rivals into collectors of reviews that help them sell products in-store.

b. *IT can erase geographical constraints.* Consumer access to a broader array of sellers increases the fierceness of competition in an industry.[29, 30] For example, your access to a dozen sellers willing to sell you this book on Amazon intensifies how low they are willing to go to be the one that sells it to you. In an excitement about reaching a larger market through the Internet, it is easy to overlook that fiercer competition can make an entire industry unprofitable. A huge market in which you lose money on every customer is unattractive, and there is no prize for being the leader in an unprofitable industry. IT also increases suppliers' bargaining power because they have more downstream firms to sell to, and potentially even directly to end customers.

c. *IT can blur industry boundaries.* The trifecta is causing a growing variety of previously independent industries to converge. Offerings from an *unrelated* industry can meet a need for your industry's core customers, increasing the threat of substitutes.[31] For example, Skype-like services substitute long-distance telephony, smartphone apps substitute photocopiers, and smartphones substitute cameras and wristwatches. Such substitution respectively wiped out once-profitable businesses run by AT&T, Canon, Kodak, and Timex.

d. *IT can enable legacy-free business models.* IT can lower conventional entry barriers such as the capital needed to enter an industry, thus enabling business models without the legacy burdens of incumbent firms (e.g., stores, sales channels, and a salesforce). This happens by substituting something costly—by tweaking a dimension of the digitization cube—that was previously needed to enter an industry. For example, Redbox's automated, Internet-enabled kiosks allowed it to meet the needs of video rental customers without the need for thousands of stores and employees. Redbox's model allowed it to charge one-fourth the price of other incumbents and, coupled with Netflix's flat-rate all-you-can-eat service, bankrupted industry leaders Blockbuster and Hollywood Video. Therefore, IT-enabled business models that shed an industry's legacy assets increase the threat of new entrants and of substitutes. IT is therefore a major catalyst for entrepreneurship.

Unlike these four industry-wide impacts that managers in an incumbent firm cannot control, they can control the last two. IT's strategic potential for existing firms boils down to these two antidotes in figure 2.2.

e. *Increased operational effectiveness.* IT can extract more productivity out of existing assets, raising the industry-wide floor for efficiency. This approach either substitutes human labor with technology or inventory with information. IT's strategic potential is in doing things better (operational effectiveness) or doing things differently (decommoditizing offerings to escape price competition). The first approach erodes margins by intensifying competition, accelerating a costly race to the bottom. For example, the US mass-retail market has profit margins of 3–4 percent, the PC business 2 percent, and online retailers (e.g., Amazon) 0.5 percent. Price competition—the worst form of rivalry—is rarely sustainable when archrivals' offerings are undifferentiated and customers' switching costs are low (e.g., with PCs, Android phones, and airlines).[32] The alternative—discussed in later chapters—is to use IT to decommoditize commodity offerings. (For example, Apple has differentiated its offerings enough so they no longer are interchangeable with its rivals' offerings.)

f. *IT enables unconventional competitive barriers.* IT enables erecting two unconventional competitive barriers that simply do not have counterparts in the industrial age. These create *value-adding*, noncoercive forms of lock-ins that simultaneously reduce customers' bargaining power and discourage new entrants. The first are *network effects* (a.k.a. the *Facebook effect*), which mean that every new customer increases the value of a product or service for all *existing* customers.[33] Customers' willingness to patronize a firm's offering therefore increases with the number of others who also patronize it. For example, each new Facebook account increases Facebook's attractiveness for all existing Facebook users. A new rival such as Google Plus would have to be so superior that Facebook's users would be willing to forego their Facebook network to switch to it. The high costs of switching away from

Facebook to a competing offering creates a formidable barrier for Facebook's rivals. The cycle voraciously feeds on itself to strengthen Facebook's lock on the market.

Such network effects shelter eBay (more sellers attract more buyers, and vice versa), Apple's iMessage platform, Uber, and Skype (more existing users attract more new users) from competition. Even Netflix exploits it; better data-driven movie recommendations increase watching, which in turn improves recommendations. Network effects discourage new rivals by making customers less willing to patronize them and by discounting what a newcomer without network effects can charge. However, network effects offer protection only when they are proprietary to your firm and not transferable elsewhere.[34] Such network effects are hard to initially create, difficult to dislodge, and have historically been restricted to software-based services. The trifecta—particularly the infusion of software into nontechnology products—is opening opportunities to create network effects in nonsoftware industries.

The second competitive barrier is analytics-driven customization, which means that a firm uses IT to develop deep insight into a customer's needs in ways that she values enough to make rivals' offerings unattractive. Netflix, for example, has successfully used deep customization to withstand assaults from well-heeled, lower-priced rivals such as Amazon's video streaming service. Deep customization involving "more like this" recommendations accounted for more than $30 billion of Amazon's annual revenue, making it more difficult for new entrants to gain a foothold.[35]

Deep customization combines proprietary data with proprietary apps to create enough value for the customer that she would not *want* to switch to a rival offering,

Box 2.3
How Uber Creates a Market for Underutilized Assets

A typical car is used 5 percent of its lifetime and at about 20 percent of its capacity.[36] That translates to about 2 percent productivity in an industry that was about 4 percent of the US GDP in 2016. Uber and its kin attempt to match idle cars to unmet demand for transportation, essentially squeezing more productivity out of underproductive assets. (Uber gets a 20 percent cut.) Its fares are dynamic, usually undercutting taxis but rising when demand goes up.[37] The rising pricing increases supply of Uber drivers precisely when demand goes up, elegantly matching supply and demand.[38] Uber's long-term competition is not with taxis but rather with car ownership. Airbnb and its like are replicating the Uber idea in the rental apartment and hotel market, matching users needing accommodations with homeowners with a room to spare. These so-called sharing economy platforms are wringing untapped productivity out of existing capital assets, making both parties in the exchange better off.

effectively increasing customers' willingness to pay more. The trifecta is now making such deep customization possible in other industries as well. John Deere, for example, can modify the horsepower of an engine already sold to a customer using software alone, resulting in more cost-effective tailoring and in situ engine upgrades. Industry-wide use of such IT-based competitive barriers simultaneously discourages new entrants and reduces customers' bargaining power.

Lens #2: Value Chains

Strategy is fundamentally about how *a firm* will deliver more value—than its archrivals—to an explicitly defined set of customers.[39] Creating value—making your firm's outputs worth more than its inputs—better than your archrivals is how you outperform them. A firm's value chain is a lens for understanding how.

A *value chain* is a series of linked activities that your firm performs, each of which ideally adds value that your customers are prepared to pay for. Think of a firm's value chain as the prevailing business model. Primary activities—shown as a generic value chain in figure 2.5—are a firm's bread-and-butter activities that create a product or service. They involve *inbound logistics* for getting raw materials, *operations* that convert them into finished products or services, *outbound logistics* for getting them to customers, *marketing* to them (e.g., pricing and promotion), and after-sales *service*. The first three activities fall under the umbrella of supply management and the last two under demand management. Secondary activities support these primary activities. They include *procuring* inputs, managing *human resources* (e.g., hiring, training, compensating), and building *infrastructure* such as accounting, financing, legal, public relations, and quality management. Each activity in a value chain can involve multiple line functions, which is why we say that a firm's business processes crosscut functions. Information technology has historically been bundled into secondary activities but should no longer be, as it has evolved into the glue that undergirds and links firms' primary activities.

A firm's value chain is part of a larger stream of value chains involving other firms, who have their own value chains. This is a firm's *value stream* (figure 2.6), which spans the entirety of the value-creation process, from getting raw materials to reaching the final consumer. (Some call this a value system; this book sticks to the more intuitive value stream.) If one firm owns the entire figure 2.6, it is called *vertically integrated*. Therefore, a value chain describes only the firm, but a value stream encompasses its partner firms. (Supply chain management is the operational representation of the flow of materials, information, and money in a value stream.)

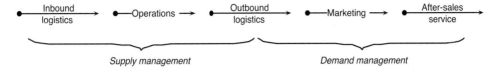

Figure 2.5
Primary activities in a firm's generic value chain.

Whenever you hear the word "enterprise" in IT discussions, it is usually referring to the firm and its constellation of upstream and downstream partners in figure 2.6. Larger constellations such as iOS and its 250,000 app developers are called business ecosystems.[40, 41, 42] Think of these simply as ginormous value streams.

The activities in a value chain are the building blocks of strategy. They are *the* source of all costs and the basis of all differentiation. Therefore, differences in your firm's costs and differentiation relative to your archrivals come from *how* they do the activities in each step in their value chain. It is at this level alone—not in the firm as a whole—that competitive advantage is created.[44] The value chains of most firms with the same strategic aspiration in an industry have comparable structures.

For your firm to earn margins, what its value chain produces must be worth more than the cost of producing it. To achieve competitive advantage, your firm must perform the same activities cheaper or it must perform them better *than its archrivals*. It must tailor its value chain to its own strategic aspiration—being cheap or different. IT is instrumental to such tailoring.

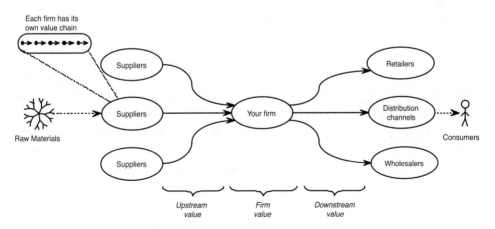

Figure 2.6
A value stream is a collection of value chains of multiple firms.

Box 2.4
Value Chains Also Apply to Services Firms and Nonprofits

Although the value chain concept originated in manufacturing firms, the idea readily applies to both service firms and nonprofits.[43] Figure 2.7 translates the value chain idea in figure 2.5 to such organizations. The corresponding series of activities to which a service firm adds value are problem recognition, project and process management to solve it, solutions delivery, customer relationship management, and postdelivery support. For nonprofits, the corresponding activities are recruitment of talent and fundraising, problem solving to address the focal social challenge, execution of the solution, outreach to secure commitment from the relevant stakeholders, and the evaluation of outcomes. The secondary activities in both service and nonprofit value chains resemble manufacturing.

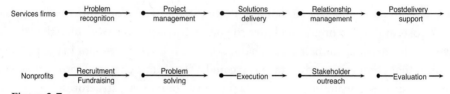

Figure 2.7
Value chain concepts that originated in manufacturing also apply to services firms and to nonprofit organizations.

You can contribute by first sketching the value chain and value stream for your own firm next to your archrivals. Zero in first on the biggest cost drivers. Do these activities matter to your customers? In which step are they underserved or overserved? What would happen if you scaled back an activity where they are overserved or invested more into one where they are underserved? Your answers are a stepping-stone to IT investments.

How IT Can Transform a Firm's Value Chain
The potential for using IT to transform a value chain comes entirely from one property: Value chains are information intensive. Every primary activity in a value chain has a physical component and an information component. Therefore, every step in figure 2.5 both uses and produces some kind of information. This information component is higher in some industries (e.g., airlines, finance, consulting, and software) and lower in others (e.g., manufacturing). The trifecta is increasing the information component in industries where it was historically low.

IT can transform a value chain in one of two places: (1) the content of individual steps and (2) their linkages (see figure 2.8).

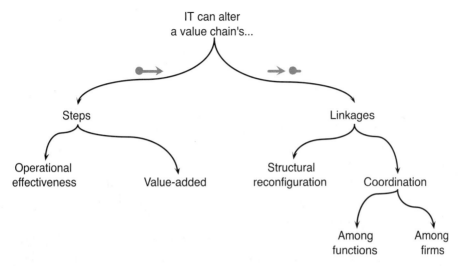

Figure 2.8
Two approaches for using IT to transform a firm's value chain.

Transforming One Step in a Value Chain

You can use IT to transform how your firm does one discrete step in its value chain either (a) by lowering costs or (b) by increasing value-added in it.

a. Lowering costs. Recall from your managerial accounting coursework that costs arise from unsold inventory sitting somewhere, running out of products that customers want, lengthy supply chains, under- or overpricing offerings, serving unprofitable customers, and service and support expenses. We can map these sources of costs back to the individual steps in figure 2.5. This approach uses IT to increase operational effectiveness, which is doing the same things as your archrivals but better. The emphasis is on squeezing more productivity out of your existing people and assets

Box 2.5
Pie-Wrangling versus Pie-Expanding Mind-Sets

A firm can approach competition with an efficiency-seeking *red-ocean* mind-set or a value-creating *blue-ocean* mind-set, which respectively are pie-wrangling and pie-expanding forms of competition. A firm with a pie-wrangling mind-set gains by taking value away from someone else in its value stream. It focuses on finding new ways to serve existing customers better than archrivals. This zero-sum form of "I win, you lose" competition dominates most industries. A pie-expanding mind-set alters the rules of competition to create new demand in underserved pockets of the market.[45]

(e.g., airplanes owned by an airline). When strategy pundits speak of execution, they are emphasizing operational effectiveness. IT can facilitate this by automating rote activities and improving one step of your value chain. For example, online ordering, automated notifications, self-checkouts in retail stores, and customer self-service tools substitute costlier human labor.

Table 2.2 shows examples of firms that have lowered costs using IT to transform just *one* such step in their value chain.[46] Walmart, for example, uses IT to reduce in-store inventory, credit card issuer Capital One to predict customers most likely to be profitable in the future, Amazon to match products that a customer is most likely to buy, Delta Airlines and Marriott hotels to price fares/hotel rooms to improve profitably, and Honda to preempt quality mishaps. IT can also help lower the costs of performing secondary activities.

b. Increasing value-added. A second way to transform the content of any *one* step in figure 2.5 is by using IT to increase the value that your firm adds to it. This produces a more differentiated offering for which customers might be willing to pay you more than to your archrivals. Consider some examples in each step, as summarized in table 2.3.

• *Inbound logistics.* The largest global auction center for fresh flowers is Royal FloraHolland in Aalsmeer, outside Amsterdam in Holland (www.floraholland.com). More than 50 percent of the world's flowers are traded there, making it 5 percent of Holland's gross domestic product (GDP).[47] (That is a larger percentage than what

Table 2.2
Examples of Firms Using IT to Lower Costs in One Step in Their Value Chain

Value chain step	Activity	How IT is used to enhance a primary activity	Example
Inbound logistics	Supply chain	Minimize stock outs and reduce inventory	Walmart, 7-Eleven
Operations	Supply chain	Matching supply with demand	Peeps (Just Born Inc.)
Outbound logistics	Supply chain	Direct global delivery from manufacturing partner to buyer	Apple and UPS
Sales	Marketing	Identify customers who will be most profitable	Caesars, Capital One
	Sales	Match products with customers most likely to buy them	Amazon
	Pricing	Price to sell most profitably	Progressive, Marriott, Delta
Service	Quality	Minimize quality problems	Honda

the auto industry adds to the US GDP.) Dutch inspectors grade flowers as they are cut in various countries and enter ratings in an online system. Increasingly, growers supply digital photos and data on length, health, and size of flowers. Licensed whole-sale bidders on the trading floor in Holland—and increasingly online—often finish bidding on lots even before the planes transporting the flowers from South America, Africa, and Europe touch down. This buyer-trusted, IT-driven approach differenti-ates it from rivals by guaranteeing the freshest flowers, which have a short shelf life within which they must be retailed (typically in North America, Europe, or Japan). Forty percent of tulips are estimated to be sold even before they are harvested.

• *Operations*. Insurance provider Progressive installs wireless monitoring devices in insured vehicles, which allows it to reduce insurance premiums to reward actual driver behavior rather than the industry's norm of pricing insurance using demo-graphic and historical factors. This created a new line of business in its existing industry by profitably insuring customers that its rivals considered too risky to touch. Similarly, Great Clips (an American barbershop chain) allows customers to join a

Table 2.3
Examples of Firms Using IT to Increase Value Added in One Step of Their Value Chain

Step	How IT is used to increase value-added
Inbound logistics	Dutch flower market inspectors grade flowers electronically, and an electronic bidding system allows entire planeloads of freshly cut flowers to be sold before touchdown
Operations	• Progressive Insurance uses in-car sensor data to price insurance premiums • Great Clips' virtual queue on its smartphone application eliminates in-store wait times • Site-to-store ordering systems used by many retailers
Outbound logistics	7–Eleven Japan uses weather predictions to determine an optimal mix of hot and cold noodles replenished across nineteen thousand stores three times a day
Marketing	• Starbucks uses card usage patterns for prospecting store locations • Japanese drink vending machines use dynamic pricing; prices change with weather • Caesars Casinos uses IT to identify potentially more profitable customers better than archrivals • Luxury shoemaker Ferragamo embeds electronic chips in its shoes to fight counterfeiters
Service	• Samsung remotely troubleshoots and diagnoses its Internet-connected washer and dryer appliances • Online support communities driven by Apple's own customers reduce problem resolution times and support costs

haircut queue using their smartphone, eliminating wait time at the store. Many retailers use site-to-store ordering systems to allow customers to preorder an item for immediate pickup, differentiating them from their online rivals.

• *Outbound logistics*. Ready-made hot (*Udon*) and cold (*Soba*) noodles are a staple Japanese lunch food whose demand varies with weather. 7–Eleven Japan integrates weather predictions to decide what mix of the two to deliver to each of its nineteen thousand stores three times a day. Accurate demand forecasting gives it one of the highest inventory turnover of any existing firm in any industry.

• *Marketing*. IT-based analytics used by marketers enable precision targeting, dynamic pricing, and behavioral insights into your customers. Even food trucks in New York City now use social media to communicate the truck's current location. (See, for example, www.treatstruck.com.) Starbucks uses card usage patterns of its regular customers to identify promising locations for new stores. Coke's Internet-connected vending machines in Japan dynamically change drink prices. (Cold canned drinks decrease in price if it is cold outside and hot canned coffee when it is hot outside.) Similarly, luxury brands that have long suffered from authentic-looking counterfeits are using IT to fight back. Italian luxury shoemaker Ferragamo embeds a chip in its shoes. When an electronic interrogator device is brought near it, only an authentic shoe can send back a correct response.[48]

• *Service*. Samsung connects its home appliances to the Internet to remotely diagnose problems before dispatching a service technician with exactly the right parts, reducing warranty repair delays and costs. Similarly, many firms such as Apple host online communities to have users of its products help each other solve technical problems. This speeds up problem resolution and lowers Apple's support costs.

Firms in these examples use IT to differentiate *just one value chain step* that matters enough to customers that it increases their willingness to patronize the firm over its archrivals. Once imitated, it becomes a consumer expectation rather than a differentiator. Analytics enables discovering previously unobvious for how firms can tweak each step in their value chain.

Linkages between Steps in a Value Chain
You can also use IT to transform the *linkages* by (1) "disintermediating" firms from your value stream or (2) coordinating steps within your firm's value chain, as well as with firms upstream and downstream in your value stream.

    1. *Disintermediation* uses IT to bypass entire sets of firms in a value stream (see figure 2.9). This can eliminate unnecessary costs and dated assumptions of legacy industry structures to leave more of the pie on the table.[50, 51] When you hear the

phrase "business model innovation," it almost always means using IT to alter the structure of an existing value stream. For example, the publishing industry had a 50 percent margin on a typical book split among wholesalers, distributors, and retailers. Figure 2.9(a) shows how the margins for a one-hundred-dollar book were historically split among firms in the publishing industry. Amazon used IT to alter this structure by bypassing all firms between publishers and the book buyer by passing orders directly to publishers (figure 2.9[b]). It then passed on most of the savings to consumers, who were happy to pay 30 percent less. This involved digitization of just one dimension—the purchase process—in the digitization cube in chapter 1.

This model of cutting out middlemen has been successfully replicated in many industries such as auto retail (e.g., TrueCar), banking, real estate (e.g., Trulia), airlines, car rental (e.g., Uber), and apparel. Disintermediation weeds out firms that no longer add meaningful value, making value streams more efficient. Firms such as Amazon are taking disintermediation a step further using platforms such as Kindle Direct books and its own TV studio to eliminate book publishers and movie studios

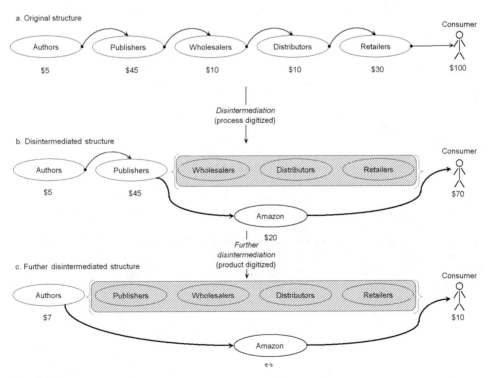

Figure 2.9
Disintermediation uses IT to reconfigure a value stream.

from its value stream. This involves digitization of a different dimension of the digitization cube, the product itself. As figure 2.9(c) shows, this *can* dramatically lower prices and increase Amazon's margins. Netflix similarly vertically integrated from being a distributor of Hollywood movies to making them. (Its $6 billion production budget for 2016 was three times larger than HBO.) The question that non-IT managers must ask is whether their own firm adds enough value to survive disintermediation from their own value stream.

Box 2.6
How IT Turned Caesars Casinos from Vegas's Ugly Duckling to Its Envy

The casino business in Las Vegas long believed in the power of "whales"—rich gamblers that it coveted. The entire industry was built on this premise. First, you have to get a gambler into your casino. So Vegas casinos redefined extravagance. One built a volcano, another a burning pirate ship show, a half-scale Eiffel Tower, a Venetian canals replication with Italian-singing gondoliers, and even a Madame Tussauds wax museum. Then there was poor Caesars Casino (then Harrah's) that could not afford to match these big-budget attractions, some costing several hundred million dollars. It had always been an also-ran.

Its fortunes changed when its CEO Phil Satre met thirty-seven-year-old Harvard professor Gary Loveman in 1998. Loveman had never been to a casino before, so he approached Caesars with a research project idea. Loveman decided to track and analyze the data collected by Caesars gaming machines. It signed up customers for a loyalty card (a simple magnetic stripe card), which they would insert into a slot machine before they played. Loveman then analyzed data on how many machines a customer played, how many separate wagers she placed, her average bet, and the total amount of "coin-in" money spent during a visit. It combined this data with age, gender, and zip code to construct a detailed profit-and-loss prediction that would help Caesars gauge its future investment in each customer. If Caesars's predictive model said that a customer was financially attractive, Caesars started mailing her customized inducements—a free steak, a free show, or a free hotel room for a night—to not spend her money at rival casinos. At its height, it sent out 250 million mailings a year. (The system was built using purchased, off-the-shelf pieces.)

When Caesars built a profile of its ideal customer—the type that generated almost all its profits—it was flabbergasted.[49] The ideal customer was a sixty-two-year-old grandma living thirty minutes away, who liked to play dollar video poker slot machines. It found that 80 percent of its revenues and almost 100 percent of its profits came from 30 percent of its customers that spent between one hundred dollars and five hundred dollars per visit. It was not the whales that its industry coveted. Caesars then started ignoring the whales and lavishing the retired old ladies, growing revenues by $100 million in two years. The system—utterly invisible to customers—then used every scrap of information it could muster to continuously refine each customer's profile. It used every swipe of a customer's loyalty card to confirm or disconfirm what Caesars

Box 2.6 (*continued*)

believed about that customer. (Fifteen years later, we call this business hypothesis testing.) Gary Loveman then quit Harvard and went on to be Caesars's CEO for twelve years, turning it into the envy of its industry. The genius was in how Caesars used commodity IT synced with its operational strategy to change how casinos compete. By the time its archrivals took notice, they were already behind in the Red Queen race. It took them about ten years to catch up, and when they did, Caesars's differentiating innovation became its industry's new norm. It filed for bankruptcy in 2015.

Non-IT managers can sometimes successfully adopt IT innovations from other industries in theirs. Over a decade later, American electronics retailer Best Buy did just that. When it found that less than 10 percent of its customers accounted for half its sales, it reorganized its stores to focus on those customers' needs. After Best Buy, Staples (an American office supply store chain) adapted Caesars's IT strategy. Staples found—counterintuitively—that it made less profits from high-margin furniture and computers than it did from inexpensive highlighters and legal pads. This led it to reallocate underproductive floor space to office supplies, leading to a multiyear streak of growth.

Using IT to Improve Coordination in Value Chains and Value Streams

a. Coordination across steps within a firm's value chain. As firms grow, departmental specialization isolates line functions into little fiefdoms. Yet because business processes crosscut line functions, there is enormous value in better coordinating to manage the dependencies among value chain steps.[52, 53] For example, marketing and service activities can be more effective if a product is built with them in mind. IT systems, particularly enterprise resource planning (ERP)–type systems that connect disparate parts of a firm that rarely communicated with each other, overlay a digital connective tissue into a firm. This can create a wholesome view of the firm that previously never existed.[54]

b. Coordination across a firm's value stream. IT can also enhance your firm's coordination with the upstream firms that supply your inputs and downstream firms that use your outputs (e.g., sales channels or retailers). IT coordinates a value stream primarily by aligning supply and demand. The idea is to produce enough of what customers will buy and less of what they will not. It mitigates two leading culprits that erode margins: stockouts of popular merchandise (firms leave money on the table) and unsold inventory (firms can lose money by discounting unsold merchandise).

To accomplish this, supply-related activities must be coordinated with demand-related activities in figure 2.5 and respectively with the upstream and downstream parts of a firm's value stream (the left and right sides of figure 2.6). IT can facilitate this by (i) substituting information for inventory and (ii) using analytics to anticipate changes in demand.

Box 2.7
Raising London's Heathrow Airport's Productivity Using IT

London's Heathrow airport is Europe's busiest airport, shuttling about seventy million passengers a year. It runs at 98 percent capacity, with flight takeoffs and landings every forty-five seconds from 5 a.m. to 11 p.m. Geographic constraints restrict its ability to physically grow, so the airport relies heavily on IT to handle more passengers without physically expanding the airport. The guinea pig was its new Terminal 2, opened in 2014. An IT portfolio with an integrated set of IT apps coordinates eighty-four airlines, their maintenance crew, baggage handling, passport control, caterers, and air traffic control.

The project's goal was increasing throughput. This, it believed, would give it an edge over other European airports for airlines to use as an efficient connection hub. The project was conceived as using IT to link steps in the airport's value stream. Beginning with a luggage drop-off process designed to take no more than seventy seconds, all the way to automated security gates and self-boarding gates, IT underpins the entire flyer experience. To ensure that everything worked robustly, it decided to use only proven technology. Attempting a novel way of linking its value stream with untested technology was too much novelty to mix well. It created a model terminal—a massive test bed to develop, test, and work out kinks before rolling it out into the real terminal. However, even the most rigorously tested technology can have undetected bugs that surface only after it goes live. So Heathrow did a phased rollout to just 10 percent of Terminal 2's operations. It then gradually scaled it to the rest of the terminal. This rollout was the foundation for future innovations such as using passenger biometrics to fully automate check-in processes and using video surveillance data to dynamically disperse areas before they became too crowded. This project illustrates how IT investments focused on a single unifying objective—here, increasing throughput—can improve the productivity of assets that an organization already owns. In Heathrow's case, it was done by using IT to integrate steps across the airport's value stream with just one goal: increasing throughput.

i. Substituting inventory with information. A typical Walmart store might sell two hundred thousand unique items; it must hold enough inventory for each item in each store. As you know from your accounting coursework, holding inventory is costly. IT can allow you to substitute physical inventory with information about it, slashing inventory holding costs. Walmart, for example, uses IT to connect its store-level IT systems directly to its suppliers. A supplier such as Gillette can track how many units—of, say, disposable razors—are on the shelves in each store and predict exactly when they are likely to sell out. Walmart makes these suppliers responsible for monitoring store-level inventory of their products and to replenish it just in time before it sells out. Such electronic coordination can be a win-win for the firm as well as its suppliers in managing inventory and forecasting production volume and mix.

Box 2.8
Enterprise Systems and Their Strategic Casualty

ERP systems are the IT industry's attempt at providing firms an IT portfolio-in-a-box. ERP systems are large, multimillion dollar firm-wide systems that include a diverse variety of ready-made IT apps that your firm can pick and choose. They can include accounting apps (e.g., a general ledger, account tracking, and billing), operations apps (e.g., supply chain management, inventory management, logistics, and shipping), customer relationship management apps, human resources apps (e.g., payroll), and production management apps. Their selling point is that if your firm buys each of these apps from the same ERP software producer, they are guaranteed to work with each other. They usually do, yet a staggering number of ERP-implementation projects fail because of problems integrating them with firms' other preexisting IT assets. In theory, they instantly enhance coordination across a firm's value chain. In practice, they increase homogeneity among rival firms.

Their strategic downside is twofold: (a) your firm's business processes become undifferentiated clones of other rivals who also purchased the same ERP systems and (b) you must modify your existing business processes to match what is preprogrammed into the ERP software. (Firms selling such software must make it generic enough to appeal to many corporate buyers.) Customizing them to your firm's business processes is limited to a menu of choices. It is like picking options in a car at a showroom, unlike custom-built apps that build a car from scratch. Costs of such customization and integration with your firm's existing IT systems can vastly exceed the cost of the software. Even though you can somewhat customize them to how your firm does things, they often require your firm to adjust its business processes to fit the "best practice" processes hardwired into them. The strategic penalty of this forced adjust-to-the-system approach is that the way your firm does things matches your rivals using the same software. Differentiation in business processes is therefore often their first casualty. The end result: streamlining of business processes but an annihilation of any differentiation in how your firm does things. ERP systems causing such competitive convergence and wiping out competitive differentiation is rarely problematic for nonprofits and government agencies.

(IoT devices are replicating this idea of semiautomated replenishment at the level of individual customers.[55])

Substituting information for inventory has also propelled new firms to the forefront of many other industries. This includes the world's largest taxi service (Uber, which hardly owns vehicles), accommodation provider (Airbnb, which owns no real estate), and media company (Facebook, which creates no content).[56]

ii. Anticipating shifts in demand. IT-enabled analytics can also give insight into what products are most likely to sell and in what quantities. Unlike static demand forecasting that has historically dominated most industries, firms can now anticipate changes in demand patterns in real time. Greater connectivity with downstream channels (e.g., retail stores) is the source of such data, and sharing it with upstream firms in your value stream can allow your market offerings to stay one step ahead of shifts in market demand.

Lens #3: The Competitive Litmus Test

Being competitive is one thing, but staying competitive is another. The *competitive litmus test* in figure 2.11 helps judge whether a discrete IT asset—a specific app, infrastructure element, or data asset—can produce a *sustainable* competitive advantage. What it takes to create a competitive advantage using an IT asset is different from what sustains it. To create a competitive advantage, an IT asset must be *valuable* in your industry and *rare* among your archrivals. To sustain a competitive advantage after you have successfully created one, your archrivals must not be able to copy it (*inimitable*) nor achieve the same ends differently (*nonsubstitutable*). An

Box 2.9
Using IT to Match Supply and Demand for Peeps, Flowers, and Pizza

Around the first Monday of each September (Labor Day in the United States), American candy manufacturer Just Born begins gearing up for its make-or-break sale season, Easter. Its best-selling candy is a little marshmallow candy called Peeps. Ever since Russian-born confectioner Sam Born opened his small candy store in Brooklyn, New York, in 1917, Peeps have been a staple of American culture. Two billion Peeps are sold in a year, mostly around Easter.[57] Just Born forecasts sales each year to buy massive quantities of corn syrup, gelatin, flavoring, food coloring, and packaging materials. And every year, it would either not produce enough to meet demand or end up with tons of unused raw materials. Just Born relied on historical sales data for its forecasts, but the data was always error prone. Some came from its salespeople but most from supermarkets, grocery stores, and independent stores that had little incentive to collect it.[58] Poor quality data could not produce trustworthy insight. Any business that has seasonal demand and a perishable product shares Peeps' problems. Pizza chains, for example, see around a 50 percent spike on Super Bowl Sunday and another spike on snowy days. Flower orders at ProFlowers grow more than twentyfold on Mother's Day week and Valentine's Day.

The solution is using IT to link the supply side of your firm's value stream to the demand side. It creates an information flow in a direction opposite to the physical flow of goods. It means getting data from your downstream partners' IT systems (e.g., point-of-sale scanners) in real time to adjust raw materials orders to your suppliers. This is the essence of IT-driven supply chain management.

Although the Internet has dropped the cost of connectivity between Just Born's IT systems and its partners' IT systems to near zero, the cost of getting various firms' disparate, proprietary systems to talk is not trivial. Firms are also protective about their

Box 2.9 (*continued*)

data. So your firm, like Just Born, must offer your value stream partners a compelling reason to invest in such connectivity and to share proprietary data (e.g., sharing of cost savings or a credible promise to increase revenues). This requires trust.

In Just Born's case, new IT investments created upstream information flows (figure 2.10). The ability to see actual sales allowed it to dynamically adjust its raw materials orders and production to reduce unsold Peeps and stockouts. The result is visible right after Easter, when fewer markdowns of unsold Peeps are now seen than a decade ago. This initiative eventually became the foundation of Just Born's experiments with year-round flavors to make its revenue less seasonal and for matching regional preferences to its growing diversity of flavors.

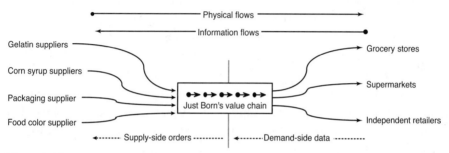

Figure 2.10
Matching supply with demand for Peeps uses IT to create information flows in the opposite direction of physical flows.

IT asset that meets only the first two criteria is a temporary competitive advantage; if it also meets the last two, it is a sustainable competitive advantage.

IT Assets That Are Valuable but Not Rare

IT infrastructure of any sort is not rare even when it is valuable, so it rarely generates a competitive advantage. It has operational—but not strategic—value. It is nevertheless a competitive necessity because it provides the foundation for *other* IT assets that might generate a competitive advantage.

The other two classes of IT assets, apps and data, are rarely sustainable competitive advantages in and of themselves. However, they can be used as tools to construct a sustainable competitive advantage. Most purchased apps used innovatively to create a competitive advantage by doing something valuable and rare can be acquired by your rivals. Successful IT-driven business innovations attract imitators; imitation destroys their rarity. Managers often suspend the imitability test under the mistaken belief that a valuable IT innovation will remain rare. Apps that are valuable

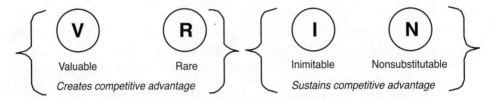

Figure 2.11
An IT asset must be valuable and rare to create a competitive advantage and inimitable and nonsubstitutable to sustain it.

but not rare can increase a firm's operational effectiveness but do not competitively differentiate a firm from its archrivals. Having them creates competitive parity.

Many analytics initiatives that are valuable are not rare, which is why they do not create a sustainable competitive advantage. Caesars Casinos' analytics-driven strategy to predict profitable customers that propelled it to industry leadership was copied within ten years by most other rival casinos. Imitation made yesterday's masterstroke today's norm. Similarly, supply chain management apps that interconnect firms in a value stream to match supply and demand are valuable but not rare. Therefore, the competitive advantage that they generate is not sustainable. To sustain a competitive advantage built on purchased IT apps, you must add valuable new IT capabilities faster than your archrivals can copy them, giving them temporary rarity. This relies on speedily identifying and constantly investing in new IT opportunities to keep a step ahead of your archrivals. However, this approach can be financially exhausting and is usually unsustainable. Purchased apps therefore can create but rarely sustain a competitive advantage.

Custom-Built IT Assets
The route to sustaining a competitive advantage is developing IT assets that your archrivals find difficult to imitate, which preserves their rarity. For example, your archrivals cannot simply buy proprietary apps custom developed in-house by

Box 2.10
Escape from the App Acronym Jungle

When firms were historically more hierarchical and less flat, a jungle of acronyms was used to describe IT apps at different organizational levels. Midlevel managers used decision support systems, top managers used executive support systems, analysts used expert systems, and frontline employees used transaction processing systems for routine operations. These distinctions now are less meaningful.

your firm. They must attempt to reverse engineer and recreate them at considerable expense. (Remember that you cannot directly patent software.) Reverse engineering software is much harder than, say, a car because a rival can observe only its behavior but not the underlying software code. However, custom building is also the riskiest and costliest route for your own firm to acquire an IT asset—enough to warrant an entire chapter later in this book. The *only* reason to custom build an app is if it inches your firm toward its strategic aspiration in ways that your archrivals cannot copy. If a determined rival does successfully replicate a custom-built app, it commoditizes a once-strategic IT asset.

Consider, for example, Citibank's mobile check-cashing smartphone application. Citibank was the first major bank to introduce a smartphone app to cash a check by taking a picture, offering unprecedented convenience to customers and reducing Citibank's own dependence on a costly, aging network of automated teller machines (ATMs).[59] Citibank's proprietary app used nonproprietary data also available to other banks—namely, a serial number and bank routing number printed on every check. Even the smallest rival banks successfully copied it within a year. What was Citibank's competitive differentiator became an industry norm, redefining the baseline to be in the banking business. Citibank was hardly surprised because it was déjà vu from having spent $100 million first introducing ATMs in the late 1970s.

A proprietary app that exploits data readily available to other firms—a serial number on a check, a product barcode, data trails left by browsers, or data produced by commodity supply chain apps in your partner firms—can make it worthwhile for archrivals to incur the expense and risk of attempting to clone a valuable proprietary app. Therefore a custom-built app by itself is at best a temporary, unsustainable advantage. Your firm cannot bet on the mythical killer app for sustainable competitive advantage; it is as real as the tooth fairy.

Blending Apps and Data

There are two ways to construct a more sustainable competitive advantage using an IT app: (a) using it to create network effects and (b) blending it with proprietary data to create an analytics-driven edge. In either case, your firm is using an app to create another asset—for example, a social network or a source of insights—that your rivals must also re-create to replicate an app's business value. However, the bigger challenge is the sparse opportunities for firms to create network effects in the first place.

A second way is combining proprietary apps with proprietary data to create an analytics-driven edge in one line function's operations or in a business process. Put differently, you use the amalgamation of apps and data either on a value chain step or link (lens #2) to create an edge over your archrivals. This *combination* is harder for archrivals to imitate. The more complex or eclectic the processing an app does on the data, the harder it is for your rivals to replicate.[60] However, the business *use* of such insight in day-to-day operations must outdistance your firm from its archrivals in ways that matter to your customers. Nest, for example, combined usage data with intelligent software *and a different business model* to deliver a product unlike anything seen before.

Firms that have successfully thwarted imitation by exploiting both network effects and analytics include the movie recommendation app in Netflix's service, the product recommendation engine built into Amazon, and Starbucks's crowd-sourced innovation hub (mystarbucksidea.force.com). Netflix's app mines terabytes of data on movie streaming behavior of millions of customers; its recommendations account for three out of every four movies watched. It has ushered in an era of binge watching among its customers. Amazon's recommendation app added $30 billion to its 2016 sales. Starbucks's crowdsourcing hub has generated more than a half million ideas for product and service innovations, several hundred of which it has implemented. In each instance, how each firm *uses* the app to further its strategic aspiration—not the app itself—is valuable. In each instance, the app is one miniscule part of their mostly commodity IT portfolio. The most commodity is Starbucks, whose app is purchased (from Salesforce.com) but is shielded by the network effects among several million loyal customers regularly using it. Netflix's service runs mostly on commodity infrastructure, services purchased from Amazon, and a small number of proprietary apps such as its recommendation app. Even if a rival could imitate Netflix's or Amazon's proprietary recommendation apps, it would still struggle to replicate their massive troves of data assets that make them potent. Time lapsed is on their side; they are far enough ahead in their Red Queen race that only a substitute can realistically erode their head start. Figure 2.12

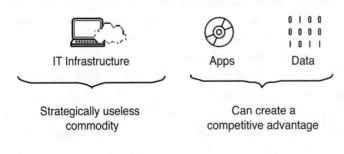

IT Infrastructure   Apps   Data

Strategically useless   Can create a
commodity   competitive advantage

Figure 2.12
Sustainable competitive advantage can come from combining apps with data but almost never from infrastructure.

summarizes the potential of the three classes of IT assets to produce a sustainable competitive advantage.

Analytics-oriented apps have mostly focused on only one branch of analytics called predictive analytics. The next section briefly describes other approaches for turning data into insight.

Four Approaches to Data-Driven Analytics

Four classes of approaches—summarized in figure 2.13—undergird software apps that extract actionable insight from raw data.[61] They allow you to see patterns invisible to a naked eye. IT infrastructure that collects, stores, and communicates data is a prerequisite because most of them are data intensive (see table 2.4).

1. *Predictive modeling.* Predictive models are the workhorse of business analytics. They use a bunch of variables to predict an outcome using historical data.[62] For example, you might have a coarse model predicting purchase and might find that age, gender, and income affect it. So if you knew that single males under thirty-three with incomes of $50K–60K living in major metro areas are more likely to buy your product, you would advertise it to precisely that demographic. Similarly, insurance companies know that males under age twenty-four are more accident prone, so they charge them more. New data allows you to refine these models to increase prediction

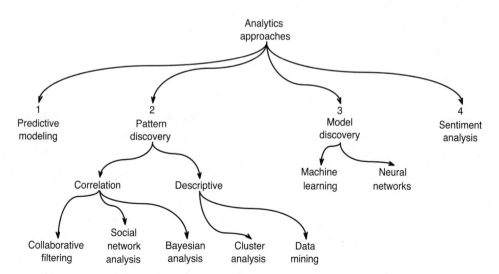

Figure 2.13
Four approaches to data-driven business analytics.

accuracy, and contextualized big-data streams allow real-time tactical adjustments (e.g., using a freebie to entice a customer who fits the profile of a predicted buyer who is walking away from your store).

2. *Pattern discovery using correlation.* Correlation-based pattern-discovery approaches search for patterns of things that move together. For example, if a thousand customers liked three movies—*Goodfellas*, *Gladiator*, and *Scarface*—and you liked the first two, it is likely that you will also enjoy the third, *Scarface*. The idea is to discover customers' preferences and customize recommendations for them. Besides these "those who liked X also liked Y" approach (called *collaborative filtering*), you can recommend things that individuals' Facebook friends like (*social network analysis*) and use attributes of historical purchases to predict what other offerings with these attributes will appeal to a particular customer (*Bayesian analysis*), to identify previously unrecognized market segments (*cluster analysis*), and to spot patterns in large data sets (*data mining*). The last two are purely descriptive approaches to make sense of large volumes of data but cannot make predictions. Netflix, for example, used cluster analysis to identify more than seventy-five thousand microgenres of movies that it now uses to make recommendations.

3. *Model discovery in big-data streams using machine learning.* It is not always possible to create a statistical predictive model. *Machine learning* works the other way around: you feed it lots of raw data, and it figures out a model to estimate an outcome variable that you care about. The more data it chews through, the better its predictions become. Hence the term *machine learning*, which includes *neural network analysis* modeled after the human brain. Their forte is prediction when you cannot articulate a prediction model. Unlike statistical models that rely on assumptions about data, machine learning can deal with all sorts of nonnumerical data. It is therefore used for image recognition, spam detection, voice recognition, drug development, fraud detection, creditworthiness assessment, and medical prognoses. The complexity of these models makes them unintelligible to humans. This approach is the foundation of the emerging artificial intelligence trend discussed in chapter 9.

4. *Sentiment analysis.* Unstructured textual data such as Facebook posts and tweets is harder to analyze using most statistical techniques. Sentiment-analysis approaches search for patterns in large volumes of text to detect emotions, attitudes, and trends.

To recap the litmus test, an IT asset creates a competitive advantage only when it is valuable and rare among your archrivals. You must first generate a competitive advantage before you fret about sustaining it. Many operationally valuable corporate IT assets are not rare and, therefore, have no strategic value. They are merely competitive necessities. If an IT asset is both valuable and rare, the competitive

Table 2.4
Four Classes of Approaches for Business Analytics

Approach	What it does	Data intensive	Domain knowledge needed
1. Predictive models	A class of statistical regression methods that uses a bunch of variables to predict an outcome (e.g., purchase, credit default, or account cancelation); this is the workhorse approach for analytics		•
2. Pattern discovery	Discovers patterns of things that happen together		
a. Collaborative filtering	Matches one customer's behaviors to others (e.g., 60 percent of people who watched *Goodfellas* also watched *Scarface*); widely used to generate recommendations for high-volume movies, books, music, and smartphone applications	•	
b. Social network analysis	Identifies opportunities, assuming that people have preferences similar to their friends'; less reliable than predictive models	•	
c. Bayesian analysis	Uses product attributes to predict other products with similar attributes that will appeal to a customer	•	
d. Cluster analysis	Uses statistical analysis to identify previously unrecognized distinctive microsegments		•
e. Data mining	Extracts patterns in large data sets	•	
3. Model discovery	Reverse engineers a predictive model from large data sets by combining artificial intelligence and statistics using machine learning–based methods	•	
4. Sentiment analysis	Analyzes unstructured textual data to spot emotions, attitudes, and trends	•	

advantage generated by it is sustainable only if it cannot be imitated by your archrivals and they cannot find a substitute for it.

Key Takeaways

1. *Humans' unwavering obsession with prediction.* We have always obsessed over predicting the future. Although the advent of ephemeral streams of big data and cheap computing are making it possible to anticipate things that firms care about, most firms struggle to harness them.

2. *Analytics-driven strategy.* Using data to anticipate and predict business outcomes.

3. *Better ingredients, better insights.* Raw facts are data; condensed and organized data creates information; actionable information is insight. Insights from analytics are only as good as the data and models from non-IT managers that go into apps, which do this conversion.

4. *The three lenses.* How IT can be strategic requires first understanding (1) how it is affecting your industry (using the five-forces lens), (2) how it can alter how your firm creates value vis-à-vis your archrivals (using the value-chain lens), and (3) whether a particular IT asset can create a sustainable competitive advantage (the litmus-test lens). You must use all three together because they zoom into different aspects of your firm's competitive landscape.

5. *Margins as a firm's oxygen supply.* If the money going out is more than the money coming into your firm, nonprofit, or government agency, it cannot survive.

6. *IT alters industry attractiveness but also provides antidotes.* IT can alter the attractiveness of an entire industry by increasing transparency, blurring industry boundaries, enabling legacy-free business models, and squeezing margins. Firms can use IT to erect unconventional competitive barriers using network effects and analytics-driven customization.

7. *Two ways to use IT to reimagine value chains.* IT can alter value chains by improving either one step in it or the connection between two steps. The latter approach extrapolates to a firm's upstream and downstream partners as well.

8. *The litmus test.* An IT asset creates a competitive advantage if it is valuable and rare; you can sustain it if your archrivals cannot imitate the asset or find a substitute. Proprietary apps and proprietary data—especially in combination—are usually the only sources of a sustainable competitive advantage using IT.

The Non-IT Managers' Checklist

☐ How is IT increasing the fierceness of competition in your industry? Is the balance of power shifting to your customers or suppliers because of increasing transparency, wiping of geographical constraints, colliding industries, or new rivals unburdened by your industry's legacy assets?

☐ If you had the ability to better predict two business outcomes in your functional area, what would you pick and why? (These are the things you want to predict using analytics.) How would this ability inch your firm toward its strategic aspiration?

☐ Is the digitization-infusion-ubiquity trifecta increasing the information content of a specific step in your firm's value chain? Which one? How?

☐ Can you envision how IT could improve either the efficiency or the value-added in a specific step in your value chain? Which one?

☐ Can you envision how IT can either reconfigure your firm's value stream or improve coordination within it? How would you induce your partner firms to cooperate?

☐ What proprietary data can you use and how can you use it to create an advantage that your archrivals would struggle to imitate? Could you use a ready-made app to analyze it, or would you have to custom build one?

Part 2

Architecture

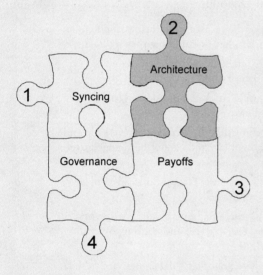

Jargon Decoder

IT architecture	A blueprint of the IT assets in a firm's IT portfolio describing what they do and how they interact.
Operational performance	An IT asset's fitness of purpose (speed and reliability), security, and maintenance costs.
Evolvability	How easily an IT asset can be adapted to do unplanned things.
DNA analogy	An app's architecture is practically irreversible and constrains how it can and cannot be changed over its life.
Enterprise architecture	How a firm's corporate IT apps, infrastructure, and data are organized.
App architecture	How an app's three building blocks are divvied up between a user's device and a more powerful central machine.
Data architecture	How and where your firm's data assets are stored.
Architectural trade-off	Tension between operational performance now and evolvability later.

3

IT Architecture

IT systems are costlier to keep running than to get, and they do not die when you are ready for them to. Every dollar spent on an IT system costs up to another seven dollars to keep it running over its lifetime.[1] They outlive their intended lifespan by up to 200 percent.[2] Most firms obsess over spending that first dollar wisely yet often overlook how choices made today will affect their IT assets' maintainability over their protracted life spans. Repeated failed attempts to replace the US air traffic control from the 1970s, predating even GPS technology, illustrate this double whammy.[3] IT systems not *designed* to evolve become costly straightjackets that handicap firms that depend on them.[4, 5]

Evolvability is predicated in architectural choices made long before the first line of code is written. IT architecture is your firm's technological DNA: irreversible and strategically preordaining. Saying that an IT asset's architecture shapes its operational performance oversimplifies reality. The bigger consequences are strategic, which without non-IT managers' contributions to architectural decisions, don't even enter the picture until it is too late.

This chapter equips you to contribute to architectural decisions in ways that your IT colleagues cannot. We begin with a few examples of the surprising business consequences of firms' architectural choices. We explain how thoughtful architectural choices pay dividends in lower lifetime IT costs and business agility. Without non-IT involvement, architectures' strategic consequences escape firms' radar screens. Left to their own devices, IT units tend to use their leeway to maximize immediate operational performance, often oblivious to the strategic handicaps they inadvertently create. We illustrate how non-IT managers can ensure that corporate IT apps, infrastructure, and data architecture decisions become catalysts for their firm's competitiveness.

Examples

Consider a few examples of how your irreversible IT architecture choices today sow the seeds of tomorrow's competitive strategy.

• *Why a new user costs Facebook a hundred times more than it costs Skype.* Adding a new user to existing tens of millions of users costs Skype about five cents but costs Facebook at least five dollars.[6] An additional Skype user adds more computing power than she consumes, making it technologically stronger as it grows. The same user requires constant upgrades to the thirty thousand "servers" on which Facebook ran in 2016. A difference in their architecture embeds scalability in Skype's DNA but not in Facebook's.

• *How Siri got its smarts.* Computers struggled with human voice recognition since the 1950s until Siri's arrival took it mainstream. Instrumental was a shift in architecture that quit trying to get a user's machine to do the voice recognition. Instead, your device captures your speech and ships it over the Internet to a remote collection of supercomputers that do the heavy lifting. An architectural tweak in Siri now gives your smartphone direct access to the brainpower of several thousand powerful computers to make voice recognition work.

• *Why Obamacare crashed on its debut.* When the US government launched the "Obamacare" site to revolutionize affordable health care, the $2 billion site designed for fifty thousand simultaneous users crashed when twenty million people tried to use it. The system intended for the entire United States (2017 population: 330 million) could not even handle 1,100 simultaneous users. The problem was in its architecture, which worsened its inherently poor scalability.

• *How Netflix streams to one hundred million viewers without a hiccup.* Netflix has almost one hundred million users in 190 countries and accounts for a third of all US Internet traffic. Yet it streams without a hiccup largely due to Netflix's "distributed" architecture explained later in this chapter.

• *How Delta Airlines turned around without retraining its eighty thousand employees.* The lynchpin of Delta Airlines' return to profitability was a $1.5 billion IT project called the Delta Nervous System that gave it a unified view of its global operations across all six continents.[7] Yet Delta largely left the software interfaces used by its employees untouched while replacing everything under the hood. This allowed it to skip retraining eighty thousand employees, who barely noticed its introduction. This strategy was possible primarily due to the architecture of the new system.

• *How UPS grows the size of FedEx every Christmas without losing a package.* Global shipping behemoth UPS temporarily grows by the size of its archrival

FedEx every holiday season. UPS's IT architecture partly enables its ability to rapidly grow and shrink. One "data architecture" decision made in the 1980s—to use a *single* package database worldwide[8]—helps ensure that no package gets lost. (UPS also operates among the world's largest private aircraft fleets and cellular networks.)

• *Why Napster died after digitizing the music industry.* Napster literally created the digital music industry that later wiped out music retail stores. It could be legally shut down because its architectural choices pinpointed Napster as the enabler of piracy. Had Napster used a more "decentralized" architecture, it—not Apple—could have evolved to dominate the legitimate music distribution industry.

• *How Target lost 110 million customers' data.* US retailer Target lost 110 million customer records and forty-two million credit cards across its 1,800 stores during the 2013 Christmas season. It had no single point of vulnerability but insufficient separation of its financial IT systems from its refrigeration support systems. The seeds of the gigantic security breach were in poor firm-wide IT architecture.

• *Why Google's million servers need to keep growing.* Google needs to keep adding to its million-plus power-hungry servers because of its architecture.[9] Its monthly electric bill to power them exceeds a quarter million homes.[10]

Architecture as a Universal Translator

Architecture serves an identical purpose for IT projects as it does for homeowners: it translates between users and builders to get them on the same page.[11] Figure 3.1 illustrates the parallels. If you want to build a home, you begin with a vision of what you want it to look like, your needs, and what matters more to you. A builder knows costs, constraints, materials, and even possibilities unknown to you. An ideal architecture reconciles the two perspectives into a design that comes close to what you want at a cost that you can afford. The conversation around architecture reconciles what's desirable and what's achievable. IT architecture serves an identical role for IT assets.

Like the Babel fish in the cult novel *The Hitchhiker's Guide to the Galaxy*, IT architecture helps translate between business functions and your firm's IT unit. The translation is from the abstract vision of business users into concrete IT capabilities.[12, 13, 14, 15] It fosters a shared understanding with the IT unit of the problems that line functions are trying to solve. Architecture is a business vision implemented *one project at a time*.[16] It begins with your firm's operational strategy and ends with an IT project (such as an app or infrastructure component).

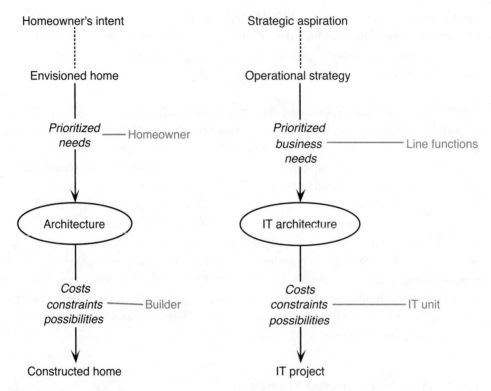

Figure 3.1
Architecture helps translate a vision of business needs into IT solutions.

On the right side of figure 3.1, operational strategy drives your line functions' business needs and priorities, which should shape IT architecture. You contribute business acumen to the conversation—your knowledge of business processes, goals, and priorities for the project. Your IT colleagues contribute insight into costs and technical constraints about what is possible and might even suggest possibilities that you have not considered. The ideal solutions might not be affordable or even technically feasible; the IT unit is better equipped to evaluate such constraints and possibilities. The architecture of a project reconciles the business and IT perspectives to ensure a harmony of purpose between them. A common purpose is a powerful synchronizer.

Shortchanging the conversation around architecture shortchanges discovery of latent business needs, often squandering money on projects that fail to deliver *business* benefits. Shortcuts in architectural decisions take on a technical sort of debt, whose interest your firm pays in greater maintenance costs and poorer business agility.[17] (Chapter 6 explains how IT projects can discover such latent business needs.) A thoughtful, firm-wide IT architecture reconciles what is desirable and what is viable for all three aspects of a firm's IT portfolio: infrastructure, individual apps, and data assets.

Architecture as DNA

Architecture is the DNA of IT systems: it is largely irreversible, imprints their traits, and influences how they can and cannot evolve.[18] Although in theory it can be changed, the prohibitive costs in practice make it almost impossible to change. Its strategic consequences manifest long after its immediate operational consequences.[19] However, IT architecture lurks in the blind spot of non-IT managers because they perceive it as a technical decision best left to IT specialists, who are unschooled in its strategic consequences. The resulting choices can constrain strategic flexibility tomorrow.

Consequences of Architecture

A choice of IT architecture is a choice among trade-offs; maximizing one desirable attribute can compromise another. Non-IT managers must be cognizant so they can proactively *make* such trade-offs rather than recognizing them after it is too late. Even when you do not make a choice, you are making a choice. By not participating in IT architecture decisions, you are choosing to delegate them to your IT folks. If you do not make the trade-offs yourself, your IT unit will make them for you. To contribute your business acumen to the conversation, you must know *just enough* about IT architecture to communicate your business vision and to negotiate trade-offs. Figure 3.2 summarizes the trade-offs between operational consequences that are immediately visible and strategic ones visible only later.

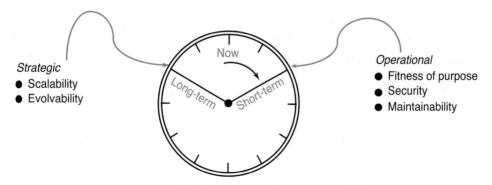

Figure 3.2
The short-term operational and long-term strategic consequences of IT architecture.

A firm can promote operationally ideal systems and pay some real strategic costs later. Or it can promote flexible systems and pay some real operational costs today. Conversations around architecture put such trade-offs on the table early on. Without non-IT involvement, the emphasis invariably is on operational performance alone. A good architecture balances economical performance today and economical change-ability later.[20] It fulfills today's requirements but plans for tomorrow's expectations.

You—as a non-IT manager—can help sacrifice the ideal in either to preserve enough of both. The strategicness of your firm's IT assets will be shaped not by any one big trade-off but by many small ones. Table 3.1 previews the consequences of IT architecture—for infrastructure, apps, and data.

Operational Consequences
The operational consequences of IT architecture shape an IT asset's ability to cost-effectively serve its intended purpose.

Fitness of Purpose
The first operational consequence of architecture is an IT asset's fitness for its intended purpose, which boils down to how responsive it is (*speed*) and how much you can count on it (*reliability*). An IT asset must be *acceptably* responsive and reliable, no more to remain economical and no less to be usable. The definition of acceptable speed and reliability for each individual system must come from non-IT managers whose line function it touches. Think of acceptable as the threshold below which it will become a liability. For example, speed and reliability trump almost everything else for a commercial video streaming service like Netflix but are less important to an order-processing system. IT functionality is not on this list because different architectures can be used to deliver the same functionality.

Table 3.1
Operational and Strategic Consequences of IT Architecture

Consequence	What it means
Operational performance	
Fitness of purpose	How responsive is it (*speed*), and can you count on it (*reliability*)?
Security	How vulnerable is it to malicious tampering?
Maintainability	How cost effectively can you make incremental improvements to keep it functioning smoothly?
Strategic	
Scalability	How cost effectively can it grow with your firm's needs?
Evolvability	Can it adapt to do things that it was never designed to do?

Security

Architecture also determines how vulnerable a system is to someone with malicious intent. Security often comes at a cost of convenience for a system's users. For example, the need for security is progressively greater for a system that handles social media, financial information, and confidential medical records. Generally, more centralized architectures have a single point of *complete* vulnerability, but decentralized architectures require widespread protection. (Chapter 8 delves into non-IT managers' contributions in making a security-convenience trade-off appropriate for your firm.)

Maintainability

Architecture also profoundly affects lifetime costs of an IT asset because some architectures are more economical to maintain than others; this adds up to several times its initial costs. Generally, more centralized architectures are costlier to build and upgrade but cheaper to maintain than decentralized architectures. We mostly think of maintainability as bug fixing, but such *corrective* maintenance is only about twenty-five cents of every dollar spent on maintaining IT systems. The bulk (seventy-five cents) of such costs are *adaptive* maintenance—tweaks to add functionality to meet evolving business needs (e.g., new business processes) or to keep it functioning with other IT assets that have changed.[21] The penalty of poorly maintainable systems is poor *business* agility. The harder it is to quickly change them, the more it will translate to squandered business opportunities.

Maintenance of IT systems often befuddles non-IT managers because it means something different from its literal meaning.[22] When you maintain your lawnmower, you clean it, oil it, and occasionally replace its spark plug. Maintaining an IT system, in contrast, largely entails changing it to adapt to evolving business needs and to keep it working with other systems in your firm's IT portfolio. Just as you cannot "maintain" a lawnmower into a sports car, there are limits to how an IT system can be changed. Architecture determines these limits.

Strategic Consequences

IT architecture shapes *business* agility by preordaining whether an IT asset becomes an enabler or impediment to your firm's competitive moves.

Scalability

The first strategic consequence of IT architecture is a system's capacity to cost-effectively handle increased usage. The hundredfold cost difference between

Facebook and Skype of adding a new user and the inability of the US Obamacare system to function acceptably described earlier illustrate how the choice of a system's architecture influences how cost effectively it can scale. Decentralized architectures are inherently more scalable and resilient. However, such scalability often comes at the cost of operational performance. Video streaming services such as Netflix, for example, use an architecture that prizes operational performance even though it makes it costlier to scale up.[23]

Evolvability

The second strategic consequence of architecture is evolvability, which is its ability to support business moves by doing *new* things that it was never designed to do. An IT asset's architecture tilts its evolutionary trajectory one way and not another. This includes adding new functionality to support changed business needs and to absorb new technologies.[24] This property—also called malleability, extensibility, and adaptability—is especially important in corporate IT apps. Evolvable IT assets enable business agility. They also have greater longevity because they are built for change. Poor architecture makes it harder to change one app because it requires recognizing and rewiring many other apps as well. It bakes inflexibility into an IT asset. Unevolvable IT architecture will eventually put you too far behind in Red Queen competition to catch up. Differences in a firm's overall IT architecture can explain why one firm's IT is more adaptable than its archrivals' and why they can harness new IT innovations faster.

Non-IT managers must rank order—in a single list from table 3.1—what matters most to their line functions. The end game is clarity.

Inside the Corporate IT Architecture Blackbox

IT architecture is a blueprint of the IT assets in a firm's IT portfolio that describes what they do, how they interact, and how they fit together.[26,27] A firm's IT portfolio is a federated system of infrastructure, apps, and data. IT architecture (a) decomposes a firm's IT portfolio into relatively autonomous IT assets and (b) facilitates integrating them so they behave as a cohesive whole. An *enterprise* architecture describes the firm-wide organizing logic of the three classes of IT assets: its IT infrastructure ①, its data assets ②, and IT apps ③. Its three layers are a firm's collection of apps, the infrastructure that supports them, and the data that they handle. As figure 3.3 shows, the three are interrelated; IT infrastructure constrains app architecture, which in turn shapes how a firm's data assets are organized.

Box 3.1
How Shanghai Mobile's IT Architecture Created a Competitive Edge[25]

The Chinese telephony market was long dominated by a landline and cellular duopoly in every region of China. That disappeared in early 2009 when the Chinese government split it into three competing nationwide carriers: China Mobile, China Unicom, and China Telecom. Competition increased markedly, and Shanghai Mobile (a flagship division of China Mobile) experienced rising customer defection. Its chief information officer (CIO) Xie Qin knew that Shanghai Mobile's complex legacy architecture would be a competitive stumbling block. Its market channels—local branch stores, retailers, an online store, and call centers—were siloed in different IT systems that led to inconsistent pricing policies and costly duplication of hard-to-maintain systems. As offerings from rivals multiplied, Shanghai Mobile was unable to change its IT fast enough to make matching moves. There was no information sharing across channels, so a store clerk would have no idea about a walk-in customer's interaction history with its online store. This led to a poor customer experience in a cutthroat market.

Qin decided to embark on a risky ten-month overhaul of its sales and service IT systems to improve the customer experience, making them cheaper to maintain and faster to tweak. The new architecture adopted a Lego-like "modular" approach, centralizing all data from all channels and unifying key business processes across all sales channels. He knew that he could not abruptly swap a live system serving millions of active customers. Therefore, Qin rolled out the new systems in phases, one marketing channel at a time. The old and new systems ran in parallel throughout the transition. The result: increased consistency in customer interactions across all sales channels, a reduction in ongoing IT costs, a drop in problem resolution from two hours to two minutes on average, and a more agile firm with a 30 percent faster time to market.

How IT Complexity Paralyzes Business Agility

Architecture is the primary source of complexity in a firm's IT portfolio. Complexity can paralyze *business* agility by making it hard to evolve a firm's business processes to its changing competitive needs. Adapting business processes requires

Figure 3.3
A firm's enterprise IT architecture has three layers: ① IT infrastructure, ② data, and ③ apps.

changing the—often multiple—apps in which they are embedded. The architecture of IT interwoven into organizations' business processes constrains how organizations can and cannot change.[28] Architectural choices therefore lay the foundation not just for IT systems but also for the business processes increasingly embedded in them. If a firm's IT architecture is not a catalyst for business agility, it is an impediment.

As a firm adds or tweaks apps in its IT portfolio, it eventually can create an incomprehensible, handcrafted tangle of intertwined systems spanning epochs and generations of technologies. As ad hoc, piecemeal connections accumulate, a portfolio that started out as figure 3.4(a) becomes like figure 3.4(b). It devolves into a variegated patchwork of apps installed over decades and connected in idiosyncratic, poorly documented ways. Ambiguity about what ripple effect a change in one app might have on others makes change harder; an update to one app might cause another one to stop working. Changing one app requires ensuring that a change does not break others that it depends on or that depend on it. (Most apps use data that originates in another app or send data to another app, so data must be able to move back and forth among them.[29]) Even Humpty Dumpty would pity their plight because they become difficult not only to integrate but also to pull apart for tweaking.

Line functions' own little fiefdoms with their own business apps and data compounds this problem. The coordination needed to tweak any app rises with the number of apps used in your firm, potentially increasing the inflexibility of your firm's IT portfolio. Such growing complexity makes apps so brittle that their unchangeability becomes a competitive liability. When apps hinder business moves, the syncing between IT strategy and operational strategy breaks. The complexity of IT systems can therefore imperil firms' ability to sync its IT strategy.[30] Such complexity does not

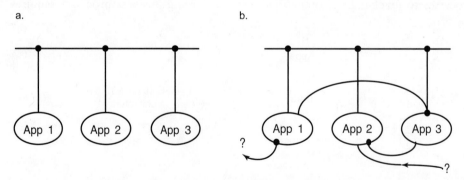

Figure 3.4
Piecemeal modifications to apps over time create an incomprehensible tangle.

magically disappear. *Unnecessary* complexity has to be surgically excised through thoughtful architectural choices that minimize such ripple effects.

Simplicity Is the Ultimate Sophistication

An antidote to complexity is imposing simplicity. A good enterprise architecture makes complexity manageable by (a) increasing the autonomy of IT assets and (b) easing their integration. Key to this is lumping together things that change for similar reasons and at similar speeds. Apps and infrastructure do not need to change at the same speed. Rapid change and variety are more important in apps, where firms' business processes usually embedded. For infrastructure, reliability and economy are more important than flexibility. So we break up a firm's IT portfolio into two major chunks: (1) IT infrastructure that remains relatively stable and is shared by many line functions, and (2) specialized business apps that can change much faster and might not be used by many line functions. This chunks a firm's IT portfolio into IT assets intended to change—like a clock's two hands—at two speeds: apps that change faster to foster business agility and infrastructure that changes slower to lower costs (figure 3.5). The stability of infrastructure supports faster-changing apps that depend on it, just as a building's trustworthy foundation supports changing what is inside it.

Lego-like Architectures Enable Change

Of all IT assets, apps—into which business processes are hardwired—are most often the daunting roadblock to change. An ideal IT portfolio lets you easily separate an app needing tweaking and then easily glue it back into the firm's IT portfolio. Gluing it back refers to its ability to continue interoperating with other apps.

The solution is to adopt a Lego-like approach—called *modular design*—where apps are designed to be relatively autonomous and interoperate only using prespecified connection standards.[31] Such connections are like using standard electrical plugs

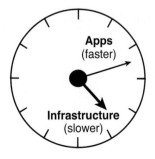

Figure 3.5
An IT portfolio is chunked into IT assets that change at two speeds: apps much faster than infrastructure.

in your home. As long as a gadget follows that standard, it is guaranteed to interoperate independent of whether it is a toaster, coffeemaker, or vacuum cleaner. Using such standards to interconnect apps is analogous to using removable Post-it strength adhesive instead of superglue that hardens over time. This ensures that apps can be tweaked independently yet continue to interoperate.[32, 33] This autonomy among apps also enhances firm-wide IT resilience by keeping glitches in one app (say, experimenting with unproven, immature, or evolving functionality) from destabilizing others. In a Lego analogy, you can freely change any brick and it will still attach to other bricks to create more complex structures as long as you keep the standard Lego attachment studs.[34]

A well-partitioned app portfolio reduces the *need* for one app's owner to understand the innards of other apps. Its hallmarks are simplicity and adaptability. To one app, all other apps appear as blackboxes; it needs to know only how to interact with them but not how they work.[35, 36] This is like driving a car, where you must know how to control it but not what is under the hood. Each app can then independently be designed and changed.[37] Disciplined use of such standardized connections to guarantee integration between apps dramatically increases the flexibility to make changes in any one without causing others to malfunction. One app can be tweaked in blissful ignorance of other apps.[38, 39]

This approach also greatly simplifies integration of activities with your partner firms. Their systems can talk to your firm's systems, without you having to disclose inside details of your own systems. You can do this by creating explicitly documented hooks—known as *private application programming interfaces* (APIs)—for your partners' systems to interoperate with yours.[40]

App connection standards can be formal data standards, APIs,[41] or even proprietary specifications made up by your firm. The only requirement is that they be explicitly documented and frozen. Such inflexibility in how apps connect creates flexibility in what they do. They act as an agreed-upon, shared rulebook—like if you and I agreed to communicate in, say, Morse code—that ensures that one app can be confident in its interpretation of what it says to and hears from other apps. However, app connection standards—like traffic lights—are useful only when everyone complies; violating them undermines interoperability.

Such partitioning allows new apps to plug and play into a firm's existing portfolio of IT assets. This Lego-like divide-and-conquer approach does not eliminate complexity in a firm's IT portfolio but makes it more manageable. It permits line function–driven innovation in IT apps without forsaking their firm-wide integration.

Architecture as a Roadmap: Lessons from Paris

The evolution of Paris over the past two thousand years offers an instructive analogy for how architecture acts as a roadmap for evolving a firm's IT portfolio over time (see table 3.2). Both span a variegated patchwork of assets spanning many eras. The challenges in both Paris and corporate IT are to preserve viable old assets (figure 3.6), to introduce new ones, and to maintain an infrastructure linking them coherently.[42]

Just as Paris has a variety of neighborhoods with different character and purpose, a firm has a variety of apps used by different line functions. Reliable and economical infrastructure links all of Paris (e.g., Paris *Métro*, *Périphérique* ring road, and *Francilienne* motorway) just as it does apps in an IT portfolio. Just as streets have a longer lifespan than individual buildings, IT infrastructure tends to outlive individual apps.

Just as Paris is chunked into specialized zones, a firm's IT portfolio is chunked distinctive operational and strategic apps. Just as the diversity of Paris's neighborhoods'

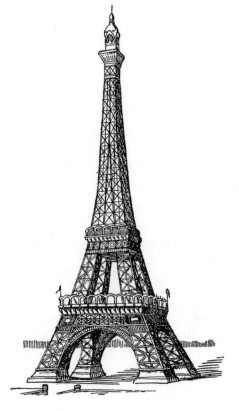

Figure 3.6
The evolution of Paris is analogous to the evolution of firms' IT portfolios.

Table 3.2
Parallels between the Architecture of Cities and IT Portfolios

Attribute	Paris	IT portfolio
Variety of . . .	Buildings	Apps
Infrastructure	Reliable roads, water, and electricity	Reliable firm-wide IT infrastructure
Zoning	Residential and commercial areas	Operational and strategic apps
Local character	Neighborhoods with unique character	Line functions with distinctive IT needs
Mix of . . .	Preserved old and new buildings	Legacy and new apps
Governance	Free citizens bound by city laws	Autonomous apps bound by firm-wide standards
Evolution	Gentrification of neighborhoods	Once-strategic apps become operational apps
Preservation	Renovation of historic buildings	Evolution of existing apps
Assimilation of . . .	New immigrants	New technologies

character is celebrated, so should be distinctive needs of line functions. Just as Paris's modern skyscrapers coexist with its historical buildings, new apps must coexist with legacy apps from earlier epochs. Both must build on them and shy away from a rip-and-replace mind-set.

Just as Parisians are free citizens bound by law, autonomous apps must still be governed by firm-wide standards. This ensures that growth in the app portfolio does not explode its complexity. Just as gentrification can make scrubby neighborhoods mainstream, strategic apps can evolve into operational apps. Just as the local needs of Parisian neighborhoods must be reconciled with the interests of Paris as a whole, line functions' unique IT needs must be reconciled with firm-wide interests.

Enterprise IT Architecture's Three Layers

The three layers of a firm's IT architecture are the architecture of its IT infrastructure, apps, and data.

IT Infrastructure Architecture

IT infrastructure is your firm's digital plumbing—its firm-wide foundation of shared IT assets and IT services used by all line functions. It includes the networks through which data travels and apps are linked and the hardware on which apps run and store data (e.g., computers, tablets, servers, and storage devices).[43] IT *infrastructure architecture* is their firm-wide arrangement.

IT infrastructure remains stable relative to apps, is mostly a generic commodity, and is rarely a competitive differentiator. This foundation—which consumes more than 50 percent[44] of corporate IT budgets—must be reliable but economical. (Constructing a transatlantic Internet cable costs about $300 million, giving you a feel for how costly some IT infrastructure can get.[45])

Reliable, firm-wide IT infrastructure improves how fast and inexpensively new apps can be implemented. Infrastructural upgrades are potentially leverageable by all apps that use it as a foundation, multiplying the payoffs from systematically separating infrastructure from apps.

The key architectural choice is *how much* to decentralize IT infrastructure or how much to centralize it. Figure 3.7 illustrates the corresponding trade-offs. *Centralization* creates firm-wide economies of scale by aggregating the IT infrastructure demands of all line functions and eases analytics-friendly firm-wide integration but also concentrates its vulnerability. *Decentralization* facilitates tailoring it to individual line functions' unique needs but also increases costs because of duplication. A *hybrid* mix of the two (which decentralizes some but centralizes other IT infrastructure) has the strengths—and weaknesses—of both.[46] Generally, more centralized architectures are costlier to build but cheaper to run than more decentralized ones.

Commoditized infrastructure increases—not reduces—opportunities for competitive advantage by freeing up more resources to invest in apps. The mantra should be

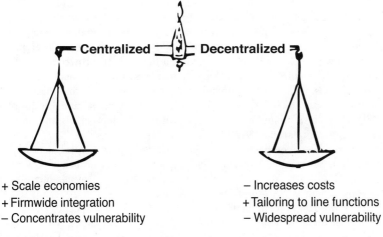

Figure 3.7
Trade-offs between centralizing and decentralizing IT infrastructure.

to buy before building. Barring strong competitive reasons favoring proprietary IT infrastructure, sticking to industry standards lowers its costs because of competition among firms that supply it. Even if your firm's IT infrastructure needs are so unusual that you cannot yet purchase it in the market, sticking to industry standards keeps the door open to reducing costs when potential suppliers catch up. Avoid investing in Esperanto.

Non-IT managers can contribute answers to two questions about IT infrastructure: (a) is firm-wide economy or tailoring to line functions more important and (b) what is considered "good enough" operational performance for their line functions? (Higher performing IT infrastructure costs more.) What is the acceptable threshold below which users within and outside the firm will experience pain? Since infrastructure does not competitively differentiate firms but can become a competitive liability if it underperforms, the objective is to minimize costs while ensuring an acceptable level of performance. This should be measured using business metrics appropriate to *your* firm (see chapter 4).

Box 3.2
How Rethinking Its IT Infrastructure Saved Delta Airlines

Atlanta-based Delta Airlines is the oldest and one of the largest American airlines in operation. Its IT systems were costing so much that they were wiping out income in an industry known for its razor-thin margins. Delta was making losses year after year. It was well on its way to join the corporate graveyard with many others of its vintage: Pony Express, Lehman Brothers, and PanAm. It was running thirty major collections of IT systems, none of which talked to each other. Each of them required a staff of about one hundred people, costing Delta $700 million a year just to keep them running. A simple question such as "at which gate does flight 74 arrive" could give you seventeen different answers depending on which IT system you queried. If a flight control tower changed gates, the flight crew, maintenance engineers, baggage handlers, and customers did not receive timely notifications. All of this kept planes on the ground longer than needed, which is the surefire way for any airline to lose money. (Airlines are estimated to lose five hundred dollars for every minute of delay in departure.) Losing bags is another; retrieving a lost bag cost Delta around $150.[47]

Interim CIO Charlie Feld compared Delta to a person whose central nervous system was broken; one physical part of Delta did not know what another part was doing. Delta embarked on a firm-wide IT-simplification process. The project—literally called Delta Nervous System (DNS)—cost Delta more than $2 billion in 2016 dollars and took five years (1998–2003). It eliminated inefficiencies from every aspect of Delta's operations by linking customer, scheduling, ticketing, and employee databases. Feld knew that attempting to rip and replace everything would be far costlier and likely to fail. Even if he managed to pull it off, retraining thousands of employees would be daunting.

Box 3.2 (*continued*)

Instead of scrapping its old apps, Delta connected all of them with new IT infrastructure. This "middleware" was like a highway that sat on top of its old apps and seamlessly shuttled data between Delta's forty-odd operational apps (e.g., flight control, ticketing, boarding, and catering). Leaving the apps untouched was the masterstroke; the employees would not even know of the new technology under the hood, and they could continue using the old systems without retraining. (See figure 3.8 contrasting the old and the new Delta IT portfolio; the changed part is shaded.) If a gate changed, the DNS would instantaneously push the information to every app that needed to know it. It also created flexibility because it standardized connections between all major operational apps. Delta now could tweak or replace one app without disrupting others in use. The simplified architecture eventually allowed Delta to add new technology simply and with minimal risk. Delta became one of the first airlines to introduce smartphone ticketless boarding. The system paid for itself within a few years by reducing annual IT costs by 30 percent, increasing employee productivity, and laying a foundation for Delta to discover that the most profitable routes are literally the less traveled ones. The nuanced analytics the new systems enabled allowed Delta to make strategic moves that bolstered its margins. Many American airlines used to believe that the US-Japan and US-Europe routes were the most profitable. Delta discovered that far more profitable were US flights to Israel and Africa and flying in twenty-two tons of asparagus each year from Lima, Peru, and attacking Alaska Airlines' stronghold on moving three thousand pounds of basil each year from Puerto Vallarta, Mexico.[48] Using data from the DNS, Delta then systematically reallocated the same planes to more attractive routes. Delta even bought its own $150 million oil refinery in 2012 to stabilize jet fuel price volatility.[49] (Contrary to the popular belief that IT leads to vertical disintegration, this is an example of how it can instead encourage vertical integration.) The DNS system gave Delta a new brain and contributed to Delta's record profitability in the years since.[50]

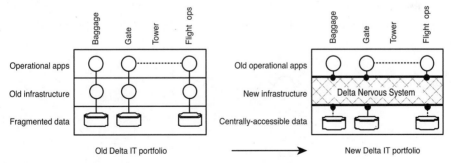

Figure 3.8
Delta Airlines' IT portfolio before and after its IT infrastructure overhaul.

App Architecture

Apps are software programs that undergird the functionality of a hardware device such as a PC, smartphone, tablet, cash register, or other Internet-connected devices (e.g., a thermostat, camera, or car systems). Such devices (called *clients*) are used to access a resource or service placed on a more powerful central computer (called a *server*). One server machine can serve many user devices, which connect to it through the Internet.

Any app consists of three building blocks of functionality (figure 3.9), which can independently be placed either centrally or on individual user devices. Their placement—on the left or right in figure 3.9—*is* an app's architecture.

1. Interaction functionality, which handles an app's interaction with users (such as receiving inputs and displaying outputs)
2. App logic, which performs the core work that makes the app useful to its users; most business innovation occurs in this block
3. Data storage, for data that an app uses and produces[51]

An app's architecture is simply how you choose to divide these three pieces between a centralized "server" and user devices.[52] Choosing where to locate these pieces is like arranging pieces on a chessboard, with irreversible operational and strategic consequences. Their arrangement—a choice that the app's designer makes—gives us three common app architectures: (a) cloud architecture, (b) client-server architecture, and (c) peer-to-peer architecture. App architectures have a striking parallel to men's neckties; a particular app architecture goes out of style only to reappear in a subsequent IT epoch.

Cloud Architecture

Cloud architecture puts all three pieces on a central server (figure 3.10). The user's device can be fairly feeble (thus inexpensive) because its only role is inputting and

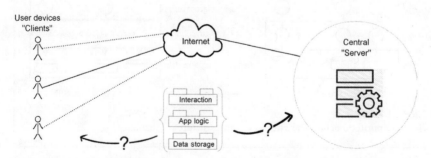

Figure 3.9
Where you *choose* to place the three building blocks of an app defines app architecture.

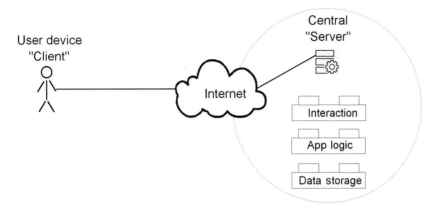

Figure 3.10
Cloud app architecture centralizes all three pieces of app functionality.

displaying information. The device is just a window into the server's work. It is called cloud computing because everything the app does is done on the server, which the app accesses through the Internet (symbolized by a cloud). Everything requires a round trip across the Internet to the central server for the user's device to do anything useful. Cloud architecture is a reincarnation of mainframe architectures from the 1960s, when computers cost several million dollars each and organizations could not afford to give each employee one. An example of cloud architecture is Apple's Siri, where your smartphone is a dumb conduit for the heavy lifting for voice recognition done on a powerful remote machine. Your smartphone does not need to be powerful because it can draw on vast number-crunching resources on the other end through the cloud. The bigger the cloud part gets, the wimpier our devices can become.

The strength and weakness of cloud architecture is that it centralizes everything. Centralization generates economies of scale, eases maintenance (only the software on the server side needs upgrading, not individual devices), and reduces the need for in-house IT staff if another firm manages the server side.[53] Maintenance is a cinch because only one centrally located copy needs to be maintained, upgraded, and bug fixed. New features can constantly and instantly be rolled out, unlike other app architectures where they are held till the next big version upgrade. Its two weaknesses are (a) a single point of vulnerability (a hacker need not break into individual devices but rather just one central server) and (b) it needs reliable Internet connectivity without which the app is useless.

From a business perspective, non-IT managers must weigh in on two considerations: (a) the sensibility of swapping variable operating costs for up-front capital IT investments and (b) whether the economy gained is worth the strategic differentiation sacrificed. Cloud app architectures precipitously lower up-front capital costs because it is a utility-like model where you only pay for usage. But there is a catch: one-off up-front capital cost savings instead become ongoing, variable operating costs. As usage grows, their performance can become sluggish. But cloud servers are typically run by outside firms who are then responsible to grow their capacity. (You typically outsource the cloud part to a specialized firm such as Microsoft, Google, Salesforce, IBM, or Amazon.) If your firm runs the servers itself, it is called a *private* cloud. Private clouds offer none of the legally enforceable performance stipulations of public clouds and are a very costly proposition to build. (Commercial-grade ones can cost billions of dollars.) Popular cloud services run huge collections of computers (called *server farms*, which act as one giant computer) to meet demand; more than a million machines power Google search. (A *data center* is a massive scale facility that functions as a giant server for an app with high usage. Apple's iCloud data center based primarily in Maiden, North Carolina, for example, serves about a billion users.) Adequate performance is guaranteed by service-level agreements (SLAs) that contractually guarantee speed and uptime, with contracts for 99.9 percent reliability typically an order of magnitude costlier than 99 percent reliability. Cloud architecture can scale to meet growing usage needs with enforceable SLAs in place. Non-IT managers can help their IT unit determine the reliability appropriate for the cloud apps that their line functions use.

Their potential for strategic differentiation is poor in practice because you are restricted to existing commoditized solutions also available to your rivals rather than ones tailored precisely to your firm's needs. Cloud app architectures are the second-most widespread app architectures used for corporate IT apps and often the most economical to operate.

Cloud architectures are therefore recommended as a capital-economizing approach for apps that do not differentiate your firm and for devices with minis-cule computing prowess (e.g., IoT devices such as smart thermostats and appliances whose intelligence is in the cloud). Flipping the cloud arrangement locates all three app functions on the user device, creating the *stand-alone* app architecture that does not require the Internet at all. (Your word processor and PowerPoint use it; it is a vestige of the pre-Internet era.) It fragments data across individual user devices. We do not delve into it further because it foregoes the entire appeal of using the Internet to integrate fragmented data.

Client-Server Architecture

Client-server app architecture—which predates cloud architectures—locates the interaction and app logic functions on user devices and centralizes only data storage (figure 3.11). The user device does all the app's heavy lifting. It blends an advantage of cloud architecture (centralizing data) yet offers considerably more potential for competitive differentiation. Client-server is the single most common app architecture used for corporate IT apps, both purchased apps and apps custom developed by firms. Their maintenance is costlier and more burdensome because upgrades require upgrading installations on all individual user devices.

Strategically, custom-developed client-server apps are competitively more valuable because a rival must first muddle through reverse engineering them and then bear the high cost of also custom-developing them. This strategic potential does not come cheap because even a small app can have one hundred thousand lines of software code, which costs $15–$40 *per line* to develop ($1.5–$4 million).[54] Their long-term costs can also be far higher because you cannot rely on a Microsoft to maintain what it never created. You must retain your own employees to maintain it, potentially spending as much as another $30 million (700 percent of its initial cost) to maintain it over its lifetime. This estimate of five to seven times is not unreasonable once you know that a railway spends twenty-one times the price of a locomotive engine on its lifetime maintenance. Similarly, lifetime maintenance costs 3.5 times the cost of an average car.[55] Only non-IT managers can answer the question about whether a custom-developed app is competitively worth such a steep price tag.

In-house IT departments historically ran the servers in client-server architectures. However, two new variants of this architecture inspired by cloud-based architectures have emerged. First, *service-oriented architectures*, where some of the server-side functionality can be purchased as a software service that is integrated into custom-built apps. This relieves the firm from some of the cost of custom-developing and

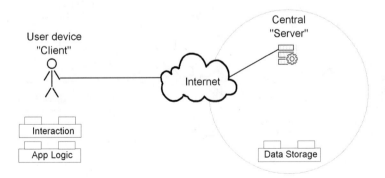

Figure 3.11
Client-server architecture centralizes only data storage.

maintaining the app. Second, *microservices* are discrete generic services that can be purchased from many different firms to assemble the application logic of an app. An app built using them might integrate hundreds of microservices invoked through the Internet alongside software code developed in-house. This can lower up-front costs and accelerate the development of custom apps.

Peer-to-Peer Architecture

Peer-to-peer app architecture (figure 3.12) takes the stand-alone architecture and then connects all user devices using the Internet. Every user device performs all app functions. There is no central server; every user device simultaneously also acts as a little server for all other user devices.[56] This architecture draws its strength from numbers; every new user device added to the "hive" increases its collective capacity, potentially giving it infinite scalability. British Broadcasting Corporation (BBC) uses it to distribute video footage that did not make it into broadcast shows, which would be cost prohibitive to distribute any other way. The hundredfold cost difference of an additional user between Facebook (a cloud architecture) and Skype (a peer-to-peer architecture) is traceable directly to their different app architectures. However, the absence of *any* control relegates this architecture to niche applications in eclectic domains. The absence of control is *the* reason firms such as Netflix needing high scalability shy away from it. Peer-to-peer architecture is therefore recommended only for

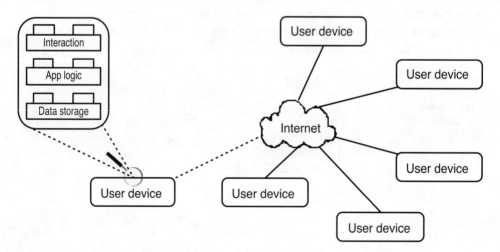

Figure 3.12
Peer-to-peer architectures do not use a central server and replicate all three app functions on each user device.

apps that require very high levels of scalability but demand absolutely no control by a firm over user devices.

Client-server and cloud-based architectures dominate firms' IT portfolios. Even when firms mix and match these app architectures into hybrids, one approach dominates. For example, Skype has a peer-to-peer architecture but incorporates elements of the client-server architecture to monitor users' availability.

Of the three app architectures, cloud is the most centralized, peer-to-peer is the most decentralized, and client-server is in between (figure 3.13).

Trade-Offs among App Architectures

No single architecture is optimal because every one of them involves trade-offs. Figure 3.14 contrasts the operational and strategic trade-offs among these three app architectures. The strength of client-server architecture is speed and reliability; cloud is the least expensive to maintain, and peer-to-peer is the most scalable. None are inherently more secure; more centralized ones centrally concentrate vulnerabilities where protection must focus and decentralized ones require protecting all individual devices. None are inherently more evolvable; evolvability has to deliberately be designed into them. An app's architecture also heavily influences whether its development and upkeep can be outsourced.[57]

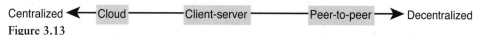

Centralized ◄────Cloud──────────Client-server──────────Peer-to-peer──► Decentralized

Figure 3.13
The three common app architectures run the gamut from centralization to decentralization.

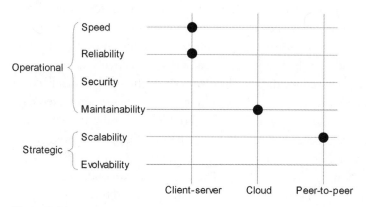

Figure 3.14
Trade-offs among the three app architectures.

Non-IT managers must weigh in on two questions to help assess what is most appropriate for their firm. These questions must be answered individually for each corporate IT app. First, how would you rank the operational consequences that are important to your business and your own function's activities? The choice of trade-offs must be mindful of the interests of not just your firm's line functions but also its business partners and customers. Second, how much operational performance are you willing to sacrifice today to avoid paying a strategic penalty later?

Data Architecture
Data architecture answers one question: Where is your firm's data stored? Integrated firm-wide data is the foundation of IT-enabled automation of business processes and large-scale business analytics. However, the prevalent problem in firms is proliferation of duplicated and inconsistent data. This problem is caused by the dispersion of a firm's data (a) across apps and (b) across geographic locations. They require different fixes.

Fragmentation across Apps
Fragmentation of data across apps is a consequence of the apps in your firm's app portfolio. Recall that a firm's IT portfolio has many apps. Although the most common cloud and client-server apps both centralize data, such centralization is only for *one* app. Every app has its own central server, and their multitude can create silos of data scattered across different apps. For example, an online ordering app will store its data on a different server from, say, a payroll or customer service app. Similar data can therefore be duplicated across apps and become inconsistent over time. This is why Delta Airlines' older systems produced seventeen different answers to a simple question about a flight's gate number. The collection of all apps—by virtue of their architectures—therefore determines how a firm's data assets are organized and where they are located. They collectively define how a firm manages its data. Therefore, data architecture—whether it is centralized or decentralized—is a direct consequence of app architectures. These fragmented data silos are integrated using *data warehouses*, which are large centralized repositories that automatically assemble *copies* of data from different IT apps scattered across various line functions in a firm. Therefore, a data warehouse is to your firm's data what the Library of Congress is to books.[58] The access to firm-wide data that it provides is a stepping-stone to business processes innovation and business analytics initiatives.

Dispersion across Geographic Locations

An app's users becoming more geographically dispersed over time can also cause its data to become geographically dispersed. Although an app might begin with one central server that your employees or customers use, its operational performance can degrade to intolerable levels if your colleague in, say, Singapore has to constantly access data to do her day-to-day job from a machine sitting ten thousand miles away in Atlanta. You can choose between two solutions shown in figure 3.15 to solve this problem. Imagine the entirety of your firm's data for an app as a cheesecake; you can either make replicas of it or slice it into pieces that you spread around. The first approach is called *replication* (figure 3.15[a]), where you make copies of an app's entire data and keep a copy at each location so users' apps make a quick local trip to access it. To ensure that the copies remain synced, you connect them using the Internet. (Such connections are easy to secure by encrypting them; anyone snooping on them will only see gibberish.) Alternatively, you can slice the app's database into smaller pieces, where each piece only keeps data for that locale (*partitioning* in figure 3.15[b]).[59] By connecting each piece to the Internet, you can still slowly send or read data from each far-off location or even assemble copies of it in a central data warehouse.

As a non-IT manager, you can help answer two questions to help your IT colleagues decide on the appropriate data architecture. First, what data can remain siloed (e.g., in a line function or in one sales channel) and what data should be centralized firm-wide either for executing your core business processes or for pursuing analytics? Second, if your firm has international operations, what type of data must be shared across your markets?

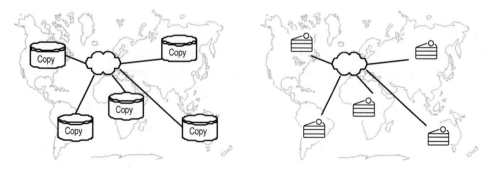

Figure 3.15
(a) Replication places a copy of the data everywhere and (b) partitioning places a different slice of it at each location.

Box 3.3
The Data Architecture That Makes Netflix Flow[60]

Netflix consumed more than a third of all US Internet traffic, serving up content to more than fifty million paying customers in 2017 in the United States alone. Video is the most data-intensive content that you can send over the Internet, and even a slight slowdown can ruin a movie experience. Netflix uses a replicated data architecture to minimize this problem, the idea being to spread out copies of its movie content on streaming servers far enough geographically so all subscribers will be close to some of them. We're talking serious amounts of content; it took twelve servers to hold a single copy of Netflix's 2016 catalog. Each film is encoded into more than fifty versions with varying video quality, audio quality, and language dubbing. Netflix places duplicates of the entire content in hundreds of data centers owned by Internet service providers and companies such as Amazon, both around the United States and in the almost two hundred foreign countries in which it operates. It provides for free its proprietary hardware to reduce costs incurred by any Internet service provider that serves more than one hundred thousand customers. The streaming app itself has a cloud architecture—independent of whether it is built into your Internet-connected TV or streaming box or installed on your iPad. This distributed, replicated data architecture is key to ensuring that Netflix flows without hiccups. Netflix sticks to industry standards for its infrastructure and even releases much of its infrastructure software code to the open-source community. It knows that the infrastructure is not its differentiator; widely sharing it encourages others to build on it and improve it. It knows that its competitive differentiator is its home-brewed movie-recommendation app combined with its trove of ratings data, which it fiercely safeguards.

Key Takeaways

1. *IT architecture as technology's DNA.* It irreversibly imprints trade-offs between immediate operational performance and future evolvability. Operationally, it drives an IT asset's fitness of purpose, security, and maintenance costs. Strategically, it shapes IT assets' scalability and capacity to evolve in not-yet-anticipated ways.
2. *IT architecture as a translator.* It translates between business-speak and technology-speak to foster a shared purpose. By transforming strategy-driven business priorities into matching IT assets, it provides a blueprint for executing business strategy.
3. *Enterprise architecture spans all three classes of IT assets in your firm's IT portfolio. App architecture* is how an app's three building blocks are split across the Internet to juggle trade-offs among speed, reliability, maintenance costs, security, and evolvability. Centralizing IT *infrastructure architecture* lowers costs, but decentralizing it helps tailor it to line functions differing needs. *Data architecture* determines data consistency and accessibility.

4. *Complexity causes brittleness.* Growing complexity—which makes apps brittle to change—can be curbed using a Lego-like approach to connect them to each other.

5. *Disengagement causes erroneous trade-offs.* By choosing not to contribute to architectural decisions, you delegate them to your IT folks. They will invariably optimize for operational performance, oblivious to any strategic consequences. Non-IT managers' inputs help dodge unintended strategic penalties.

The Non-IT Managers' Checklist

☐ For *each* major IT app used by your line function . . .

Is it a strategic differentiator or needed just to keep up with your archrivals?

Rank order its desirable operational and strategic properties in table 3.1.

What is the threshold of speed and reliability below which it is a liability?

How much should you sacrifice operational performance today to avoid a strategic penalty later?

☐ What data must be local versus centralized firm-wide?

☐ What IT infrastructure must sacrifice economy to better tailor it to which line function?

Part 3

Payoffs

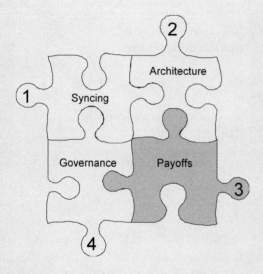

Jargon Decoder

IT payoff clock	A sequence of steps—each of which must go right—for an IT project to deliver financial benefits.
IT funding dilemma	Funding corporate IT can be simple, accurate, or fair; pick any two.
80/20 rule	20 percent of the metrics provide 80 percent of the insight into IT's business value.
Operational IT metrics	Short-term metrics used to judge improvement in a particular business activity resulting from an IT project.
Financial IT metrics	Long-term metrics used to judge IT's financial impact on your firm's bottom line.
Capital versus operating costs	The one-time costs of new IT assets versus the much larger ongoing costs of keeping them running.
Real options	Flexibility without the obligation to do something in a project.

4

Dollars and Sense

With annual IT spending eclipsing $4 trillion, firms are questioning whether they are getting their money's worth from their single biggest capital expense. Eight out of ten firms struggle to estimate the benefits of their IT investments.[1] They are notoriously difficult to financially value, but that is hardly an excuse for not attempting to put a dollar value on them.[2,3,4,5] Your firm can avoid misguided IT investments and discover valuable opportunities with tenacity and fiscal discipline, but only with non-IT managers' inputs.

This chapter explores how non-IT managers can help ensure a healthy return on IT investments. Sensibility in IT investment boils down to four questions:

1. How much does it cost and who foots the bill?
2. Are we investing in the right places?
3. Are we getting our money's worth?
4. How do we tread when the payoff is potentially huge but uncertain?

The end goal of fiscal discipline is neither keeping up with the Joneses nor being a cheapskate, but spending your IT dollars more wisely. We begin with the *IT payoff clock*—a sequence of steps through which an IT investment gradually translates into bottom-line financial returns. We then explore four tricky properties of IT that good IT metrics must tackle, ways of figuring out how much IT actually costs your firm, and deciding who should foot the bill.

IT investments proceed one project at a time, which requires judging individual projects' business impacts using short-term *operational metrics* drawn directly from its functional domain. Any such operational improvements should eventually have a tangible financial impact, which we measure using long-term *financial metrics*. Financial metrics make the leap from individual IT projects to the bottom-line impact of your firm's IT portfolio. They assess what happened as well as what we expect will happen. Metrics for IT's impact in this chapter directly connect IT strategy to your coursework on managerial accounting and corporate finance. Finally, we explore how you can use *real options* thinking to tread into high-risk, high-return IT projects without losing your shirt.

The IT Payoff Clock

Any IT project's financial benefits emerge through a sequence of intervening steps, each of which must go right. The *IT payoff clock* in figure 4.1 summarizes them. You must grasp it to pick metrics appropriate at each step to keep an IT investment on track to deliver a financial return. The payoff fails to materialize if even one step goes awry. You initiate the clock by investing in a new IT project.

1. *Implementation.* The initial investment begins a project's implementation cycle. This phase can be short if you purchase the system and integrate it into your IT portfolio or can take several years if you custom build it. Project management (chapter 6) is all about getting this part right, irrespective of whether you do it in-house or outsource it (chapter 7).

2. *Adoption.* Once you flip the proverbial on switch after rolling out a completed system, your employees must *use* it for it to generate value.[6, 7, 8] A widespread dysfunction is that corporate IT units focus on delivering software rather than business value.[9] So measurement stops at this point. The rest of this chapter focuses on the

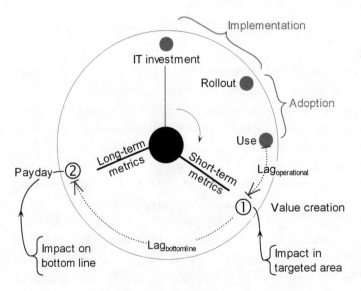

Figure 4.1
The IT payoff clock.

next two steps in the IT payoff clock where the operational and financial benefits of IT surface.

3. *Business value creation* (①). An IT system in full-fledged use can begin generating value by impacting—after a delay (Lag$_{operational}$ in figure 4.1)—the functional area(s) that it targets.[10, 11] The *short-term* operational metrics in this chapter measure this operational impact. They must relate directly to just *the activity that a project targets*. The time lag after which it is appropriate to attempt to measure them (Lag$_{operational}$) is crucial; measure too early and you will incorrectly conclude that it was a dud.

Many firms do not even get this far, focusing instead on *IT* performance metrics. Operational metrics for corporate IT must judge desired business outcomes, not technical achievements.[12] If left to their own devices, IT units gravitate toward technical performance metrics uncorrelated with business benefits.[13] They track many technical metrics for their own consumption (e.g., system uptime, transaction processing speed, user satisfaction scores, timeliness of projects, and help-desk response times). These should be of little interest to non-IT managers because they do not measure IT's *business* impact.

4. *Payday* (②). Operational improvements—better, faster, or cheaper—in a project's targeted area must eventually improve revenues or reduce costs, thus improving a firm's bottom-line margins. The *long-term metrics* discussed in this chapter measure this financial payoff. They involve a second delay—Lag$_{bottomline}$ in figure 4.1—which also requires non-IT managers' insight.

Challenges Unique to IT Investments

IT investments differ from other capital investments such as buildings and factories in four ways: (a) many of their benefits are intangible, (b) their impact lags investment, (c) it is difficult to be sure that they *caused* observed improvements, and (d) they can demand complementary investments to realize an impact.[14, 15, 16] IT metrics must account for these idiosyncrasies, which table 4.1 summarizes.

a. *Intangibility of benefits.* Some benefits of IT can be intangible: for example, increased customer satisfaction, faster decision making, brand awareness, or improved collaboration inside and outside your firm. Their intangibility can never be an excuse for poor fiscal discipline because intangible benefits are benefits *only* if they eventually show up in the bottom line or in its *measurable* future prospects. Non-IT managers can help make that connection using both operational and financial metrics.[17]

b. *Lags in impact*. The observable impact of IT investments is rarely immediate. It can take time for apps to be absorbed into a firm's operations, and IT infrastructure can have long payback periods involving complementary IT investments that leverage it. The time frame for IT metrics must explicitly recognize such lags for each major IT investment.

c. *Attribution challenge*. It is often difficult to attribute improvements in an organizational outcome to IT investments. If your sales increased next year, you would be hard pressed to be certain that it was caused by a website overhaul and not because the economy improved or a rival dropped the ball. The longer $Lag_{operational}$ and $Lag_{bottomline}$ in figure 4.1, the more difficult it is to attribute improvements to your firm's IT investments. The length of time appropriate for both of them must come entirely from non-IT managers. Judgments of IT must therefore track year-on-year *changes* in key business metrics and benchmark them against your archrivals where possible. Are they getting better or worse over time?

d. *Complementarities*. IT investments often exhibit complementarities; one IT investment can be worth more in conjunction with another. For example, Starbucks's smartphone ordering system was more valuable when Starbucks also invested in new in-store cash registers that could process orders received from it. This requires IT metrics to track the impact of a firm's portfolio of IT assets, not just individual projects.

Choosing a Few Good IT Metrics

Measurement drives behavior. You must be careful in your choice of IT metrics because you encourage what they measure. Firms often use too many metrics for IT, which drowns them in a sea of meaningless data. Simpler is better, and a thoughtful few are better than many. Like gauges in your car, simultaneously trying to track too many will cause a wreck.

Table 4.1
Properties of IT-Appropriate Metrics

IT investment attribute	IT metrics must . . .
Intangibility of benefits	Translate into measurable business consequences
Lagged impact	Span an appropriate time span
Attribution challenge	Track *changes* in metrics, benchmarked against archrivals
Low payoff without complementary IT investments	Monitor an IT *portfolio's* impact on business outcomes

IT metrics are appropriate if they nudge IT to solve the *right* problems that move your firm toward its strategic aspiration. Follow the 80/20 rule for selecting metrics: strive to find the 20 percent of the metrics that provide 80 percent of the insight into the business value of IT. Use three criteria to select just a few IT metrics: (a) cost-effectiveness, (b) competitive insightfulness, and (c) objectivity.

a. Worth more than they cost. The value of a metric must be worth more than the cost of tracking it. As figure 4.2 illustrates, measurement costs of metrics eat into the financial benefits of an IT investment, leaving fewer of them as measurable business value (the shaded area). You do not need pinpoint accuracy for them to be useful; close enough suffices.

b. Competitively insightful. To be strategically relevant, an IT metric must be business centric, not IT centric. It should help you intuitively gauge how your IT assets are moving your firm toward its strategic aspiration (e.g., squeezing costs if you are a cost leader or increasing customers' willingness to pay if you aspire to differentiate). It should also help you benchmark against your archrivals the business value that your firm is getting from IT.

c. Objective, spanning the short and long term. The excuse that IT's benefits are intangible lacks credibility because IT costs real money. If IT metrics are subjective, IT proponents and opponents can construct their own narrative, untroubled by facts. Having verifiable, agreed-upon measures of IT success dodges a guessing game that no one can win. Such metrics must be objectively quantifiable; subjective IT satisfaction ratings cannot substitute for objectivity. They also provide a reliable way to compare IT investments with each other and from year to year.

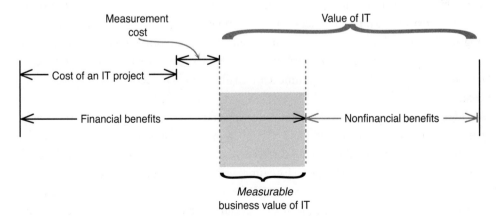

Figure 4.2
Metrics' measurement costs reduce the project's measurable business value.

Box 4.1
The Hawthorne Effect: Separating a Blip from a Real Improvement

Operational IT metrics often judge employees' work. Sometimes simply knowing that they are being watched can alter their behavior. It might have nothing to do with an IT project you might have rolled out. This phenomenon—the Hawthorne effect—was observed in the 1920s in Western Electric's Chicago plant. The experimenters simply changed lighting levels, and it caused workers productivity to rise. However, the increase in productivity was short-lived. The blip had nothing to do with the lighting but everything to do with the change. This is why you need an appropriate delay—$Lag_{operational}$ in figure 4.1—between introducing a new IT system and measuring an operational metric to remove the Hawthorne effect from its actual impact.

The financial benefits of an IT project can take several years to materialize, even after you have completed it and know the actual costs incurred.[18] The few metrics that you use must therefore span the short term (① in figure 4.1) and the long term (②) and be explicit about their time lags (the two arrows $Lag_{operational}$ and $Lag_{bottomline}$ in figure 4.1, measured in months or years).

How Much Does IT Cost?

All IT funding approaches require knowing the *costs* of IT, which can be tricky because they can have both capital expenditures and operating cost components. *Capital expenditures* are the costs of purchasing or building new IT systems. Capital expenditures, unlike operating expenses, pay off in the future and therefore compete with other immediate investment priorities of firms. *Operating expenses*—the ongoing cost of running IT assets—are the lion's share of corporate IT costs. Such ongoing costs include salaries, support, licensing fees, maintenance, training users, and ensuring that evolving IT systems continue to talk to each other. Operating expenses over an IT asset's lifetime can easily approach several times its initial cost.

Investing in IT is susceptible to the same mistakes as you buying a car. You might spend less up front on a car but could pay much more in maintenance and repair costs. A more expensive car might actually cost less over its lifetime. Unless you know the total costs of ownership over its expected lifetime, you cannot reliably compare one car to another. This challenge is aggravated in IT investments because their estimated lifetimes can turn out wrong in hindsight. Many corporate systems—like the electronic learning system you are likely using for this course—outlive their intended lifespan by years.

The approach used to reliably estimate the actual costs of any IT asset is its *total cost of ownership* (TCO). It is the total cost of getting *and* running an IT asset over its lifetime. Besides an IT asset's up-front cost, TCO includes human costs such as IT staff salaries, operating expenses (e.g., electricity, network connectivity, and technical support), training, and maintenance. Tracking these costs can itself be a costly endeavor. The upside of TCO is the widespread availability of industry benchmark data that allows you to see how your costs compare with averages in your own industry for specific types of IT assets.

Will a Project Be a Worthwhile Investment?
You can use three approaches to judge whether a prospective IT project is likely to be a worthwhile investment: net present value, the hurdle rate rule, and return on investment.

Net Present Value
The workhorse approach that helps decide whether an IT project is likely to be a sensible investment is its *net present value* (NPV). You know from your accounting coursework that NPV is a project's benefits minus costs, accounting for the time value of money. Time value of money comes into play because a project's costs and benefits can span multiple years.[19] NPV's appeal is its intuitive simplicity and understandability to managers in any department in a firm. The heuristic—*the NPV rule*—is simple: pursue projects with positive NPV and reject those with negative NPV.

NPV, however, cannot directly help choose between two projects if they have different costs. To wisely use your firm's limited capital, you need insight into which IT project would be more valuable to *your* firm. You can compute each project's *profitability index* from their NPVs to do such a project-to-project comparison. It allows an apples-to-apples comparison because it represents the value created for each dollar invested. A project with a higher profitability index is preferable.

You must be careful in overrelying on NPV for judging IT investments for three reasons. First, NPV requires calculating costs and benefits in dollars, both of which can be notoriously difficult to even guesstimate reliably for IT projects. Costs are often underestimated by 50–100 percent and often overlook installation, debugging, and training costs.[20, 21] Benefits can be even harder to quantify in dollar terms. Unrealistic projections of a project's financial benefits invariably result in bad IT investments.[22] Second, NPV works well when there is little uncertainty involved in an IT project. This scenario rarely exists outside accounting textbooks. Third, NPV cannot account for intangible costs and benefits.

Hurdle Rate Rule

Firms set their own *hurdle rate* threshold, which is a preset percentage return that a prospective project must exceed for it to be considered a sensible investment. For a project to proceed, its own projected return (*internal rate of return*) must exceed your firm's predefined hurdle rate. Hurdle rates are set with good intentions to discourage squandering money on poor projects, but they can penalize the pursuit of strategically promising IT projects whose benefits are difficult to quantify. Real options thinking discussed later in this chapter allows such projects to demonstrate their potential through small, staged investments.

Return on Investment

A much simpler yardstick is *return on investment* (ROI), which is the percentage return that your investment in a project pays back. A $100,000 project that increases revenues by $120,000 has a 20 percent ROI. Knowing this number allows you to decide whether you are better off spending that money on a particular project instead of other ways you could have spent it (the project's *opportunity costs*[23]). Firms also use a project's *payback period*, which is how long it will take to recoup its cost. This should only be used as a rule of thumb to compare projects that deserve further consideration and to weed out ones that will realistically never recover their costs.

The downside of all these project payoff metrics is that they are more about the price that you pay but not the business value that you get. They focus more on recovering an IT project's costs but not on how it—or your firm's IT portfolio—enhances your firm's competitiveness beyond the payback period. IT projects with the highest ROI are also not necessarily ones that advance your firm toward its strategic aspiration.

Who Foots the Bill for IT?

Any approach for funding corporate IT can have only two of three desirable properties: simple, accurate, and fair (figure 4.3). You can pick any two. It can be simple and accurate but not fair, accurate and fair but not simple, or fair and simple but not accurate.

Who foots the bill for IT—which encompasses both capital investments and operating expenses—depends on which of the three common accounting approaches is used: corporate funding, allocation, and chargeback summarized in table 4.2:

1. *Corporate funding* pays for IT expenses out of corporate coffers. It encourages big, ambitious IT projects since no one line function foots the bill. Its downside is that IT can become technology driven rather than business driven, with IT managers pursuing

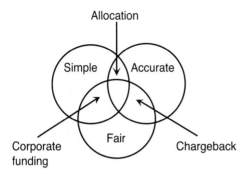

Figure 4.3
Simple, accurate, or fair: pick any two for funding IT.

technology for technology's sake. This can encourage poor business decisions about IT and do more damage sustaining IT budgets in the long run when the annual corporate budgeting process subjects IT expenditures to a harsh competition with other corporate spending priorities. Corporate funding of IT is therefore simple and fair but not accurate. Line functions foot the bill for other two funding approaches, typically monthly.

2. *Allocation* divides up IT costs among line functions based on some count such as the number of user accounts and bills them based on that count. If a thousand-person company spent $100,000 on IT last month, a line function with fifty users gets a five-thousand-dollar (50 × $100) bill. It does not matter that some employees in that line function (e.g., a parking deck attendant) do not even use these systems; their department still foots the bill. Therefore, the approach is simple and accurate but not fair because it ignores actual usage.[24]

Table 4.2
The Three Approaches to Funding Corporate IT

Funding approach	Mechanism	Who pays	Upside	Downside	More appropriate for . . .	
					Apps	Infrastructure
Corporate	Fixed annual budget	Corporate coffers	Encourages ambitious projects	IT competes with other priorities	•	
Allocation	Costs per user	Line functions	Low bookkeeping overhead	Unfair because it overlooks usage		•
Chargeback	Usage billing	Line functions	Fair	Onerous bookkeeping		•

3. *Chargeback* charges line functions for actual usage to recover IT costs.[25] This approach is fairer than others because your line function is charged for what it uses, and it sensitizes managers to how much IT is costing their department. Its downside is the onerous bookkeeping overhead to compile detailed usage data for every IT asset. Chargeback is therefore fair and accurate but not simple. In smaller firms, the bookkeeping overhead can exceed the actual costs of IT.

Knowing which approach to use for what IT asset is important. Some approaches work better than others depending on the type of IT asset. Corporate funding is typically more appropriate for funding app-development projects and allocation or chargeback for IT infrastructure. The rationale is that IT infrastructure consumes about half of corporate IT budgets but is rarely a source of competitive advantage. Therefore, the accuracy of both allocation and chargeback disciplines spending on IT infrastructure and encourages frugality. In contrast, apps are a venue for IT-driven business innovation that can competitively differentiate your firm. The corporate funding approach is more likely to encourage ambitious IT app projects.

Business Value: Are We Getting Our Money's Worth?

Quantifiable data trumps blind faith in credibly demonstrating IT's business value. Quantifying forces accountability and precise thinking. Any IT investment promises to make a specific operational activity better, faster, or cheaper. Operational metrics capture such operational impacts in the short term; they are how you measure the IT unit against its promises to the line functions. Eventually, any operational improvement either increases revenues or reduces costs. An improvement in an operational metric must therefore eventually show up in a firm's margins, which are the difference between revenues and costs. Therefore, improvements in short-term operational metrics should lead to improvements in long-term financial metrics. You need both to judge IT's payoffs.

Operational Metrics: The Stepping-Stone to IT's Financial Benefits

You often hear claims about how IT enhances business agility; it is operational metrics that gives them substance. After a completed project is put to use, it must improve the functional activity that it targets before it can produce financial returns. *Operational metrics* tied directly to a project's business objectives quantify objectively whether it is on a trajectory to deliver its promised financial benefits. Their practical utility is more than just an intermediate reality check. Operational metrics can provide clues about where to focus attention and what to change to realize

Box 4.2
How Obsession over Operational Metrics Linked to Strategic Aspiration
Fostered a Century of Growth at UPS

UPS is a leading American package delivery company that has been in business since 1907, employing about a half million people with operations in more than 220 countries (www.ups.com). It has repeatedly survived dramatic shifts in its business over a hundred years by focusing on just the one thing it does well and aspires to get better at: efficiently getting a package from point A to B. In 1913, it was the advent of automobiles (particularly Ford's mass-market Model-T) that threatened the future of UPS messenger boys. In the 1970s, it was the fax machine that threatened its overnight business. In the mid-1980s, it was FedEx's acquisition of airplanes. In the late 1980s, it was e-mail. In the late 1990s, it was the Internet. And today it is 3-D printing. Relentless focus rather than jumping on the latest fad helps UPS grow stronger and more dominant with every disruptive innovation that threatened its existence.

UPS and its smaller rival FedEx both annually spend about $1 billion on IT, but differently. IT plays a different strategy-driven role for them. UPS's IT strategy is an offshoot of its industrial engineering roots. Over the years, it has optimized little details such as which foot a UPS driver puts first in her truck, keeping truck keys on her pinky finger, and minimizing left turns in countries that drive on the right side of the road (it saves fuel burned waiting at a red light). Its IT investments focus on consistency, reliability, and efficiency in getting a package from point A to B. Its centralized IT environment focuses on its aspiration to be low cost and dependable for a mass market. In contrast, FedEx's IT focuses on flexibly serving specific segments of the mass market but not all of it. This is reflected in FedEx's costlier, decentralized IT portfolio conducive to meeting the distinctive needs of the diverse market segments that it serves. Its decentralized IT portfolio reinforces its strategic aspiration to differentiate itself through local innovations appropriate to its many global markets. Both UPS and FedEx are successful because their IT investments match their distinctive strategic aspirations.

When the Internet came into the scene, UPS was a late bloomer. It ramped up its IT investments long after FedEx had online package tracking capabilities. UPS decided to build a single package-tracking database fed by cellular-connected handheld scanners given to all UPS drivers. This was done to make it almost impossible to lose a package along the way. This IT project eventually became a platform (i.e., provided growth options described later) for entirely unrelated lines of business. The data collected by its handheld devices became the basis for new high-margin services such as guaranteed delivery, financial services for corporate customers, an international customs clearinghouse, and reverse logistics (e.g., handling store returns).

It also provided the foundation for UPS to later build several IT innovations that lowered its costs. These included IT-driven route optimization for delivery trucks that increased UPS's capacity and reduced fuel costs, reducing accident-prone reverse gear shifts, and a system to coordinate its delivery truck fleet with its 500-plus aircraft, its smartphone application, and an API that allows thousands of retailers to directly integrate UPS services into their websites.

Box 4.2 (*continued*)

UPS measures the business value of its IT investments using operational metrics that match its strategic aspiration of cost efficiency for a mass market. Each UPS delivery truck drives about one hundred miles each day. Sensors embedded in them monitor data on speed, direction, braking behavior, reversals, and fuel performance.[26] UPS analyzes such data to refine routing and optimize package pickups and deliveries; each mile saved on average reduces its fuel costs by $50 million a year.[27] For such IT investments, it uses operational metrics such as fuel savings and minutes of employee labor reduced. Its operational IT apps even monitor individual UPS trucks to help load each most efficiently and alert the maintenance crew using actual wear-and-tear data to preemptively repair a truck part before it breaks. UPS systems—using a GPS chip built into UPS drivers' equipment—even alert a truck driver if she is about to drop off a package at the wrong address.

The moment an incoming package is scanned into UPS's automated sorting hub in Louisville, Kentucky, its IT systems kick in to activate automated sorting machines to route it on 110 miles of conveyor belts to get it to the appropriate plane among the hundred scheduled to depart each night.[28] Its custom-built apps combine data from radars and weather systems with data from plane-door lock sensors that indicate that the plane is loaded, reducing taxi time enough to save a quarter million gallons of jet fuel each year. The operational metric used to judge this IT-centric facility is the speed with which an incoming package gets on the correct plane. UPS's IT investments paid off because they obsessively focused on its strategy of aspiring to be a reliable and cost-effective shipper.

the full potential of an IT investment after the money has been spent. If a project's operational metrics raise a red flag, you can tweak IT systems, better train users, and incentivize its use.

Such metrics help your IT colleagues see their work in the big picture of your firm. Measuring—and publicizing—your IT colleagues' contribution to business success using such operational metrics is a powerful syncing mechanism. Tying their compensation to operational business metrics is a powerful way to hold them accountable for business results.

Non-IT managers in a project's targeted functional area are the primary source of appropriate operational metrics for IT. Such metrics must be communicated transparently to your IT unit, preferably involving it in creating them. This is an opportunity to broaden your IT colleagues' understanding of how their work fits into the whole.

For example, inventory turns is a cost-effective, insightful, and objective metric for an inventory management system project.[29] However, a raw operational metric by itself does not tell you much. If your inventory turns is 4.6, is that good or bad?

You need a frame of reference for it to make sense. There are two ways of doing this: (a) examining *change* (Δ) vis-à-vis its previous values in your own firm and (b) comparing it to your archrivals where possible. Such before-and-after comparisons contrast an operational metric's level before and after an IT system became widely used.[30] Focusing on such changes simplifies judging a project's impact. It also separates correlation from causation attributable to an IT investment. For example, you cannot be certain that an inventory management system project completed last year *caused* an observed improvement in your inventory turns this year. It could have been a slew of other factors such as an economic boom, an increase in consumer confidence, the demise of a rival, better advertising, or a sheer fluke. This is why you must carefully pick a Lag$_{operational}$ interval. The change had better be in the intended direction for the project to eventually deliver its promised financial benefits.

A good operational metric must explicitly articulate the following:

a. *The project's promise.* Whether it will help do something better, faster, or cheaper. Will that reduce costs or increase revenues? An improvement in an operational metric eventually must lead to at least one of them.

b. *The measure.* Dollars, percentages, or a raw number?

c. *Time to impact.* How long will it take to see the change, measured in years? This is Lag$_{operational}$ in figure 4.1.

Try writing a one-liner crux of a project's measurable value (e.g., project X will increase inventory turns by 10 percent within two years). If you struggle to write one, the project has shaky ambitions and will struggle to deliver concrete business value. (We discuss the three major reasons IT projects fail to deliver business value in chapter 6.)

Operational metrics is where IT strategy meets managerial accounting and operations management. Operational metrics must focus on a project's intended business *outcomes*, not what a project does. Table 4.3 provides a few illustrative examples of operational impacts and their corresponding metrics for IT projects. Focus on changes for each operational metric before and after an IT project is rolled out. In table 4.3, two operational metrics predominate how IT adds value to a firm irrespective of its strategic aspiration. These are how IT raises the productivity of both your firm's employees (which matters most in service industries) and the non-IT assets that it already owns (which matters most in asset-intensive industries).[31, 32] Even an IT investment intended to reach new customers, create new revenue streams, or enter new markets can be measured using operational metrics. The last two in table 4.3—better decision making and improved strategic agility—are often cited as holistic motivations for IT investments. Their operational metrics must be devised for and by the line functions where you expect these impacts. Eventually, *every* improvement in any functional area must impact your firm's margins. Table 4.3 also shows whether we expect them to impact margins by increasing revenues or decreasing costs.

You, as a non-IT manager, can help identify (a) a measurable operational metric in the domain targeted by a particular IT investment and (b) the appropriate Lag$_{operational}$ in figure 4.1 before changes in it are measured.

Financial Metrics: IT's Long-Term Bottom-Line Impacts

Operational metrics gauge the functional impacts of an IT project, but not of the firm's whole IT portfolio. Your IT metrics must also gauge how well your IT portfolio as a whole is moving your firm toward its strategic aspiration. If you aspire to be a cost-leader, IT must help do things more efficiently (e.g., lower costs or optimize pricing). If you aspire to differentiate your offerings, IT must increase customer willingness to pay (e.g., an increase in margins per customer).

The bottom-line impact of IT on your firm's performance is measured by *changes* in your firm-level financial metrics; this is where IT strategy meets corporate finance.[33] Table 4.4 summarizes them. Such metrics can be retrospective or prospective. Retrospective ones help assess how earlier IT investments have affected your firm (e.g., changes in operating margins and return on invested capital), and forward-looking ones help assess how it is improving your firm's future prospects (e.g., changes in

Box 4.3
Moneyball: How Choosing Different Operational Metrics
Helped Create a Baseball Powerhouse

The legendary fame and fortune of the lowly Oakland Athletics team in US Major League Baseball was triggered by breaking away from indoctrinated practices of using scouts and batting averages to pick players. Team manager Billy Beane shifted instead to using data on on-base percentages and slugging percentages to pick baseball players. The right operational metrics can focus organizations to deliver what really matters. The shift in metrics was not a groundbreaking shift, but its consequences were. The result was turning the middling team into a powerhouse with an unrivaled record showcased in the 2011 Hollywood movie *Moneyball*. Eventually, the New York Mets, Yankees, San Diego Padres, St. Louis Cardinals, Boston Red Sox, and Arizona Diamondbacks all copied Beane's approach. The analytics-driven differentiator became the new norm. This means that Oakland Athletics' operational metrics must now help judge how much it outperforms these rivals.

Table 4.3

Illustrative Examples of Common Operational Impacts and Metrics for IT Projects

Project's promise			Operational impact	Operational metric	Effect on margins	
					Increase revenues	Decrease costs
Better	Faster	Cheaper				
•			Employee productivity	Δ Revenue per employee	•	•
•			Capital asset productivity	Δ Return on invested capital	•	•
•			Collaboration	Δ Forecasting errors	•	•
•			Supply chain management	Δ Inventory turns	•	•
•			Value added to offerings	Δ Unit selling price	•	
•			Customer loyalty	Δ Revenue per customer	•	
•		•	Reach new customers	Δ Customer base	•	
•			Enter new markets	Δ Revenue	•	
•			Create a new revenue stream	Δ Revenue	•	
		•	Reducing ongoing IT costs	Δ IT spending per employee		•
•	•		Decision making	—	•	•
	•		Strategic agility	—	•	

Tobin's q and P/E ratio, which can only be used in public firms). We eschew the popular balanced scorecard approach because it is subjective and economic value added (EVA) because it is often inappropriate for innovative IT applications.[34]

Retrospective Bottom-Line Financial Metrics

You could argue till the cows come home for IT's operational impacts, such as speedier decisions, more efficiently executed business processes, superior service, customer loyalty, added value, and better collaboration. However, they are only means to a financial end. That end is creating more business value using your people and assets. Any IT project worth its salt and the IT portfolio that it is part of must therefore eventually improve your firm's margins, which are your proverbial bottom line. This

Table 4.4
Four Long-Term Financial Metrics for Judging IT's Bottom-Line Impact

Bottom-line metric	Definition
Retrospective	
Operating margins	Difference between revenues and costs.
Return on invested capital (ROIC)	Ratio of profit generated and the capital invested in generating it.
Forward-looking	
Tobin's q	Ratio of your firm's market value and the replacement value of all its assets.
P/E ratio	Ratio of share price and earnings per share.

is measured as improvements in your firm's *net operating margins* (a) over time and (b) relative to your archrivals. IT's impact might fail to show up in margins if competition in your industry forces you to pass on the savings to consumers as lower costs or higher quality.[35] This makes it even more important to compare *changes* in your margins to your archrivals and to triangulate them using other financial performance metrics.

Firms often use growth, market share, and common financial ratios (ROI, ROA) as bottom-line metrics. However, these alone can be misleading metrics for strategy.[36] The goal—irrespective of your firm's strategic orientation—is to earn better returns on your invested resources, which is measured by ROIC. ROIC is the ratio of profit generated by the capital invested in generating it. Operational metrics that correlate with ROIC are improvements in labor productivity (*Δrevenue per employee*) and in asset productivity (*ΔROA*).

Forward-Looking Financial Metrics
Margins, ROIC, and their accounting-based kin are backward-looking measures of value creation.[37, 38] They cannot offer insight into how your IT investments are strengthening your firm's *future* performance potential.[39] In public firms—but not private firms or nonprofits—you can complement them with two forward-looking indicators: (1) Tobin's q and (2) P/E ratio. Both are aggregate and noisy predictors of future firm performance because sources other than IT can affect them. Therefore, you must track *changes* in over time (Δs) to connect them—imperfectly—to IT investments.

Tobin's q is the ratio of your firm's market value and the replacement value of all its assets. A Tobin's q greater than one means that the market values your firm's intangible assets that aren't recorded in its books or reflected in accounting ratios (e.g., IT capabilities, social networks, intellectual property, brands, or customer goodwill).[40] For example, if your firm's market value (stock market capitalization) is $125 million and its assets would cost $100 million to replace, the market is signaling that it places a premium of $25 million on the future performance potential of your firm's intangible assets including IT. *Changes* in Tobin's q over time signal IT's contribution to your firm's performance potential (e.g., through improved service, the appeal of its market offerings, improved coordination, and market agility). Tobin's q is sensitive to industry, so you should also benchmark it against your Red Queen cohort of industry archrivals. (Temper your enthusiasm; such benchmarks get decimated when IT innovations begin to blur industry boundaries as chapter 9 describes and as has already happened in, say, camera versus phone industries.)

A second forward-looking metric is your firm's *P/E ratio*—share price divided by earnings per share—both over time and relative to your archrivals. It represents the market's expectations about your firm's future ability to grow profitably. Watching it safeguards firms from mindlessly growing revenues with unsustainable margins and focuses them on profitable growth.[41] P/E ratios are not entirely speculative because they are based on track record and the confidence of a large number of outside investors. An increase in P/E ratio signals that these outside observers consider your firm to have high growth potential; this could partially be attributed to your IT investments (which are a big chunk of firms' capital investments). Watching the P/E ratio is not a dysfunctional appeasement to shareholder value but rather an actionable gauge of whether your previous IT investments are strengthening your firm's future prospects. Be cautious that IT investments cannot be isolated from other things that can increase a P/E ratio (e.g., a hit product or a market boom). It is a mistake to rely on just one number; triangulate it with other aggregate metrics such as Tobin's q.

Are We Investing in the Right Places?

Analyzing your IT portfolio is key to understanding whether your firm is investing the right amounts in the right places. You must examine your entire portfolio of IT assets including (a) apps and (b) IT infrastructure that provides a technology foundation such as Internet connectivity, hardware (e.g., desktops, tablets, handheld devices), and data storage used by apps. Apps can be operational (which streamline and automate core business operations) or strategic (which foster competitive advantage over rivals by helping enter new markets or innovate in products, services, or business processes).

Your firm's mix of IT assets must be appropriate for its industry and for its strategic aspiration within its industry. Given *your* firm's strategy, how does your IT portfolio disadvantage you vis-à-vis your archrivals? The ideal portfolio varies by industry, with some industries where better performing firms are more IT infrastructure heavy and others where they are more apps heavy. Figure 4.4 shows the ballpark mix of these IT assets for manufacturing, services (e.g., finance and insurance), and retail firms (both consumer and business-to-business).[42] The large bars show the mix of IT assets in the portfolio of the top-performing firms in each type of industry. The skinny bar next to each of them shows the industry average. Even though their actual percentages will change over time, two patterns in figure 4.4 are striking. First, the proportion of IT investments in infrastructure, operational apps, and strategic apps varies considerably across industries. Manufacturing firms dedicate the largest apps percentage to operational IT apps (25 percent of their total IT portfolio), whereas services firms dedicate theirs to strategic IT apps (19 percent). Manufacturing is also slightly less IT infrastructure heavy than other industries. Second, notice in each industry which IT assets the top-performing firms invest less in and more in than their peers. Top-performing manufacturing firms invest *less* than their industry peers in IT infrastructure but more in operational IT apps. No such differences are striking in services firms. However, top-performing retailers invest more in IT infrastructure but less in strategic apps relative to their industry peers. A surprising theme in figure 4.4 is that as much as 70 percent of IT assets are infrastructural—precisely the kind of IT assets that offer no competitive advantage. Yet messing up this part of the IT portfolio always is a competitive liability.

The total amount of money that firms spend on IT as a percentage of revenue also varies across industries. In 2016, this figure was about 7 percent in financial services, 4 percent in health care, 3 percent in utilities, and 2 percent in retail and manufacturing.[43] Although you can benchmark your firm against your industry's norms, remember that how much you spend on IT is less important than how you spend it. IT is not a spending race. For example, top-performing firms in financial services spend 10 percent *less* than average, but their portfolios are weighed more toward IT infrastructure.[44] Top retailers spend 10 percent more than their industry average but lean more heavily toward operational apps.

One size does not fit all firms. Firms in the same industry within each sector in figure 4.4 can compete either on cost or on differentiation. They require different IT portfolios that match that focus. IT investments in low-cost firms must focus singularly on increasing operational efficiency. They must invest more in infrastructure and apps that automate core business operations. In contrast, firms pursuing a

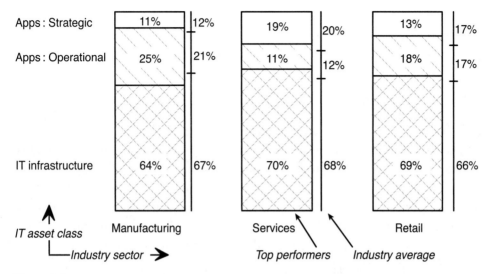

Figure 4.4
The blend of IT assets in a corporate IT portfolio varies by industry sector.

differentiation strategy must singularly focus their IT investments on differentiating themselves from rivals. They generally must invest more in strategic apps than their cost-leader counterparts.

Real Options Thinking

Firms often must contend with IT investments that *might* give them substantial advantages over their archrivals but are also fraught with technical and market uncertainty. Real options thinking is an IT investment mind-set for reducing the downside risk of such high-risk, high-return IT investments. A fifteen-year evolution of a Starbucks IT project subsequently illustrates these ideas.

The Perils of NPV

Uncertainty has no place in NPV math, the workhorse accounting metric widely used to judge IT investments. NPV can lead you astray when uncertainty in an IT project prevents you from reliably estimating its benefits or costs. The risk of misestimating either of them increases with uncertainty, along with the risk of rejecting a promising IT project.

All strategic management frameworks assume that you have a reliable crystal ball to predict your firm's future competitive environment. Real options thinking is an antidote that assumes that you cannot predict the future. It provides a way to embrace and exploit uncertainty without discarding NPV's power. It is a way of disciplining IT initiatives to cap losses on potentially bad bets while preserving their upside potential.[45] Real options thinking attempts to quantify the value of flexibility associated with an IT project on the top of its NPV.[46, 47, 48, 49]

Flexibility is plentiful in IT because of its inherent malleability, its versatility of not-yet-possible future uses (e.g., using broadband networks to stream video that no one had originally envisioned), its near-zero reproduction costs unlike any other capital asset, and not having to discontinue its use when a copy is put to a different use.[50]

A *real option* is simply the flexibility to do something in the future without being obligated to do it.[51] The options-accounting $NPV_{options}$ is conventional NPV ($NPV_{conventional}$) plus the value of the bundle of real options present in a project.

$$NPV_{options} = NPV_{conventional} + \{\text{value of all real options present in a project}\}$$

When the value of options—the part in the brackets—is zero, $NPV_{conventional}$ is identical to $NPV_{options}$. When it is not, conventional NPV underestimates a project's value and risks rejecting a promising project. It is less important to quantify the part in the brackets; at least one Nobel Prize was won just for trying.[52] Instead, it is options *thinking* that non-IT managers must appreciate to exploit it. Real options thinking views uncertainty is an unavoidable but manageable part of IT strategy. It accepts uncertainty and then tries to deliver business value on top of that uncertainty. Paradoxically, acknowledging uncertainty increases certainty.

A project can have multiple types of real options simultaneously present in it, as figure 4.5 summarizes. Some exist naturally, but deliberately restructuring a project at the *outset* can create more. Different types of real options let you do different things without having to do them. This can be the flexibility to stage project investments into results-driven baby steps, grow an IT project's scale, morph it into something that it was never intended to be, or even kill it. The more uncertain and lengthier a project, the more valuable real options become. Real options tend to be plentiful in complex, large-scale IT projects involving evolving technologies in unpredictable markets.

Two Sources of Uncertainty: Technologies and Markets

Uncertainty in IT projects can be technical uncertainty or market uncertainty.[53] *Technical uncertainty* relates to immature technologies with unclear future trajectories, competing technologies without a predictable winner, and the difficulty of

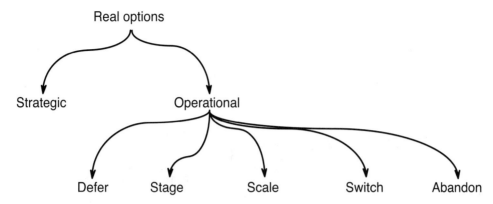

Figure 4.5
Six types of real options that can be present in an IT project.

integrating complex technologies in new ways. Will an emerging technology you are betting on be a blockbuster or a dud? The IT industry has a history of consistently producing both. *Market uncertainty* arises from being unsure how the market will react to your project. Will your customers or business partners want it and use it? Will your rivals retaliate with matching investments?

Raising your firm's hurdle rate for IT projects does not fix the problem because it simply cannot reduce market uncertainty.[54] For example, retailers reluctant to support Apple Pay adopted a wait-and-see approach; no amount of tinkering with it would have reduced market uncertainty about mass adoption by stores or consumers. You must separate these two sources of uncertainty because you must tackle them differently. Reducing technical uncertainty requires cautious baby steps, but reducing market uncertainty requires a wait-and-see approach.

Real Options Come in Six Flavors
Real options can be strategic or operational.[55] A project has a *strategic growth* option if it provides a foundational platform for *unrelated* follow-on projects that cannot yet be anticipated. Strategic options exist primarily in infrastructural IT investments that serve as a platform for other projects.[56] Such options are obvious in hindsight but can be difficult to foresee. *Operational* options create flexibility in how you implement a project. They come in five flavors summarized in table 4.5:

1. *Defer.* Such flexibility exists in a project if you can delay it without forsaking a market opportunity. It allows reducing market uncertainty before you make a commitment to

Table 4.5
Recognizing Operational Options and How They Create Value

Option	Present if a project can be . . .	How it creates value
Defer	Delayed without losing a market opportunity	IT reduces the risk of being a first mover when market receptivity is uncertain.
Stage	Broken into a sequence of independent baby projects	Completing each baby project reduces ambiguity about the value of doing the next. Each is pursued only if outcomes of the preceding one warrants it.
Scale	Scaled up or down	A small-scale version produces insight into the value of additional investments in the project.
Switch	Repurposed for a different use from one for which it was created (switch use) or swapping of a key technology building block (switch inputs)	A project can be more valuable in a different use or if one of its key technology building blocks can be replaced with a new one.
Abandon	Terminated, possibly with some salvage value	Terminating a failing project cuts losses.

a project. A common trap is misjudging deferability in that delaying a project will make your firm fall irrecoverably behind its rivals or lock you out for good.

2. *Stage.* This option exists if you can implement a project in smaller stages, the functionality of each of which is independent of the subsequent stages.[57] New information generated at the end of each stage provides a better idea of whether it is worthwhile to proceed to the next stage. It replaces risky big-bang projects with smaller subprojects with demonstrable benefits after each stage. You embed stage options by restructuring a larger project as an incremental sequence of smaller baby projects. A common snag is failing to make a baby subproject independent of later ones.

3. *Scale.* This option exists if you can cost-effectively scale up a project without dramatically increasing its complexity. App architecture choices described in chapter 3 often create this option.

4. *Switch.* This option exists if you can switch a project to an unintended serendipitous use (called switching *use*) or swap out a foundational technology building block in it for a newer or competing one (called switching *inputs*). Unlike physical assets, such as a factory, you can simply clone a software asset for a switched use without discontinuing its original use. For example, when Apple used MacOS as its foundation for creating iOS and then WatchOS, it could concurrently keep alive its original uses.

Box 4.4
The Sixty-Year Options-Powered Journey of American's SABRE Powerhouse

American Airlines created the first airline reservation system called SABRE (semiautomatic business research environment) in the 1960s to track its unsold seat inventory. It is a classic example of the switch-use option, where it was redeployed for a purpose different from the one for which it was built. Flyers make connections on other airlines, so American had to add information about their seat inventories. Eventually, American allowed partner airlines, travel agents, car rental companies, and hotels to access SABRE for a fee. Airlines and travel agents loved it because they could mine SABRE data for buying patterns to optimize seat pricing, do yield management, use it as a foundation for frequent flyer programs, and help their customers find bargain fares. This was the exercise of a growth option. By 1990, it had grown so popular in the airline industry that American Airlines was making more money from selling SABRE information than flying its planes. It spun it off into a separate company in 2000. Instead of challenging it, the arrival of the Internet made SABRE even stronger because it became the foundation of many online travel sites. Besides major airlines such as American and JetBlue, leading online travel services including Expedia, Travelocity, American Express Travel, and LastMinute.com now run on SABRE.

A switch inputs option can be embedded by using a Lego-like modular IT architecture (see app architecture in chapter 3). The key difference between a switch and strategic growth option is that the latter uses the original project as a foundation to create an *unrelated* new asset.

5. *Abandon.* This option exists if a project can be terminated midstream and its resources salvaged for other uses. Although in theory you can abandon any project, sunk costs, loss of face, and political pressure can make it harder to kill even a doomed project. Escalation of commitment to doomed projects is common because human nature fights rationality.[58] The single best way to embed an abandonment option is for non-IT managers to predefine project exit criteria using objectively quantifiable milestones and then hand over its kill switch to a non-IT manager outside the project team.

Applying Real Options Thinking in Practice

Practicing real options thinking requires non-IT managers' vigilance to both actively embed real options in IT projects and use their judgment to exercise the flexibility that they provide. To apply options thinking in practice, you must decompose a project into a series of smaller, shorter baby projects. For example, think of a hypothetical shopping application for smartphones that your firm believes will bring $3 million in additional sales. Figure 4.6 illustrates this. For simplicity, assume that you want it to have three chunks of functionality: (1) online ordering, (2) in-store inventory checking, and (3) returns management. Assume that you expect the project to take three months and to generate $3 million in additional revenues, equally attributable to each of these chunks of functionality. The traditional way to do it is a big-bang approach shown on the left side of figure 4.6. If all goes well, the project would be completed after the third month, after which it would deliver the $3 million payoff (the shaded area). But all going well in IT projects is as rare as the abominable snowman and the tooth fairy combined. If something went awry after the first month of the project (e.g., an insurmountable technical problem), your firm would have nothing to show for the money already spent. Staging is low-cost insurance against such risks.

You can dramatically lower risk if you decomposed the same project into three sequentially-staged baby projects as shown in the right panel of figure 4.6. Of these,

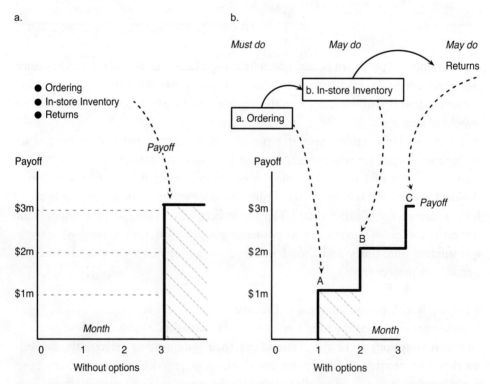

Figure 4.6
Illustration of the same project before and after it is decomposed into baby projects to embed options.

only the first stage is a *must do*; the later *may-do* stages depend on it. You must unbundle the *must-do* and *may-do* elements of a project, saving the riskiest part of the project for later stages. After the first stage is completed, the app can immediately be turned on and the first $1 million payoff realized. The next two stages are *may-do* elements; your firm can choose whether to pursue them, but the previous stage does not depend on them. If an insurmountable technical glitch surfaces after the first stage is completed and kills the rest of the project, the firm will still be able to show the first million dollars in benefits (the shaded part of the payoff curve).

All of the options value is in the may-do stages; the must-do stages have none. The must-do part is a stand-alone, minimum viable system that helps prioritize the rest of the larger project so you do not waste resources on functionality that simply proves technically unrealistic. This approach allows flexibility in pursuing high-risk projects without overcommitting to new, unproven technologies or ideas whose business benefits are uncertain. It also reduces the time to realize the low hanging fruit.

The simplest way to apply real options thinking is therefore to increase the ratio of *may-do* to *must-do* stages in an IT project. Besides capping losses in high-risk IT projects, it also discourages overengineering that breeds IT complexity.[59] Non-IT managers' contributions to a real options mind-set are threefold: (a) ensuring that the baby projects into which a project is broken up make *business* sense, (b) ensuring that the flexibility created by them is exercised in a timely manner, and (c) gatekeeping with the kill switch if a project veers off course.

An Illustration of Real Options Thinking: The Fifteen-Year Evolution of the Starbucks Card

The fifteen-year evolution of Starbucks's prepaid card from 2001 to 2016 illustrates how real options *thinking*—even without formal quantification—can guide IT investments under technical and market uncertainty. The foundation laid by this project in 2001 was responsible for almost $7 billion of its $16 billion annual US revenue in 2016.

Figure 4.7 shows the chronology of this project, most of which Starbucks could not have anticipated. Instead, it was a fifteen-year culmination of serendipitously seizing business opportunities opened up by emerging new technologies. The initial project had all six types of options—defer, stage, scale, switch, abandon, and grow—embedded in it. (The real option exercised at each step appears in italics on each arrow.)

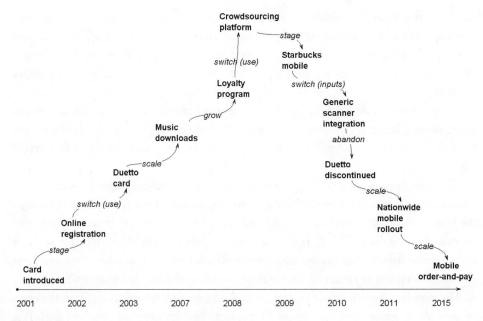

Figure 4.7
A fifteen-year chronology of the evolution of the Starbucks prepaid card.

In the early 2000s, 80 percent of all Starbucks transactions were in cash. Store employees knew the regular customers, but the company did not. A bigger problem Starbucks was then facing was slow lines, which led revenue losses because of line attrition. In 2001, Starbucks introduced a prepaid card intended simply to speed up lines.[60] Google was then barely three, the iPhone was still six years away, and broadband was not yet mainstream. Starbucks was unsure about whether such a card would resonate with its customers, so it began with a minimalist implementation using a tried-and-tested magnetic swipe card (a *must-do* baby project in real options lingo; everything else was a *may-do*). Customers would load money on the card in a store and use it to pay. The only IT infrastructure investment Starbucks needed was a minor software upgrade to its cash registers to read the new card. If the card failed to appeal to its customers, all Starbucks would be out of was that relatively small investment. The card took off better than expected: customers bought 2.3 million cards worth \$32 million in the first month.[61] It reduced transaction time by ten seconds, eliminating time-in-line by almost a million hours in the first year. It immediately lowered Starbucks's operational costs as well as line attrition. The market demand was now clear, as was the payoff. So in 2002, Starbucks introduced online registration. Customers could now replace misplaced cards, verify balances, and add more money to their prepaid card. Starbucks could have anticipated this, yet deferring it to a separate stage embedded a stage option that capped losses had customers shown no interest in the card.

The following year, Starbucks partnered with what is now JPMorgan Chase bank to introduce a Starbucks-branded Visa credit card, *Duetto*, that also combined the functionality of the Starbucks prepaid card. (Customers accumulated points for their non-Starbucks purchases that they could redeem for free drinks at Starbucks.) This represents a switch use option since all the functionality of the original Starbucks card could be repurposed for the Duetto card without discontinuing the original card. This illustrates how switching an IT asset to a new use—unlike most non-IT assets—does not require killing its original use because of the near-zero reproduction costs and malleability of software. In 2007, it introduced card-linked music downloads for albums being played in its stores; this represents a scale option.

By 2008, Starbucks realized that the card had become much more than a payment method. It had become a platform for insights into customer behavior, patterns in different geographical markets, and store-level foot traffic patterns. Therefore, in 2008, it introduced a loyalty program tied to the Starbucks card to reward loyal customers with free coffee refills and other drink accoutrements. This step created an entirely new asset—a loyalty program—and therefore represents a strategic growth option. Starbucks gained all sorts of actionable insights such as when it sold the most cake pops (Fridays) and where it sold the most Frappuccinos (San Fernando, California). This program provided Starbucks new insights into not just individual stores but also individual customers. It helped Starbucks develop an evolving profile of an ideal customer from a financial standpoint. (Starbucks found that about 20 percent of its customers that visit it more than eighteen times a month generate more than 60 percent of its revenue; those that visit one or two times a month contribute about 10 percent.)

The same year, Starbucks created its own crowdsourcing platform (www .mystarbucksidea.com). Starbucks figured that the most engaged source of new ideas for Starbucks to innovate was to get its loyal customers to suggest and vet ideas online for new products, services, and store improvements. When CEO Howard Schultz proposed the idea to its corporate board members, he made them come up with starter ideas to seed it. All customers with a Starbucks card could participate, propose, and vote on other customers' ideas. This represents a switch use option because it created an unrelated new asset—the crowdsourcing platform—while keeping intact all the assets that it built on. Within the first five years, customers had proposed 150,000 ideas, voted two million times, and led to 277 new ideas that Starbucks implemented (including new flavors, a summer happy hour, a branded line of clothing, and new services). (By 2016, the number was about two hundred thousand, of which more than seven hundred ideas had been implemented.) Perhaps the single most profitable idea was idea #1: the "splash stick." (It is a little green plastic plug that prevents coffee spills while driving.) This had such an impact on drive-through coffee sales that by 2016, many Starbucks stores—such as in the author's hometown of Athens, Georgia—did more business at the drive-through than in the store. (Drive-through transactions accounted for 50 percent of Starbucks's sales nationwide by 2015.[62])

As smartphones were beginning to take off in early 2009, it rolled out Starbucks Mobile for iPhone in just sixteen stores. Since this—a smartphone interface to the Starbucks card—simply added to the original project, it represents a stage option; its nationwide rollout in 2011 following a successful test run exercised a scale option. In 2010, it added software on the backend to allow existing generic scanners at Target stores to work with its mobile barcodes. (This is a switch inputs option at work.) The same year, it discontinued the Duetto card after seven years, exercising an abandon option. By 2015, more than 40 percent of all Starbucks transactions occurred through its card rather than cash or credit cards, saving the company considerable transaction fees. The humble magnetic stripe card intended only to speed lines accounted for almost $7 billion of its annual revenue.

In 2015, as other electronic payment systems such as Apple Pay and Google Wallet struggled to attract users, Starbucks introduced its mobile order-and-pay application for smartphones. This allowed customers to preorder a drink in a specific location, skipping the line in the process. It reduced a déjà-vu customer irritant: long waits in line at Starbucks. In our cube framework in chapter 2, this is digitization of the purchase process. This was not novel, but its success was unrivaled.[63] Within a year, it accounted for more than 20 percent of all Starbucks revenue ($3 billion in 2016), shortened lines, improved throughput, reduced line attrition, and improved the productivity of its existing capital assets and employees. It had twelve million *active* users among its forty-five million US customers by 2016, of which nine million used it every week.[64] In 2016, Starbucks had more interest-free money on circulating cards—$1.2 billion—than many companies have in the bank.[65] All of this improved Starbucks's margins, which it reinvested in employee benefits, raises, and support to coffee farmers in poor countries. Starbucks is iconic of socially responsible capitalism. A milestone in Starbucks's evolution was the opening of its first store in Italy in 2017, reexporting the Starbucks concept to the very nation that germinated its founder's idea for Starbucks.

The Starbucks case illustrates how a small, narrowly focused IT project created a foundation for a fifteen-year stream of IT-based business innovations using an incremental commitment process. The payoff from that first step in 2001 was not a sure thing, and neither could Starbucks have anticipated much of what followed. By focusing the initial step on just what could be credibly justified financially, Starbucks avoided a common overambition trap in the first step that is often met with skepticism and rejection. Real options thinking offers a powerful mind-set for taking a baby step—here the barebones magnetic stripe card project—to invest in IT under uncertainty.

Key Takeaways

1. *IT's payoff is messy*. Many of IT's benefits are intangible, their impact lags investment, you cannot be sure that an IT investment caused an improvement, and they often demand complementary investments. Because it is hard to attribute any improvement to IT, you track *changes* in a metric vis-à-vis its previous level in your firm and relative to your archrivals. IT's ongoing operating costs often exceed its upfront costs; you must count both.

2. *The IT payoff clock guides tracking IT's benefits*. An IT investment progresses through a sequence of intervening steps, each of which must go right for it to deliver financial benefits. Its operational impact begins after it has been implemented and is in widespread use. Its financial bottom-line payoff comes last.

3. *The 80/20 rule*. A few business-centric IT metrics that are cost-effective, competitively insightful, and objective are worth more than many.

4. *Short-term metrics measure IT's operational impact*. A project's promise—doing something better, faster, or cheaper—requires a short-term operational metric from the domain of the activity that it targets.

5. *Long-term metrics measure IT's bottom-line impact*. An improvement in an operational metric either reduces costs or increases revenues, which eventually must show up both in your firm's margins and projections of its future prospects.

6. *Real options create flexibility under uncertainty*. Real options thinking caps losses while preserving the upside potential in projects with high business or technical uncertainty, where NPV thinking can be dysfunctionally conservative. You can inject six types of flexibilities in a project by decomposing it into smartly sequenced baby projects, some of which you must do but others that you may do.

The Non-IT Managers' Checklist

□ Which two do we prefer for funding IT apps and infrastructure: simplicity, accuracy, or fairness?

□ For each major IT investment or project touching your own line function . . .

What metric from your functional area can measure its operational impact?

What is its promise (better, faster, or cheaper) and for which activity?

How long before the impact of its widespread use shows up in an operational metric?

Will this operational impact increase revenues or decrease costs? How soon?

□ Are we investing in the right places, given our industry and our strategic aspiration?

□ Where does our IT portfolio disadvantage us vis-à-vis our archrivals?

□ How can we decompose a project with high uncertainty into a more justifiable series of baby projects to lower risk? What criteria do we use as kill switches for each of them?

Part 4
Governance

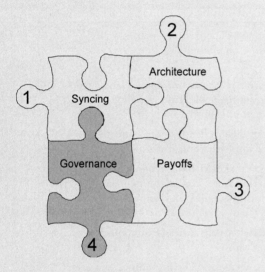

Jargon Decoder

IT governance	Who—IT or non-IT managers—makes what IT decisions? Accountability accompanies such authority.
IT governance structure	IT governance is *decentralized* if non-IT managers in line functions make an IT decision and *centralized* if your IT unit does.
Governed IT assets	Your firm can independently choose how to govern its IT infrastructure, apps, and data.
Governance trade-off	Centralization makes IT more economical and better integrated, but decentralization makes it a force for business agility and innovation; firms need both.
Infrastructure governance	Who decides what your firm's IT infrastructure must accomplish?
Apps governance	Who decides what your IT apps must accomplish?
Data governance	Who decides what your firm's data assets must accomplish?

5

IT Governance

Firms demand—and expect—their IT assets to be economical yet strategically impact-ful.[1] They loathe spending more on IT yet want it to be a catalyst for strategy. Some industry pundits find these expectations hopelessly contradictory and equate them with expecting IT to perform miracles.[2] Yet some firms perform just such miracles. IT governance—who decides what about IT—is the secret sauce for simultaneously achieving these seemingly irreconcilable goals. It is *the* pivotal determinant of the business value that your firm gets from its IT assets.[3] Firms that govern IT better get more for their money, leverage it far better in pursuing new business opportunities, and financially outperform their rivals.[4, 5] IT governance is what provides non-IT managers the mechanisms to influence their firm's corporate IT decisions.[6]

Effective IT governance is the Holy Grail of IT strategy because it goes to the heart of a perpetual tension: tailoring IT to line functions' diverse priorities without forsaking firm-wide economy and integration. Fine-tuning IT apps to individual line functions' work gives them strategic oomph. It syncs IT strategy by running IT around the priorities defined by line functions. Yet firms' core business processes span multiple line functions, so these apps must "talk" to each other and do so eco-nomically. Firms therefore need IT that is well-tailored to individual line functions but at minimal cost. Achieving this balance is the province of IT governance. Effective IT governance allows simultaneously tailoring IT to line functions' business needs only where it is critical and economizing everywhere else.

This chapter delves into IT governance, explaining how choosing who decides what about IT infrastructure, apps, and data can make your firm's IT assets simul-taneously economical and strategically forceful. For well-synced IT, neither the IT unit that creates technology nor your line functions that use it ought to have the sole responsibility for IT decisions. They must share responsibility, but not in a demo-cratic manner. They must be responsible and accountable for *different types* of IT decisions.

IT Governance Is Allocation of IT Decision Rights

IT governance simply is about who makes what IT decisions. The goal is using direction setting and oversight over IT to ensure desirable business outcomes. Firms implement IT governance by assigning *decision rights*, which refer to the authority and accountability for IT decisions.[7] Figure 5.1 illustrates the gamut of choices for any IT decision right. You perfectly *centralize* a decision right by assigning it exclusively to the IT unit; you perfectly *decentralize* it by assigning it exclusively to a line function.[8] You get a *federated* governance structure when both of them equally share it. In practice, perfect centralization and decentralization are rare, and firms locate IT decision rights somewhere between these two extremes. IT governance is about not whether your IT *assets* are centralized or decentralized but rather whether *decisions* about them are; the former is the province of IT architecture (chapter 3).

It is entirely your firm's *choice* where on the centralization-decentralization continuum in figure 5.1 it decides to locate any IT decision right. When firms do not deliberately *make* this choice, they have still made a de facto choice of centralization by relinquishing IT decisions to their IT unit. To actually govern their IT assets, firms must purposefully make this choice. Unlike IT architecture, IT governance choices can be changed over time.

Authority and Accountability Go Hand in Hand

Authority and accountability for IT decisions go hand in hand. Those who call the shots must also bear accountability for realizing its business impact.[9] When firms overlook the accountability aspect—which they often do—unproductive finger-pointing

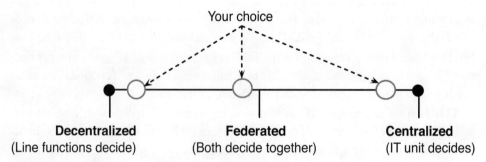

Figure 5.1
Where on the decentralization-centralization continuum you choose to locate an IT decision right defines IT governance.

ensues when an IT initiative goes awry. For accountability to have teeth, non-IT and IT managers' performance evaluations—even compensation—should be tied to IT's business outcomes.

If no non-IT manager is willing to bear responsibility for the business benefits of a particular IT investment, that alone is a red flag of its business value. The process of assigning IT decision rights ensures that IT expenditures are directly linked to your firm's IT strategy and will produce real business value. It also ensures that groovy yet nonessential IT projects are jettisoned.

IT Governance Focuses on the "What," Not the "How"

Every major IT decision encompasses two types of decisions: *what* IT should accomplish and *how* it should be accomplished. (Some firms call them strategic versus implementation decisions.) The *what* decisions—the sole focus of this chapter—are direction-setting decisions for IT activities. They are where non-IT managers' contributions to IT strategy should concentrate. The *how* decisions are operational decisions about IT implementation—that is, how the IT unit must accomplish the objectives once the direction is set. For example, should it build or buy a system, what programming language should it use, and should it should outsource? Such implementation decision rights for all classes of IT assets are best left to IT specialists in your IT unit (i.e., centralized).[10] Since they are technical decisions, non-IT managers can contribute little to them beyond holding the IT unit accountable for delivering the outcomes prespecified by the *what* decisions.

Should You Centralize or Decentralize "What" IT Decisions?

Decentralization's upside is that line functions that will use an IT asset every day decide what it should accomplish. Letting business users set the direction for IT allows tailoring IT decisions to their own needs and priorities. Decentralization's downside is that piecemeal decisions by different line functions focused on their own IT needs can potentially make firm-wide integration of IT assets a nightmare. What is good for one line function or business unit might not be good for the firm as a whole.

Centralization, in contrast, eases firm-wide coordination and integration of IT assets. Its weakness, however, is that the one-size-fits-all approach that it espouses struggles to account for the differences among various line functions' IT needs. When non-IT managers in line functions abdicate decisions about what IT should do, they allow the IT unit to set the business objectives for IT investments. This can disconnect IT decisions from business needs and priorities, resulting in IT investments ill-tailored to frontline business users. For some IT assets, the cost of poorly tailored IT can be too high a price to pay. You need both tailoring and economy.

It is tempting to assume that the midpoint in figure 5.1 (federated governance) will combine the strengths of both centralized and decentralized IT governance. It does. However, it also inherits the weaknesses of both, and the combined weaknesses often outweigh the combined strengths. Instead of making IT economical and agile, federated IT governance makes IT costly and lumbering. Too many departments must agree on an IT decision, bogging it down with no one department clearly accountable for it.[11, 12] It is reminiscent of federal and state governments working together as equals—an idea good in theory but clumsy in practice.[13] Federated IT governance therefore struggles in practice.

Degrees of Centralization and Decentralization

Let us just take the federated option off the table, given how much firms struggle with it. This means you can locate any IT decision right in the decentralization band (left of the midpoint) or in the centralization band (right of the midpoint) in figure 5.2.

The first choice you must make for any IT governance decision is choosing the appropriate band in figure 5.2. Where within the chosen band you locate an IT decision right requires understanding the notion of *input* rights. Any decisions about what IT should accomplish *always* need inputs from the other side, no matter how you choose to govern them. Consider the decentralization band in figure 5.2, which means that the line functions rather than the IT unit will be assigned that IT decision right. The IT unit does not simply disappear; any IT decision requires a fusion of business and IT expertise.[14, 15] When you choose the decentralization band, the IT unit contributes its input into the decision even though the line function primarily has authority and accountability for it. The input of this other group increases as you slide a decision right closer to the midpoint in figure 5.2. The IT unit would have more input in the decision if the decision right were located at point B rather than at point A in figure 5.2. Similarly, in the centralization band, the line functions

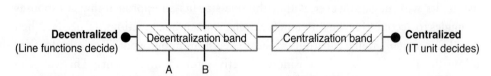

Figure 5.2
Your firm must first pick either the centralization band or decentralization band for an IT decision right.

contribute inputs to the decision even though the IT unit has authority and accountability for it. It takes two to tango.

The Three Classes of IT Decision Rights

You must appreciate what is being governed before you can help decide how to govern it. Central to this is the distinction among the three major classes of IT assets—infrastructure, apps, and data—from chapter 1. IT governance therefore spans all three (figure 5.3). Your firm's IT governance structure is therefore how you choose to divvy decision rights for your firm's IT infrastructure, apps, and data between your firm's IT unit and line functions. A firm can *independently* assign each of these three classes of IT decision rights.

The rest of this chapter focuses solely on the direction-setting decisions about *what* each class of IT assets should do (the top row in figure 5.3, each cell of which is the slider scale from figure 5.2). You can safety leave to your IT unit implementation decisions about *how* those objectives are met (the bottom row). The essence of corporate IT governance is then choosing the level of centralization or decentralization of *what* decision rights for each of the three classes of IT assets that meets line functions' needs without forsaking economy. (Figure 5.4 summarizes the optimal pattern, which we describe next.)

IT Infrastructure Governance

IT infrastructure governance refers to whether your line functions or IT unit are responsible for deciding what your IT infrastructure must accomplish. IT infrastructure serves the entire firm and is not unique to individual line functions. This firm-wide backbone provides the scaffolding for all business apps used by various line functions. It is the firm-wide technology substrate that weaves them together.

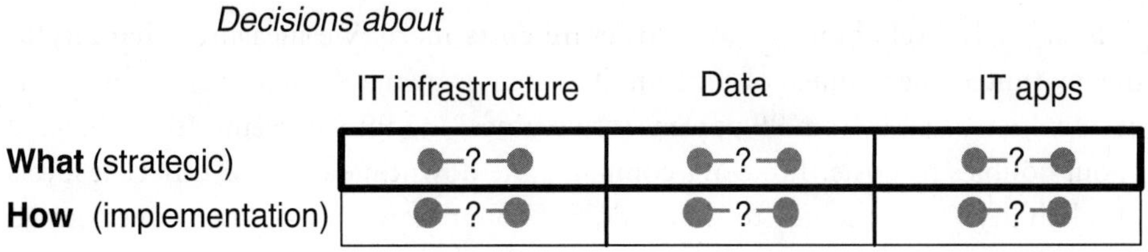

Decisions about

	IT infrastructure	Data	IT apps
What (strategic)	●–?–●	●–?–●	●–?–●
How (implementation)	●–?–●	●–?–●	●–?–●

Figure 5.3
A firm's IT governance structure separately specifies decision rights for IT infrastructure, data, and apps. Non-IT managers must focus only on the top row.

IT infrastructure does not competitively differentiate firms. It is costly, yet it is a competitive necessity. Economy and reliability matter more than tailoring for IT infrastructure.

IT infrastructure decisions draw on deep technical knowledge as well as a holistic understanding of your entire firm's portfolio of IT assets. Therefore, centralizing IT infrastructure decision rights with the IT unit—where such knowledge is concentrated—speeds up IT infrastructure decisions.[16] This also fosters economies of scale by aggregating firm-wide IT infrastructural needs across all line functions. A stable, economical firm-wide infrastructural foundation positions your firm for rapidly adopting new business apps.

If IT infrastructure decisions were decentralized, piecemeal infrastructural decisions by many line functions would aggravate IT infrastructure complexity, making apps progressively harder to implement or tweak. Further, it can create a motley of systems using different standards running across different parts of a firm, causing IT infrastructure costs to run unjustifiably rampant. IT infrastructure therefore demands frugal adequacy; costly mediocrity bankrupts.

However, IT infrastructure decisions must remain cognizant of line functions' varied IT needs. This requires non-IT managers in the line functions to contribute their inputs into IT infrastructure decisions (described next). The optimal location of IT infrastructure governance is therefore in the centralization band in figure 5.2: primarily the IT unit but with input from non-IT managers in the line functions.

Non-IT Managers' Contributions to IT Infrastructure Governance

Non-IT managers alone must answer two questions about IT infrastructure: How good is good enough? How much reliability and responsiveness is a *must* for the IT infrastructure on which your line function depends? Pause before you succumb to the temptation to say *very* good. "Better" is costlier than "good enough" in two ways.

First, higher reliability IT infrastructure costs more. We measure reliability as the guaranteed percentage of time an IT system is available in a twenty-four-hour period. Increasing it from 99 percent ("two nines") to 99.9 percent ("three nines") about doubles its costs. Table 5.1 compares the downtime caps for different levels of reliability. (Performance contracts do not count maintenance downtime toward this percentage.) To decide on the level of reliably you want and can afford, ask your IT unit for a priced menu of choices for the IT infrastructure components important to your line function's operations. As a benchmark, know that banking

Table 5.1
Downtime Caps for Different Levels of Reliability

Availability (%)	Label	Downtime per day
99	Normal norm	14.4 minutes
99.9	High availability	1.44 minutes
99.99	Fault resilient	8.66 seconds
99.999	Fault tolerant	864.3 milliseconds

systems and streaming services such as Netflix target 99.99 percent; most commercial websites and enterprise systems 99.9 percent; and internal corporate systems 99 percent. Use the Goldilocks rule: when the car you need is a Honda, you want neither the cost of a Mercedes nor the unreliability of a Kia. By not answering the question about what is considered good enough, your firm risks paying for overkill.[17]

Second, imperfect technology greases innovation. Contrast your smartphone to the Bell company landlines of the yesteryears, which were engineered for 99.99 percent reliability. You picked up one of those heavy black receivers and the dial tone was always there; there were no dropped calls or noisy connections common in smartphones. However, your smartphone costs a lot less and does a lot more. Overinvesting in more reliability than is truly essential simply raises the financial barriers to replacing an infrastructural technology when its successor comes along. (It takes longer to recoup sunk costs.)

Honestly and thoughtfully defining what is good enough reduces your firm's IT infrastructure costs and increases your firm's ability to absorb future infrastructural innovations.

IT Apps Governance

IT apps governance refers to whether the line functions or IT unit decides what business objectives your IT apps must accomplish. Whosoever has this authority must also bear accountability. Unlike IT infrastructure, business apps must be uniquely tailored to various line functions. IT apps decisions therefore draw on the business knowledge of line functions' specialized activities, business processes, and problems.[18] Recall from chapter 1 that IT apps are business analysis and operational systems that your firm's line functions use for performing their core functional activities and business processes. They include customer-facing apps, production-support apps (e.g., supply chain, logistics, and warehousing), and business-support apps (e.g., accounting and payroll).

Responsiveness to business needs matters more than economy for IT apps; clumsy apps decisions will blunt your firm's ability to execute its strategic moves.[19] Decentralizing IT apps decision rights to the line functions—where such business knowledge is concentrated—speeds up decisions about what business objectives various IT apps should accomplish. This is more likely to advance your firm's competitive priorities. This authority comes bundled with accountability, which decentralization places with non-IT managers in the line functions. This is appropriate because only non-IT managers can be responsible for making the *organizational* changes needed to generate business value from new IT systems after they are deployed. Centralizing apps decision rights can instead make them disconnected from line functions' needs, slow down IT decisions, and make them less likely to deliver business benefits.

However, IT apps decisions cannot be oblivious to how apps will integrate with your firm's existing IT assets and fit within firm-wide technological constraints. (Such firm-wide integration of IT apps is needed to execute business processes that often crosscut line functions.) Line functions are more likely to have knowledge of only their part of the IT portfolio, not the entire firm's IT portfolio as the IT unit usually has. This requires the IT unit to contribute its holistic, firm-wide knowledge of your firm's IT portfolio to IT apps decisions. The optimal location of IT apps governance is therefore usually in the decentralization band in figure 5.2, primarily with non-IT managers in the line functions but with input from the IT unit.

Non-IT Managers' Contributions to IT Apps Governance
Where within the decentralization band in figure 5.2 should your firm locate app decision rights? Closer to the left end or the middle? Non-IT managers' answers to two questions can help pick a spot appropriate for your firm.

Which IT Capabilities Should Be Firm-Wide?
Non-IT managers alone can answer the question about which IT capabilities should be firm-wide. IT capabilities—the ability to use IT to consistently do something—are implemented through operational apps and to a lesser extent by the IT infrastructure that supports them.[20] The moment you choose to make an IT capability firm-wide, you stretch the implementation of the associated app(s) across multiple line functions; you are implicitly nudging toward also centralizing its *architecture*. While this fosters synergy and integration across line functions, it also reduces the autonomy of any one line function. Your firm must explicitly commit to deciding what's *more* important: firm-wide synergy or line function autonomy.[21]

Increasing firm-wide IT capabilities demands *reducing* apps governance decentralization. The chosen point in the decentralization band in figure 5.2 will have to move closer to the center of the decision rights assignment scale (i.e., more B than A). There is no right or wrong choice—only better or worse for *your* firm. Your firm's choice of the trade-off between firm-wide synergy and line function autonomy must match its strategic aspiration. (The UPS versus FedEx contrast in chapter 4 illustrated this.)

Which Business Processes Should Receive IT Dollars?

Top-performing firms in many diverse industries are rarely the biggest IT spenders, yet they extract more business value out of their IT dollars by spending them on the *right* things. Business goals define *right*. How much your firm should spend on IT puts the cart before the horse. You must begin with crystal-clear *business* goals for IT apps and then set IT funding levels to achieve them. Ill-defined goals lead to IT spending that produces little business impact.

Non-IT managers must also play a lead role in prioritizing investments in a firm's *portfolio* of apps. What are the two most important gaps in your firm's existing IT capabilities vis-à-vis what you ideally need to execute your operational strategy? Think in terms of both line function–specific capabilities and firm-wide business processes that apps enable.[22] Fund only those higher up on the prioritized list and skip the rest. The more firm-wide this list, the more toward the middle of figure 5.2 your app governance structure moves. Not explicitly prioritizing IT investments delegates prioritization to the IT unit, which might try to pursue every request that it receives. This is a recipe for spreading your IT investments too thin and for losing focus on business value.

Data Governance

Data governance is about who—the IT unit or line functions—has the authority and accountability for decisions about what your firm's data assets must accomplish. Line functions' activities both generate and use a firm's data, which means that they are better suited than the IT unit to make direction-setting decisions about a firm's data assets. Data governance is trickier than infrastructure and apps governance because you cannot directly govern data; rather, line functions' preferences about data influence how the IT unit executes the other two classes of IT governance decisions. Remember that data governance is about *who decides* how data will be organized, not about whether the data itself is centralized or decentralized. Do not confound data governance here with data architecture in chapter 3.

Non-IT Managers' Contributions to Data Governance

Non-IT managers can contribute answers to three questions about governing your firm's data assets:

1. *What data is needed faster.* What data does your line function need instantaneously rather than for record-keeping? What data—especially big data streams—is not worth capturing or attempting to analyze at all?

2. *Firm-wide versus local data.* What data ought to be available firm-wide versus locally (e.g., within one line function or geography)? What fragmented data from what sources must you integrate—at considerable cost—to improve firm-wide decisions?

3. *Stewardship.* Which line function will be the steward of what data? Who should be allowed access to what data? What can they do to it (e.g., alter or read)? Stewardship entails responsibility for ensuring acceptable data quality, which is best done by preempting errors rather than fixing them.

How your firm's IT systems implement these choices is your IT unit's purview.

Box 5.1
Nestlé's Transformation in the Era of Global Megaretailers

Nestlé, a Swiss multinational founded in 1866, is one of the world's largest food products companies. It operates in almost every country that exists, where it runs about five hundred factories. Its twenty-nine major brands—including Beneful, Body Shop, Carnation, Gerber, Häagen-Dazs, L'Oréal, Lean Cuisine, Maggi, Nescafé—generate annual sales more than a billion dollars each. Historically, brand owners such as Nestlé held enormous sway over retailers until the arrival of global megaretailers such as Walmart and Costco in the United States, Tesco in Britain, and Carrefour in France shifted the balance of power.[23, 24] These retailers introduced their own store brands of competing products and started demanding discounts in exchange for the massive volumes of Nestlé products that they moved. Nestlé knew that it could not ignore them. It knew it had to reduce costs to protect its margins, without losing its ability to tailor its products to customers in different countries. (For example, flavors of its Maggi brand of noodles sold in the United States, France, India, and Nigeria are completely different.) Until then, Nestlé operations in each country operated like independent local companies. Nestlé knew that it had to create global scale in purchasing raw materials and managing product lines to reduce costs. IT was going to be central to this.

In the early 2000s, it began an IT project to consolidate its many enterprise systems used in different countries into one. The idea was to build a common IT-based operational template for its worldwide operations that still accommodated differences in local markets. The project was geared to reap economies of scale by globally consolidating sourcing of raw materials and product development without losing the local touch that made Nestlé successful. Its IT governance strategy mirrored this approach. It was geared

Box 5.1 (*continued*)

toward economizing IT infrastructure while allowing tailoring of apps that enabled country-by-country strategy execution. The project first focused on standardizing data used to track product variations and sizes worldwide (e.g., sizes of Kit Kat chocolate bars). It consolidated its one hundred data centers worldwide to just four. Before the project, Nestlé did not even know for sure how much of each product it was selling globally.

A key IT governance decision the project team made was to gather all country managers for a meeting to set the project's direction and to get buy-in. These were the decisions rights about what an IT project should do. The project pitch was not technical features; it was the immediate expenses and foregone revenues of not pursuing the project. To ensure that all country-specific offices affected by it also had a say in the project's implementation, Nestlé handpicked into the project team top-performing employees from different counties and colocated them to the project site for up to a year. Put differently, it increased the centralization of IT infrastructure governance and data governance while decreasing the decentralization of IT apps governance.

It standardized data management, operating practices, and systems at 90 percent of its worldwide locations by 2007, saving it almost $2 billion in annual costs. The new system provided Nestlé's country managers a level of analytical insight that they never previously had. To Nestlé's top management, it provided a worldwide view of its portfolio of business operations that it could use to leverage its global footprint, particularly for centralized worldwide purchasing. This allowed Nestlé to remain globally competitive in the age of powerful megaretailers without losing the local connections that had made it successful in the two hundred countries in which it operated.

Overall IT Governance Structure

Figure 5.4 pulls together these ideas into a pattern for guiding the governance of IT infrastructure, apps, and data. Neither centralization nor decentralization dominates it. It is generally a bad idea to centralize all IT decisions; it disconnects IT from line

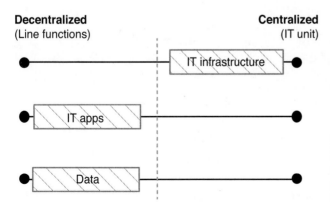

Decentralized
(Line functions)

Centralized
(IT unit)

IT infrastructure

IT apps

Data

Figure 5.4
A firm's overall IT governance structure encompasses how it governs its IT infrastructure, apps, and data.

functions' business needs. It is a worse idea to decentralize them all; it sacrifices economy and firm-wide integration.

Instead, you must *individually* decide on the governance structure appropriate for each of the three classes of IT assets, deciding first whether it belongs in centralization band or in the decentralization band in figure 5.2. The mere fact that IT decision rights *are* assigned is at least as important as how they are assigned. Your firm can simultaneously economize infrastructure and tailor apps to line functions by governing them differently. Put differently, syncing IT requires giving the IT unit some decision rights and taking away others.

Figure 5.5 summarizes the different combinations of apps and infrastructure governance options available to your firm. The ideal combination is cell 4 (shaded), where line functions drive apps decisions and the IT unit drives IT infrastructure decisions. This results in a corporate IT portfolio that is simultaneously economical and synced. IT governance is therefore a powerful—but often underused—lever for achieving both. Any other combination in figure 5.5 makes IT costlier than it needs to be or unsyncs it.

IT Governance Must Match the Architecture of What Is Governed

Good architecture only takes your firm partway to syncing IT; matching it with IT governance takes it the rest of the way. Therefore, IT governance must also match a firm's IT architecture.[25, 26] Figure 5.6 summarizes the crux of the idea: the more decentralized a class of IT assets is, the more its governance should be decentralized. Mismatches between the architecture of a class of IT assets and how you govern them squanders the advantages of your architectural choices.[27, 28, 29] For example, although decentralizing app architectures gives apps the autonomy to evolve with

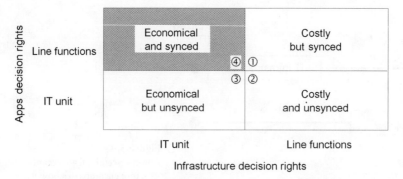

Figure 5.5
IT governance is a powerful lever for making IT both economical and synced.

changing business needs, you must simultaneously decentralize how you govern your apps to leverage this autonomy (cell 1 in figure 5.6). Centralizing the governance of decentralized apps overcontrols them, stifling their inherent evolvability (cell 4). Similarly, centralizing IT infrastructure architecture potentially facilitates a firm-wide integration and scale economy. However, you must also centralize how you govern it to leverage the advantages of its centralized architecture (cell 3). Decentralizing infrastructure governance undercontrols it, replacing firm-wide decision making about IT infrastructure with the chaos of reconciling conflicting IT infrastructure decisions by myriad line functions (cell 2). Generally, the two shaded cells in figure 5.6 are the optimal locations for apps and infrastructure governance. Mismatched IT governance choices can stifle the things your firm is already doing well; matched choices magnify their impact.

Key Takeaways

1. *IT governance means who decides what about IT.* It is implemented by explicitly allocating IT decision rights to the IT unit or the line functions. A decision right is authority plus accountability.

2. *IT governance as the secret sauce.* Effective IT governance lowers IT costs and simultaneously makes IT a catalyst for business agility. To achieve both ends, you govern IT infrastructure to lower costs by centralizing its governance and IT apps to bolster business agility by decentralizing their governance. Federated governance structures—good in theory—only lead to a stalemate and finger-pointing.

3. *IT governance spans all three classes of IT assets.* It encompasses decisions about *what* business objectives each class of IT asset—infrastructure, apps, and

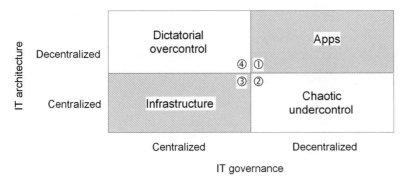

Figure 5.6
IT governance must match the architecture of what is governed as illustrated by the shaded cells.

data—should accomplish and *how*. Non-IT managers contribute primarily in setting the direction for *what* IT should accomplish.

The Non-IT Managers' Checklist

☐ Which of your major IT systems impede your firm's ability to compete with your archrivals?

☐ How much reliability and responsiveness in IT infrastructure is *good enough* for your line function?

☐ Which IT capabilities—implemented in apps—should be firm-wide?

☐ Rank the top three business processes that should receive future IT dollars.

☐ What data does your line function need instantaneously? What data siloed in various line functions is needed firm-wide, enough to justify the expense?

☐ Which line function ought to be the steward of what data?

Jargon Decoder

IT project failure	A project's *execution* can be botched by failing to meet cost, schedule, or quality expectations; it can fail to deliver promised *business* benefits.
Triple constraint	An IT project can be only two of the following: cheap, fast, and good.
Causes of failure	Imprecise business intent, unnecessary complexity, and lack of explicit trade-offs in cost, schedule, and scope.
Antidotes to failure	Discovering latent business needs, curbing scope, and explicit accountability for business benefits.
Waterfall approach	The classic linear approach for IT projects (specify requirements→design→code→test→rollout).
Lean principles	Active business involvement, rapid iteration, and less code.
80/20 rule	A heuristic that 80 percent of a project's business needs are met by 20 percent of its features; the 20 percent are identified by applying the MoSCoW mnemonic to its requirements.
Rollout strategy	How a completed project is rolled out to users; you can abruptly replace an old system, run both in parallel for a while, or roll it out in small chunks.

6

Managing Projects

The one consistency in the IT business is that barely one in three IT projects succeeds. More than half never deliver their intended business benefits. This pattern persists year after year (see figure 6.1).[1] Larger projects—with a five to ten times higher failure rate—fare the worst.[2] These problems afflict small and large firms,

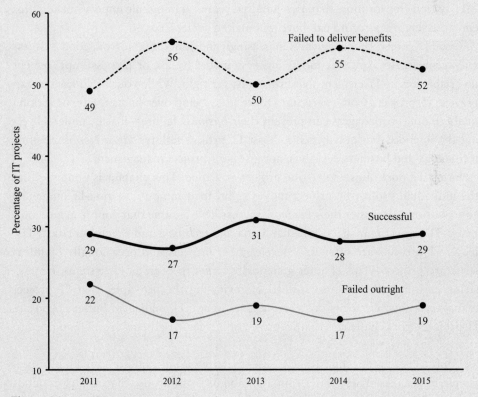

Figure 6.1
More than one in two IT projects consistently fails to deliver business benefits and one in three succeeds.

nonprofits, and governments worldwide. As IT projects grow larger, touch more parts of firms, and are baked into more products, something going wrong in an IT project afflicts greater damage.[3] And something often does go wrong.

In a large skyscraper, you would have to remove thousands of bricks to make it collapse. In a large IT system, one bad line of code suffices.[4] Even the most rigorous testing regimen leaves half the bugs undetected. The inherent fragility of IT systems is worsening because their bigness begets bugginess. Software is still painstakingly handcrafted by humans, who make ten to fifteen mistakes in every hundred lines of code. This bugginess shows up in malfunctioning products, stalled business processes, failed firms, and preventable deaths. Programmers have not become sloppier; how software is developed has failed to keep pace with its growing complexity. The solution is not better humans but better processes that bake in quality.

If we conservatively assume that 25 percent of the $4 trillion spent on IT annually went into IT projects, we waste $700 billion *in one year*. That would run the vaunted MIT tuition-free for more than two hundred years.[5] A miniscule improvement in this embarrassing track record can have an outsized societal payoff.

Good IT project management is increasingly indistinguishable from good business management. Any strategic move, business model tweak, or process improvement invariably has an IT element that firms must get right. While your IT colleagues can prevent IT projects from *execution* failure (e.g., being over budget, late, or lacking quality), non-IT managers can prevent their *business* failure—that is, underdelivering the intended business benefits. Most IT project failures are a *combination* of technology and business decisions, not just poor project management.

Firms' IT portfolios evolve one project at a time. This chapter is about getting the individual project-by-project moves right, focusing on how non-IT managers contributions can foster their *business* success. (We assume that your firm has competent IT project managers skilled at managing *technical* and execution risks.) The major IT projects are often app development projects and occasionally IT infrastructure projects. This chapter generically refers to both as IT systems, emphasizing custom-built IT apps. Instead of reviewing the principles that IT project managers know, we focus on where and how non-IT managers buffer corporate IT projects from challenges that IT project managers are themselves ill-equipped to tackle.

IT projects—even technical successes—that are *business* failures often repeat preventable mistakes. These arise from an ambiguity of purpose that results in building the wrong system, from unnecessary complexity, or from non-IT managers not being explicit about the one thing among cost, schedule, and quality that they are willing to compromise. We then describe antidotes to these three problems: using a lean approach to discover a project's true business purpose, curbing scope creep, and creating accountability for business results without micromanaging a project. Non-IT managers' contributions in each facet increase the likelihood of building faster and cheaper the *right* system of acceptable quality.

It's Déjà Vu All over Again

Ironically the problems that most often derail IT projects are predictable and preventable. Forgetting history condemns firms to repeat old mistakes instead of making new ones. Think of ambitious, unprecedented projects in recent history with massive scale, uncertainty, and bickering stakeholders: the railroads, the electric grid, the Interstate Highway System, moon landings, and the Hoover Dam. They offer timeless lessons for IT projects today.

Consider one massive infrastructure project that promised to speed the global flow of goods, mark the death of distance in commerce, wipe out inefficiencies, and be a win-win for all involved.[6] Unexpected glitches stalled progress for years, its investors became paupers, and the promised payoff was nowhere to be found. The project eventually was completed, but it was six years behind schedule and, at four hundred million French Francs, cost twice as much. The promised payoff came a hundred *years* behind schedule. The project was the 101-mile long Suez Canal started in 1854 that connected the Red Sea to the Mediterranean Sea. The idea was to give ships a five-thousand-mile shortcut around the treacherous Horn of Africa through the Egyptian desert (figure 6.2). The seventeen thousand ships with a billion tons of cargo passing through it each year now net the Egyptian government $6 billion in revenue.[7] Reaching these figures however took a hundred years—in spite of the shorter, safer trip bypassing pirates—because shippers were slow to change their habits. The lesson for IT projects: building a better mousetrap—if it ever gets built—can cost more and take far longer. Do not expect it to sell itself to its intended users on its "dead obvious" technical merits, and expect no payoff unless it is actually used.

Another failed technology project was electric vehicles in London (figure 6.3).[8, 9] More than a hundred years before Tesla Motors, the London Electrobus Company tried it in 1907. The buses were well engineered, had a thirty-eight-mile range, and used ingenious battery swaps to keep them running all day. The gasoline engine was not yet inevitable; its competition was the horse-drawn buggy. The buses

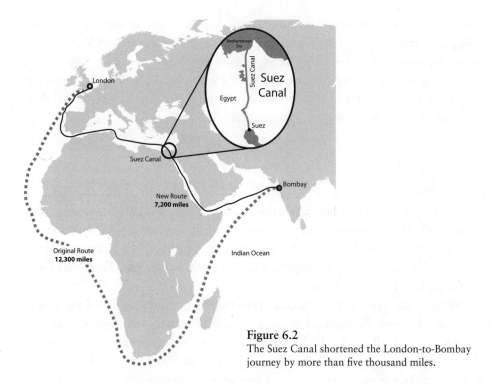

Figure 6.2
The Suez Canal shortened the London-to-Bombay
journey by more than five thousand miles.

were 300 percent over budget and plagued by a range-killing three-thousand-pound battery, and thirty of the fifty buses were never completed. Cost, quality, and schedule—it flunked all three. The project simultaneously involved too many new, unproven technologies. The Electrobus project offers three oft-forgotten lessons for IT projects: The best technology does not always win. It must outdo its *real* competition, which is not always obvious. For the Electrobus, it was not the automobile but the horse, whose staying power it underestimated. Trying to integrate many unproven technologies and introducing it before the complements that make it attractive have arrived (here, charging stations) can also doom projects.

Contrast these to the unprecedented Hoover Dam project completed in 1934. A key to its success was that its managers created the master plan but gave engineers discretion over their part of the job. The lesson for IT projects: do not micromanage specialists but clearly communicate the *results* expected from their work. Direct what they deliver, not how. These historical analogies are imperfect yet informative. The lessons from the Suez Canal, Electrobus, and Hoover Dam projects are every bit as relevant today as they were to managers three generations ago. Do not repeat the same mistake once.

Figure 6.3
The London Electrobus at its charging station circa 1907.

Three Reasons Why IT Projects Fail to Deliver Business Value

IT projects often fail to deliver business value because they lack a clarity of purpose, are unnecessarily complex, or do not explicitly choose trade-offs.

Hazard #1: Ambiguity of Purpose

The first reason that IT projects do not deliver their intended business benefits is—not faulty execution but—poor communication between business and IT that leads to building the *wrong* system. If a project team accidentally builds an IT system that nobody wants or needs, it does not matter if the project is on time and budget. It is practically useless. It is like an elegant car that is uncomfortable to drive; it belongs in a museum, not in your driveway. Unfortunately, 60 percent of all IT projects do not even define the criteria for judging their success.[10] An IT project's intended business benefits—not technical features—define its purpose. Clarity of purpose might exist implicitly right under the team members' noses, but it often does not make it into the team's work. You must appreciate the notion of *latent* needs to understand why this happens so often.

In the late 1990s, a major US chemicals firm recognized a huge opportunity: there was not a single brand of bug spray that thrilled consumers.[11] This firm invested millions in research and development to create *the* perfect bug spray formula. The company then redesigned the can to eliminate back spray that irritated customers, picked colors that would stand out on crowded supermarket shelves, priced it low, and launched with a huge advertising blitz. The product flew off the shelves, and production could barely meet demand. Until the following week, when sales plummeted and the company's warehouses were overwhelmed with returns. Managers were flabbergasted. The company tested the returned cans; each one was chemically perfect. Puzzled, its managers talked to consumers to figure out what went wrong. To their surprise, when consumers used the bug spray, the sprayed bugs scurried away and died within minutes. However, that is not what consumers wanted. To perceive it as being effective, they wanted to *see* the bugs die. Their *latent* need was not an effective bug spray but to see the bugs squirm and die. Perception mattered. The company then tweaked the formula and added a paralyzing agent, which paralyzed the bugs, made them stumble and topple over, and then slowly killed them. The revised formula went on to become *the* dominant brand of bug spray. The firm could not discern its consumers' latent needs by asking them what they wanted. Yet IT projects attempt to do exactly that every day by attempting to "elicit requirements."

A *latent* need is one that is present and capable of emerging but is not yet visible. You cannot elicit business users' latent needs; they have to be *discovered* collaboratively with them. Meeting users' latent business needs defines the purpose—the raison d'être—of any corporate IT project.

Even the most skillful IT project team cannot build what you cannot describe. Unarticulated business goals lead to a lack of clarity about project requirements and forces IT project teams into a guessing game. This leads to a kitchen-sink mentality of overengineered, feature-bloated systems that do a lot of things but do nothing well. It is futile to worry about the details until you understand what the end point is. You would not let me get away with asking you to "meet me at $%!& at 11 a.m. tomorrow," so why should we be puzzled when an IT project team with an unclear destination stumbles. *The* cardinal sin in IT project management is non-IT managers not articulating a *business* goal. An unclear destination therefore dooms many corporate IT projects even before the first line of code is written. The antidote comes solely from non-IT managers.

Hazard #2: Unnecessary Complexity

The second reason IT projects fail to deliver is *unnecessary* complexity. As a project grows larger, so does the risk of failure.[12] (Software defects rise in proportion to program size.) A modern car, for example, has 250 times the amount of software code that landed man on the moon (100 million versus 0.4 million lines of code). The small minority of unnecessarily complex projects that get completed are more likely to be ridden with costly glitches and overshoot budgets and schedules.[13] The source of growing complexity is ballooning scope; one system tries to do too much. As complexity of an IT project grows, more subsystems need to be integrated into a whole, which can increasingly be incomprehensible to any one person. Non-IT managers' contributions can help whittle *unneeded* complexity so that the unavoidable complexity that remains is more manageable.

Complexity without Purpose: A Double Whammy

A project's overall risk is a combination of its clarity of purpose and its complexity, as figure 6.4 illustrates. The two shaded cells are lethal combinations. A low complexity project without clarity of business purpose (rudderless boat; cell ③) is a solution searching for a problem. It is unlikely to deliver business value. A complex project without clarity of business purpose is like the Titanic (cell ④): a costly endeavor without realistic business benefits. You must avoid this gamble unless you can move it from cell ④ to cell ① by better articulating requirements.

Viable projects fall into the other two (unshaded) cells. Both have clarity of requirements; ones with lower complexity (cell ②) have lower risk, and ones with higher complexity (cell ①) have higher risk. Non-IT managers can help shift projects from cell ① to cell ② by prioritizing requirements to break down a large project into a sequence of smaller, less-risky projects. (We subsequently explain precisely how.)

Hazard #3: Absence of an Explicit Choice of Trade-Offs

The third reason IT projects fail to deliver business value is a failure to make trade-offs explicit. An IT project can be fast, cheap, or good—pick any *two*.

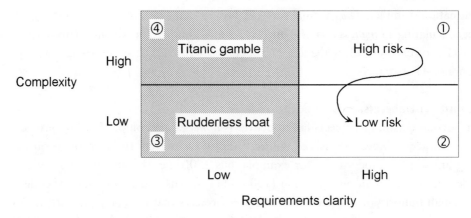

Figure 6.4
Reducing an IT project's complexity and sharpening its business requirements lowers risk.

Figure 6.5—the *triple constraint* model—illustrates this. *Good* here is the project's quality defined in terms of its scope of features and functionality. The decision about which two matter most for a project must come from non-IT managers in the line functions involved, not from the IT unit. Put differently, which one of these three can you compromise without forfeiting a project's business value? Clarity of the project's business purpose and a matching project scope drives the answer. A clear articulation of a project's objectives—not technical content—should therefore drive project trade-offs and scope. Trying to achieve all three dimensions often achieves none.

Projects usually are constrained by time or money. Up-front agreement on which one of these can be compromised determines a feasible project scope. This prioritization process is indispensable in unmasking project priorities. If your firm can compromise neither time nor money, it must rein in project scope, as we subsequently explain.

Figure 6.5
An IT project can only have two of these triple constraints.

Sources of Risk beyond Non-IT Managers' Direct Control

Non-IT managers must accept the project risks that they cannot change, change the ones they can, and have the wisdom to know the difference. Two risks can be beyond their control: (a) a project's use of immature technology and (b) underestimation of time and money.

First, no amount of project management rigor can overcome uncertainty that stems from the immaturity of technology used in a project. There is an enormous difference between such uncertainty and ambiguity. This chapter tackles ambiguity, but uncertainty requires real options thinking described in chapter 4. Second, how well a project is executed operationally is judged by how far off it was from its initial cost and schedule estimates. Initial estimates that are too low can make a well-executed project look like a financial disaster. Unfortunately, IT units tend to consistently underestimate IT project costs and schedules for two reasons. First, projects that ask for smaller commitments of time and money are more likely to be approved. To lower what they ask for, they often build in insufficient slack into schedules. (Imagine a CFO's reaction to an IT manager asking for a slack of three months in a six month IT project.) However, overpromising at the outset invariably leads to underdelivering. Second, IT project estimation is more an art than a science. The heuristics of even the most experienced IT experts cannot extrapolate reliably to unfamiliar market contexts and novel problem domains that an IT project might involve. Project complexity worsens underestimates of project completion times; the more interdependencies a project's pieces have, the more a multiplier effect can derail its schedule. (For example, a less complex project with a 70 percent chance of success is less risky than a more complex one with four interdependent pieces that each have a 90 percent chance of success. The latter's success likelihood is about 65 percent [a product of the four 90 percent figures] because it must successfully deliver all four pieces.)

The antidote to such pathological underestimation is to triangulate initial project estimates using multiple estimation techniques to reliably arrive at close enough approximations of person-hours of effort needed. (Schedule and costs can be derived from this estimate.) Aspire for roughly right ballpark estimates using the *T-shirt sizing rule* (i.e., small, medium, and large rather than pinpoint accuracy of dress shirt sizing [e.g., 16½–35]). It is better to be roughly right than precisely wrong. (Modern IT project management methods can systematically refine initial estimates as a project proceeds, but you don't want them to err by a huge margin.)

Box 6.1
How IT Project Management Botched Obamacare

It is ironic that the United States is home to the most Nobel Prizes in medicine of any country and has the world's most advanced medical care available, yet Americans can least afford health care compared to any other developed nation. Sick people die in developing nations because they do not have access to health care, but Americans die because they cannot afford it. The United States introduced legislation—popularly called Obamacare—in 2011 to fix this. The idea was to use IT to create a one-stop marketplace for health insurance plans subsidized by the US federal government. The intent was sound; as the peoples that gave the world transformative marketplaces such as eBay, Google, Facebook, and Amazon, we could surely use it to bring the same level of efficiency to our own health care. Central to this plan was the national HealthCare.gov site that was going to help match hundreds of millions of Americans with hundreds of health insurance companies. The execution of the entire plan rested on one IT system, HealthCare.gov

It took three years to build it, which is quite reasonable, considering the Manhattan project took six and the Apollo moon landing project took eight. Even with the weight of the entire US federal government behind it, its launch in 2015 was disastrous. The problems that wrecked the project were the predictable litany described earlier in this chapter.

a. *Clarity of purpose*. The Centers for Medicare and Medicaid Services, the agency responsible for the system, started building the system before its key requirements were fleshed out. The project's statement of purpose—to implement the new law—was too abstract to be actionable. The Obamacare legislation ran nine hundred pages with an additional ten thousand pages of rules. It also lacked a precise measurable organizational value (MOV) to focus the project team's work in the form of tangible measurable benefits, their timeline, and a change metric that would result directly from the system. A lack of agreement over the project's priorities among project stakeholders in this volume of legalese created an ambiguity of purpose as well as unrealistic expectations. The project's initial estimate of $56 million was immediately off by 300 percent and quickly ballooned to $209 million. New and changing requirements caused expensive rework. In a rush to meet the launch deadline, the service launched without adequate testing or phased rollouts. Major parts of needed functionality—such as the mechanism to pay insurance companies—had not even been built on launch day. The cost of a $56 million project had escalated to $840 million—a 13,000 percent cost overrun. Later estimates put the total cost at $2.1 billion—a 34,000 percent cost overrun.[14]

b. *A neglect of the triple constraint*. The project did not explicitly choose the two dimensions of the triple constraint that it most valued: schedule, cost, and scope. Managers need the humility to accept the triple constraint, given that even the might of the entire US government could not achieve all three. The schedule was inflexible since the site had to be operational on the day the new law came into effect. That left either cost or scope that ought to have been explicitly considered compromisable up front. We can assume that money was no object; the difference between a $100 million or $5,000 million IT project is pocket change for a government that collected $1.5 trillion

Box 6.1 (*continued*)

in federal taxes in 2016 alone. However, a failure to explicitly make that trade-off up front compromised the project's quality as well. A system meant for a nation of 320 million Americans could not handle more than eleven thousand simultaneous users on launch day.

c. *Integration problems.* The project depended on tax and payroll systems of many different participating states and federal agencies (e.g., the Internal Revenue Service) for individuals' records to process insurance coverage. A federal data hub created to aggregate such information for the system turned out to be more complex than anticipated. The cost of this part alone rose from $30 million to $80 million.[15] Integration with a variety of other existing systems simply did not work by the time the site was launched. The next chapter describes how firms often underestimate the costs of integrating a new IT project with existing systems and how this imperils outsourced projects even more than ones done in-house. It did not help that the Obamacare project used sixty different IT contractors, whose work became a nightmare to coordinate. The project's complexity was so huge that finger-pointing by these contractors was all that resulted after a national embarrassment.

The lesson is that the project repeated avoidable mistakes to end up delivering right on schedule an unusable system. Botching the execution resulted in an operational failure that prevented it from even reaching the point of judging its business success.

Antidotes to IT Projects' Business Failure

Antidote 1: Discovery of Purpose

IT projects traditionally follow a sequence of activities that figure 6.6 shows. You begin by gathering project requirements, then design the software (including its architecture), then write the code to implement that design, test it, and finally roll it out. This classic *waterfall* approach is the de facto way of doing IT projects (notice figure 6.6's shape). The shaded part is the realm of IT specialists. Every undergraduate with an IT degree is formally trained in an IT project management course to get the shaded part right. However, the programmers interact with future users only on the front-end (①) and the tail-end (②). Many corporate IT projects falter at these two points; they either don't get the requirements right or fail to gain traction with their intended business users.

Two major problems can—and often do—occur in the intervening window of isolation (the shaded part in figure 6.6). First, the waterfall approach erroneously assumes that a project team *can* identify business users' latent needs at the outset (i.e., at ① before the shaded steps in figure 6.6 begin). The risk in pressuring business users to articulate their needs early on is that they might overspecify project

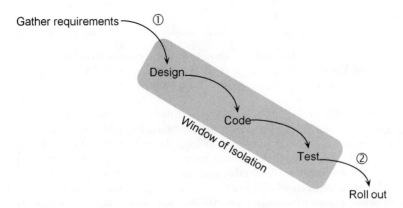

Figure 6.6
The linear *waterfall* approach used in IT projects.

requirements or a solution; a project team is likely to give them what they asked for but not necessarily what they needed. This dramatically increases the risk of building a system around a flawed or incomplete understanding of business needs. The textbook term for the first step in figure 6.6 is *requirements elicitation*, which caricatures business users as a turnip out of which a programmer must squeeze out requirements. Even the term is disingenuous to the spirit of the IT-line relationship as a two-way conversation espoused throughout this book.

Second, a lot can change during the window of isolation—which can stretch into years for large IT projects—where the system's programmers and future users have little interaction. Line functions' business needs might change, competitors might alter their strategies, technologies can evolve, or regulatory agencies may impose new rules. If a new requirement is discovered during the window of isolation, the waterfall approach requires redoing—at huge cost—the work done in all the completed stages.

The waterfall approach, therefore, simply lacks the flexibility to hit a moving target and the mechanisms to incorporate feedback. The completed project then meets the business needs that the firm once possibly had in the past, not the ones it now has. This inflexibility can lead to a project's obsolescence before completion.

The Lean Approach to Managing IT Projects

A rival philosophy is the *lean* approach to project management, which nerdier folks call *agile methodologies*. A lean approach assumes two things that put business users at the center of a project. First, future users find an IT project's requirements difficult to articulate up front. You cannot tap on a future user's shoulder to ask them what they want and then expect to get a good answer. You must integrally engage them to discover their latent needs. Second, their requirements will change over time. A project's value in the lean approach is in the eyes of its users; it is successful only if they find it useful. People come before the technology.

When you hear terms such as *Scrum, extreme programming, pair programming*, or *prototyping*, they are all permutations of three principles. If you grasp these three ideas, you can make sense of any lean or agile methodology.

Lean Principle #1: Active Business Participation
The first lean principle is actively involving *throughout* the project those who will use the new system. It makes business users integral participants in the process, unlike the waterfall approach that views them as passive sources of project requirements needed only at the outset.[16] The premise is that a good project prioritizes what they *actually* need—their latent needs. This comes from a convergence between a project's business users' objectives and the IT unit's technical knowledge of what is feasible (see figure 6.7).

You do not need communication channels between IT and line functions when business users are *in* the project team. They are the channel. Active business participation therefore increases the prospects that a project will deliver intended business benefits. Lean approaches therefore often designate a non-IT manager from a line

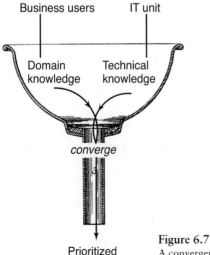

Figure 6.7
A convergence of business and technical knowledge prioritizes project requirements.

function as the project owner. (This is neither the project manager nor the project sponsor.)

A side benefit of active business involvement is the *IKEA Effect*: building something yourself fosters ownership, no matter how imperfect it is. IT projects often fail to deliver business value because a "build it and they will come" mind-set often pervades IT units.[17] A finished system cannot deliver any business benefits if it is not used. An unused IT system is an expensive paperweight. Getting people to use a rolled-out system involves the human side of IT.[18]

When you look past the technology itself, IT projects intentionally attempt to change how people in line functions do their jobs. Such change threatens to wipe out their attained skills in using the old systems.[19] If you mandate the use of a new system, users often will find creative workarounds to circumvent it and resist even more. The resistance is rarely to the new technology but to its menacing effect on their job security and power. Getting line-function employees to *use* a new system requires more than just a better mousetrap; it requires their buy-in. Buy-in that results from their active participation, in a project *they* helped create, makes them more likely to champion its use in their line functions after its rollout. They develop a personal stake in its success. A project's non-IT team members are the more credible messengers to emphasize how their colleagues will personally benefit from using it.[20]

The business-side participants best suited for inclusion in an IT project team have five characteristics (remember the mnemonic CRACK[21]):

Collaborative
Representative of users in their line function
Authorized to make decisions
Committed to delivering business value
Knowledgeable of their line function's operations and business processes

Lean Principle #2: Short Iterations
The second lean principle is to do the project in a series of iterative sprints of two to six weeks each. Each iteration hands over to the users a crude *but functioning* version of the system with only a small subset of the project's functionality. Feedback on a prototype in users' hands is worth more than a thousand presentations. When they see intermediate prototypes, they can tell the project team whether what they see is what they want and what it is missing. Such iteration forces IT designers to repeatedly test their beliefs about users' needs and correct inaccuracies in their own understanding, reducing lags between discovering a user need and addressing it in a project.[22] Working features become the project's milestones, and the users'

environment becomes the project's laboratory. Such iterative sprints integrally engage business users in a constructive conversation with the project team.

Figure 6.8 contrasts how a six-month project with a single iteration typical of the waterfall approach provides zero feedback opportunities until delivery; however, the same project with monthly iterations provides five feedback opportunities. This is analogous to breaking a marathon into a series of hundred-meter sprints. Short iterations increase an IT project's likelihood of delivering business benefits in two ways. First, by clearing up misunderstandings earlier when they are cheaper to fix, they reduce the risk of building the wrong system. Such trial-and-error iteration enables the whole team—technical and business—to reach consensus on what the end result might look like. Second, by focusing the team on just what users need most, it zaps wasteful overengineering and gold-plated functionality. Shorter delivery cycles also prevent projects from getting stuck at the proverbial *90 percent complete* state, which can sometimes escalate into years. The time constraints of each iteration do not repress innovation; they direct it.

Lean Principle #3: Less Code

The third lean principle is to reduce the amount of software code in a system. Every line of code must be explicitly justified for how it directly furthers the project's business objectives. Not one line of code without justification is allowed in. (I subjected every sentence in this book to the same principle: it had to help non-IT managers contribute to corporate IT decisions.) The two ways you implement this idea are (a) by following another 80/20 rule—that is, focusing on 20 percent of a system's features that can meet 80 percent of its users' needs—and (b) lean principle #2 (shortening iterations to under six weeks).

The *less code* principle bakes quality in and curbs costs in two ways. First, software with more code is buggier. Historical data shows that an average programmer makes ten to fifteen errors in every one hundred lines of code; even the most rigorous testing cannot catch more than 50 percent of them. Translate this: A small million-line piece of software will have ten thousand errors of which five thousand

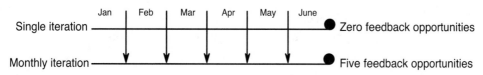

Figure 6.8
Short iterations increase feedback opportunities for cheap and fast course corrections.

errors will remain undetected before release. The more code, the more errors. The cost of fixing an error is about *one hundred times* greater after the software has been deployed. (For example, Toyota's 2009 braking software glitch cost the company around $10 billion in repair costs.[23]) Therefore, systems with less code are less buggy and cheaper to maintain. Second, less code lowers up-front development costs, which run between fifteen to forty dollars per line of code.[24]

Two additional practices complement these three lean principles: (a) *constant* automated testing and (b) *continuous* integration (which automatically runs every night to fit together all project team members' day's work). Automated testing takes the grunt work out of testing and continuous integration eliminates surprises from misfitting parts at the end of the project.

Figure 6.9 summarizes how the three lean IT project management principles help build the *right* system around a firm's real business needs faster and cheaper and with quality baked in.

Lean or Waterfall?
Figure 6.10 shows that no matter what methodology you use, larger projects are the most challenged in delivering their promises (fewer than 20 percent succeed).[25] However, their success rate triples if they are broken into smaller projects, where the benefits of lean approaches also become pronounced. Lean project management does not mean that the linear waterfall approach does not have its place. A mismatch between the project and the choice of lean versus waterfall unnecessarily

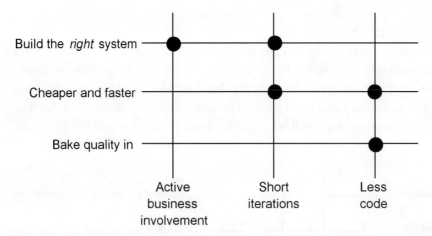

Figure 6.9
How the three lean principles help build the right system better, faster, and cheaper.

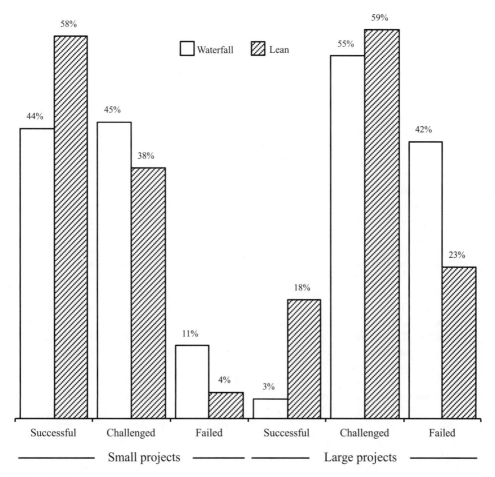

Figure 6.10
Breaking a larger project into smaller projects increases their likelihood of success, irrespective of the methodology used.

increases project risk.[26] The general rule of thumb is to prefer lean for projects where business users' needs would be hard to gather. In such projects, the solution is initially unknown and requirements are likely to change. Close interaction between business users and programmers mitigates both these challenges. The lean approach is appropriate for custom-built business apps and for software embedded in products. In contrast, the waterfall approach is appropriate for projects with clearly definable, stable requirements and proven technologies or in projects of large scale. Most IT infrastructure projects and implementation of purchased commercial

Box 6.2
How Lean IT Project Management Revitalized Denmark's Economy

Government agencies around the world are often stereotyped—sometimes unfairly—as models of red tape and inefficiency. They are under constant public pressure to become more efficient and transparent using IT. Many large-scale IT project failures have been government projects with nothing to show for the wasted taxpayer money. The challenge is acute enough that in 2016 the British government created an agency—Infrastructure and Projects Authority—charged with preventing IT failures. The same sort of problems that plague corporate IT projects plague government IT projects: antiquated methodologies, volatile project requirements, squabbling project stakeholders, and integration problems with other existing systems. Yet high-profile failures mask the many government IT projects that are resounding successes (e.g., the US Internal Revenue Service digitizes all individual tax returns and the US Postal Service automatically routes every piece of snail mail by reading ZIP codes).

The Danish Business Authority (DBA)—responsible for registering corporations that do business in Denmark—is such a success.[27] The agency's mandate was to make it easier for foreign firms to do business in Denmark, detect money laundering, and ensure tax accountability. The legacy "system" was error-prone paper forms sent by snail mail. The process took months as employees manually entered data into fourteen different antiquated computer systems. The bar for the new IT project to exceed was pretty low. The IT modernization project began in 2009, and by 2011, the waterfall approach used had completely stalled the project for reasons now familiar to you: the system's requirements were constantly changing, and the involvement of many Danish government agencies slowed down decisions. It then switched to a lean project management approach in 2011 in an attempt to break the logjam. The pitch for the switch was (a) to begin delivering some functionality even before all requirements were completely known and (b) to directly involve the project stakeholders outside DBA that were constantly changing project requirements.

DBA broke the mammoth project into a sequence of thirty smaller, more manageable projects. This piecemeal approach reduced both complexity and risk. It then placed individuals with appropriate authority and gave them decision rights (chapter 5) over what their miniproject ought to accomplish. This eliminated the bottleneck of having to wait for answers to project decisions from outside. DBA designed each of the thirty miniprojects to have no dependencies on ones that came later. DBA then transparently outsourced some of the initial miniprojects to four different IT vendors. This implicitly promoted competition among them by promising more contracts (including future maintenance) to vendors who met cost, schedule, and quality expectations. This led vendors to overinvest in their work, knowing that it would ensure future business from DBA.

The project was complete by 2014 and immediately began delivering business benefits. Business registrations became faster and less error prone, the new system automated much of the grunt work, it dropped help-desk call volume by 40 percent, it reduced an eleven-page registration process to one page, and new employee training took one month instead of five. Denmark's ranking for being easy to do business with shot up into the top three globally as did its ranking on the World Bank's digital government services benchmark.

apps (including large enterprise systems) are leading candidates for using the water-fall approach. Generally, a lean approach works best for smaller projects. You must decompose a larger project into smaller subprojects before you can use a lean approach.

Antidote 2: Curb Scope
The biggest threat to IT projects almost always is trying to do too much, often too fast or with too few resources. Trying to cover 100 percent ground can mess up the 20 percent that matters most to your business. The only way to prevent such complexity from overwhelming a project is to focus on one or two *really* important business ends that you hope a project to achieve. You can tame a project's scope by using the *80/20 rule*, the heuristic that 20 percent of a project's features can meet 80 percent of its business needs. A system that gets this 20 percent right is what Herbert Simon would call *satisficing*, or good enough to be acceptable.[28] The tricky question is which 20 percent? Non-IT managers can help identify the 20 percent by classifying each major project requirement into one of the following four categories, colloquially called the MoSCoW classification:[29]

Must-have requirements
Should-have requirements
Could-have requirements, but not critical
Won't have this time, but maybe later

The must-have requirements are the 20 percent requirements that a project must prioritize. Such prioritization focuses the project team and ensures that line functions do not make impossible demands. Ideally, the ranking must be a consensus of all line functions that have a stake in the project. This prioritization process also makes explicit what the project is *not* trying to do. The lower-priority requirements can become later subprojects; they are the *may-do* options in real options thinking explained in chapter 4. An explicit, consensual prioritization of requirements by business users safeguards projects against scope creep that leads to unnecessary complexity (e.g., one line function requesting additional functionality after development is already under way). Adding more people to a project team however is not an antidote to complexity. Adding more people only makes a late project later; there are more people to bring up to speed and coordinate.[30]

A side benefit of such business-driven prioritization is that the project is more likely to gain upper management support. Its absence can damn a project.

Antidote 3: Accountability without Micromanagement

There are two ways to judge a project's success. First, was it *executed* well in terms of it schedule, budget, and quality? Second, did it deliver the desired *business results*—measured by an operational business metric in chapter 4? Many IT projects falter in the second aspect when non-IT managers are not involved at a few critical junctures.

The third contribution from non-IT managers is holding the project team accountable for delivering desirable business benefits. Such benefits are a project's *measurable organizational value* (MOV), which must come from line functions (i.e., the business side rather than the IT unit).[31] Begin with the intended impact and emphasize desirable outcomes, not features. Any MOV statement deserves a cold, hard look at how it will further your firm's operational strategy. This value has to be *measurable* and to your *organization*. A MOV statement for any IT project must have four elements:

1. *Intended impact.* What operational, strategic, or financial impact will the project have?
2. *Promise.* Will it help do something better, faster, or cheaper?
3. *Change metric.* What is the unit for measuring impact (e.g., dollars, percentages, or time)?
4. *Time to impact.* What is the time to impact after project completion, measured in years or months?

Details of how you will achieve the MOV do not belong in the MOV statement. If a project's entire MOV cannot be expressed in one line, its scope is too scattered. Try making your project MOV pass the tweetability test by fitting it into a short sentence structured as follows.

Project X will *<promise> <targeted impact>* by *<change metric>* within *<time>*.
Good example: Project X will increase inventory turnover in our US stores by 1.6 days within two years.
Bad examples: Project X will . . .

create ubiquitous new channels to target mobile customers through real-time analytics.
strengthen our ability to deliver an industry leading experience to customers.
lower distribution costs by 10 percent.
lower IT costs by 10 percent by rationalizing our global platform.
implement the Obamacare law.

Developing a project's MOV should collaboratively involve all project stakeholders. The contributions of diverse project stakeholders help balance what's ideally desirable and

Box 6.3
How Walmart Prioritizes IT Projects

Walmart had over eleven thousand stores in twenty-seven countries in 2017, yet it manages all new IT projects centrally as part of a single IT project portfolio. Walmart's centralization of its previously decentralized project planning intended to apply its business philosophy of efficiency and fiscal discipline to the way it manages its IT investments. Previously, project managers did not prioritize many of its IT projects with an obsessive focus on Walmart's business goals and often struggled to articulate their project's business intent, and duplication of effort across countries was rampant.[33] Walmart was the largest IT spender worldwide, spending more than $10 billion in 2015 alone.[34] It depends on IT to maintain its competitive edge, which is an operational strategy that blends low margins (under 3 percent) and high volume. The shift to centralized project control was Walmart's attempt to ensure that its huge IT investments sharpened its competitive edge.

The new centralized project prioritization process is data driven, reducing leeway for managers' politicking and pushing for their pet projects unless they objectively furthered Walmart's competitive goals. Walmart assigns weights to all proposed projects using corporate goals, sorts them into a prioritized list, and then matches them with available in-house IT employees and funding. Once the resources for the current evaluation cycle are exhausted, the bottom part of the list goes on the backburner. This ensures that its limited resources are invested in IT projects that most advance Walmart's strategy of lowering costs to offer its customers low prices. The larger lesson in Walmart's approach is that firms should manage IT projects as a unified portfolio driven by their strategic aspiration, even though the portfolio evolves one project at a time.

realistically achievable. Project team members should also be informed up front that it is how the project's ultimate success will be judged. This creates accountability for delivering business results without micromanaging *how* the IT unit executes the project.

The bottom line is that any IT project must have clear non-IT ownership for *what* business objectives it will accomplish and clear IT unit ownership of *how* it will, coupled with mutual accountability. This holds the IT unit responsible for the project's business results without dictating how they ought to do their work. This MOV-centric approach—rather than overemphasizing technical metrics—ensures that your IT employees are evaluated first as business people.[32]

The overarching themes in these three antidotes to the business failure of IT projects are making projects smaller and actively involving business stakeholders.

Rollout Strategies

How you roll out a completed project to its business users affects its reception.[35] IT units often pay insufficient attention to rollouts out in a rush to get a completed system up and running. A poorly chosen rollout strategy can hurt users' receptivity, potentially jeopardizing the project's business payoff.

Figure 6.11 illustrates the three rollout strategies. *Direct cutover* (①) is the fastest; the old system that is being replaced (if there is one) is simply turned off and the new one simultaneously turned on on the rollout date. (Migration of any data from the old system must be completed before the rollout date.) The risk is that any bugs or glitches in the system can have a widespread impact. Technology glitches often lurk even if completed projects are pilot tested with a small group of actual users. Direct cutover is appropriate if the old system is unusable and if the new system is not mission critical to your firm's core operations.

The second rollout strategy is *parallel rollout* (②), where the old and new system are simultaneously available to users for an extended period and the old one is subsequently turned off on the rollout date. This approach provides a safety net for technology glitches. However, it prolongs the rollout period and requires reconciling data from the overlapping period between the old system to the new system. A *phased rollout* approach (③) takes the parallel rollout one step further, gradually introducing the new system in less-overwhelming, bite-sized chunks of functionality. Although a phased rollout is preferable, business pressures to get a new system quickly up and running can make it less feasible.

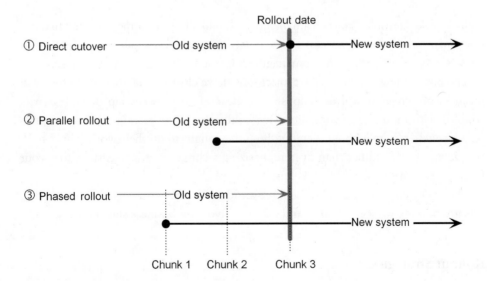

Figure 6.11
The three strategies for rolling out a finished project.

Key Takeaways

1. *IT projects have dismal success rates.* Most IT projects either fail to get completed within the firm's constraints or fail to deliver intended business benefits. The business cost of this is escalating as IT infuses into more business processes and products.

2. *Three reasons why IT projects disappoint firms.* Having an imprecise purpose, having more complexity than necessary, and failing to make an explicit cost-schedule-scope trade-off jeopardizes them. Their antidotes are using lean methods to discover a project's latent business needs, curbing scope, and creating clear accountability for business results without micromanaging the project team.

3. *Why lean often beats waterfall.* The waterfall approach cannot accommodate evolving business needs and new requirements. Its lean rival espouses flexibility, assuming that business users cannot articulate project requirements early on. However, it works better for smaller projects.

4. *Three principles undergird lean project management.* Lean approaches to IT project management espouse active business participation, short and frequent iterations, and minimal code.

5. *MoSCoW mnemonic.* To focus an IT project, identify 20 percent of its features that will meet 80 percent of its business needs. Non-IT managers can use the MoSCoW mnemonic to classify project requirements into *must have* (the 20 percent), *should have*, *could have*, and *won't have*.

The Non-IT Managers' Checklist

> For any IT project
>
> ☐ What is the single most important business outcome that it must deliver? How will you measure it? How long after project completion will it materialize?
>
> ☐ If you had to delete 80 percent of the project's requirements, which 20 percent would you keep? Would other project stakeholders—excluding your IT unit—agree?
>
> ☐ Classify its requirements using the MoSCoW classification. Will reducing its scope solely to the *must-have* requirements deliver most of its intended business benefits?

Jargon Decoder

IT sourcing	The decision about whether you develop and maintain your IT assets in your own firm or outside it.
Strategic sourcing decisions for IT	IT sourcing decisions for the software embedded in your products, custom-developed business apps, and nonrecurring IT tasks need non-IT managers' inputs. This excludes outsourcing of business processes enabled by IT as well as commodity IT infrastructural services and software packages.
Offshoring	Outsourcing to a foreign vendor or using your own employees in a foreign facility.
Community outsourcing	Using open source, crowdsourcing, or creating iOS-like ecosystems of partner firms.
Tapered outsourcing	Doing the up-front design of a project in-house before handing off the rest to an outside vendor.
Concurrent sourcing	Simultaneously insourcing and outsourcing the same sort of IT activities.
Backsourcing	Bringing back outsourced IT activities in-house.
Outsourcing challenges	The outsourced system does not play well with your existing IT systems, or you end up with a system that you never wanted.

7

IT Sourcing

Many nontechnology firms faithfully followed admonitions to stick to their knitting and decided that developing IT systems was not one of them. Seduced by the promise of higher quality at lower cost, they outsourced IT wholesale. However, they are now realizing that everything they make or sell is becoming so entrenched in IT that executing their core competencies is inseparable from their firm's IT. IT is literally becoming *the* knitting. The customer experience of the cars produced by an automaker such as General Motors, pacemakers made by Medtronic, insurance offered by Progressive, burritos sold by Taco Bell, or the streaming services offered by Netflix are *shaped* by the software embedded in their products and the software in which these firms embed their business processes. For many firms, IT outsourcing was an unexpectedly one-way street that left them unable to bring it back in-house.[1] How can firms outsource IT projects without hurting their *business* agility or creating a competitive liability? How can they be prepared when the insourcing-outsourcing pendulum swings? This chapter explores these questions.

We begin with three nonstrategic IT-related decisions that do *not* require non-IT managers' inputs in *how they are sourced* (business processes enabled by IT, commodity IT infrastructure and services, and commodity-packaged software). This leaves on the table sourcing decisions for custom-built and embedded software, where non-IT managers' inputs matter strategically. We briefly explore the many forms of sourcing that stretch beyond the defunct insource-outsource dichotomy. We then describe the two challenges—integration costs and receiving the wrong system—that perpetually wreck outsourced IT projects. We also illustrate whether, how, and where to outsource what IT to preempt these problems.

What IT Sourcing Decisions Strategically Matter?

IT sourcing broadly refers to where—in your own firm or outside—are your IT assets developed and maintained. Let us begin by taking off the table three IT-related activities that firms often *incorrectly* consider corporate IT sourcing decisions. Your IT managers have to get them right, but decisions about how they are sourced are neither strategic nor require non-IT managers' attention.

a. *Business process outsourcing.* Sourcing of *business activities* that are enabled by IT—such as business process outsourcing,[2] customer support outsourcing, call centers, using remote workers to do grunt work such as data cleansing, or crowdsourcing—are outside the purview of strategic *IT* sourcing decisions. They are *consequences* of IT use rather than the production of IT assets themselves. They are the purview of operations sourcing, not IT sourcing.

b. *Commodity IT infrastructure and services.* Commodity IT infrastructure implementation and IT services (such as Internet connectivity) are routinely outsourced; thinking about doing them in-house is as nonsensical as asking if you should generate your own electricity instead of buying it from your local utility company. (All IT hardware purchases, operating systems, and networking gear fall under IT infrastructure.)

c. *Commodity software.* Commoditized software packages—whether an inexpensive spreadsheet or a multimillion-dollar enterprise system—that you purchase in the market are outside the realm of IT sourcing decisions. Irrespective of whether you buy such software and install it ("on-premise" software) or rent it over the Internet as a service ("cloud sourcing"), coordinating with its seller, negotiating pricing and service levels, and managing contracts are your IT unit's responsibilities. All of these are routine, nonstrategic IT management activities that merely demand competent employees in your IT unit. The IT sourcing decisions that require non-IT managers' contributions therefore exclude sourcing of work enabled by IT, infrastructure and services, and commodity software purchases.

This leaves sourcing decisions for three types of IT activities that have strategic consequences and need non-IT managers' involvement: (a) software that is embedded *into* your firm's products or services, (b) custom-built business applications into which your firm's business processes are baked, and (c) one-off, nonrecurring IT tasks. All three are primarily IT activities involving *custom* IT apps. The rest of this chapter focuses on non-IT managers' contributions to these three types of IT sourcing decisions.

The Ins and Outs of Insourcing and Outsourcing

Insourcing is the practice of using your own employees to accomplish IT activities, and *outsourcing* is the practice of using outsiders instead (called *IT vendors*).[6] The advantages of insourcing are threefold. First, in-house IT employees have a natural

Box 7.1
Why General Motors Backsourced Its IT

General Motors (GM) is among the world's oldest automakers. It produced ten million vehicles in thirty-seven countries in 2016 under brands such as Chevy, Buick, Cadillac, Opel, Jie Fang, and Baojun. In 2013, it abruptly ended a $3 billion a year IT outsourcing deal with Hewlett Packard, replacing it with eight thousand new in-house programmers. GM realized that software had become too important to the auto business for it not to be doing it in-house. Software is a rising proportion of the cost of a new car, and a flurry of expensive software-defect recalls by its rivals was only the tip of the iceberg. Customers' perceptions are increasingly being shaped by their car's user interfaces, touch screens, integration with their smartphones, and a mind-set that a $25,000 car ought to live up to expectations framed by customers' less-expensive personal technology. Software has also become more instrumental in how cars are purchased and maintained. GM also did not like the idea of being stumped by a new breed of technology-savvy rivals such as Tesla Motors and Google that were slowly making inroads into its industry. GM's CIO felt that bringing the IT work back in-house would let GM discover new business possibilities—for making cars, in car content itself, and in selling them—that would otherwise remain unrecognized. GM believed that custom-building the software embedded into its vehicles and for its own use could also differentiate it from its existing archrivals Ford and Toyota in responding to evolving customer preferences. GM's calculus for backsourcing IT was to give up money saved by outsourcing IT in exchange for the much larger gain in revenue.

American laws mandate that new vehicles be sold through a dealership, not by a manufacturer or a third party such as Amazon. So how does an automaker sell online when it legally cannot sell online? Most automakers had been using the Internet as an interactive product brochure—hardly an innovation by any standard. GM's epiphany came from watching Tesla Motors' lead, which was hardly a rival. (Tesla sold fifty thousand vehicles in 2015, unlike GM's ten million.) Therefore, GM created an online service called Shop-Click-Drive in late 2013 that it offered for free to all its 4,300 American GM dealers. The intent was to make it easier for prospective customers to do almost everything to find, price, finance, and insure a GM vehicle online. A customer could even schedule a home delivery of a purchased vehicle, but the actual purchase was from a dealer because of legal restrictions. The project took two years to build from scratch. Its home-brewed nature meant that its rivals could not easily replicate it. The system acted as a glue for GM's vast dealer network, routing buyers to the nearest dealer that has in stock a customer's preferred GM vehicle configuration. The site also automatically pulled data on the trade-in value of customers' old vehicles (from the used-car pricing benchmark, Kelley Blue Book). The sophistication and cost of the system would have been prohibitive for any GM dealer. GM building it and then deploying it on thousands of dealer sites created scale that combined the technological prowess of GM and a vast dealer network.

The bet paid off. Within the first two years, GM dealers received a quarter million sales leads through the system. The dealers were receptive to the idea because Shop-Click-Drive did not attempt to circumvent them; instead, it became a new source

Box 7.1 (*continued*)

of sales. Thirty percent of the individuals that used Shop-Click-Drive ended up buying a GM vehicle, a number almost 10 percent higher than any rival online automobile-finding service. It was also attracting a new group of customers that GM never had. (Forty-three percent had never owned a GM vehicle before.[3])

The success of Shop-Click-Drive convinced GM that writing its own software would be a small price to pay for taking "the lid off what is possible," as GM CIO Randy Mott put it.[4] Next came growing GM vehicles' software content. In-house developers are more likely to understand GM's customers, their latent needs and wants, and details about GM's inner workings better than outsiders.[5] The potentially higher costs to do the IT work in-house could be well worth it if a better IT-driven integration between the mechanicals and electronics resulted in more reliable vehicles that customers wanted more than Ford's or Toyota's. This trend of backsourcing IT to custom develop software is growing as more firms in diverse industries realize that IT is increasingly integral to what they do, what they make, and how they sell it (the three faces of the digitization cube in chapter 1).

alignment of interests; what is good for your firm is also good for them. Second, insourcing retains IT skills and expertise within your firm. Insiders will often have a better appreciation than outsiders of your firm's culture, ways of doing things, and idiosyncrasies. This is conducive to better *using* IT to further your firm's aspirations and generating business value. Third, your firm's intellectual property and inner workings are better protected when they do not venture out of your firm.[7] Insourcing therefore deters—or at least slows down—imitation of IT assets that might give your firm an edge over its archrivals. The downsides of insourcing are (a) your firm might not have some needed IT skills and (b) an outside firm could do the same work at a *potentially* lower cost.[8, 9]

The attractiveness of cheap labor fueled a fifteen-year outsourcing boom to countries such as India, Philippines, and Ireland at the turn of the century, but rising wages, integration problems, and the trifecta have since wiped out the cost advantage. The more enduring upsides to outsourcing IT are twofold. First, firms can access IT skills that they lack in-house. Second, it is more economical to outsource than to hire in-house IT expertise for *some* one-off IT activities with intermittent demand. These include data migration from an old system to a new one, data cleansing, maintenance of a legacy app, and integration of two systems from different IT epochs or merged rival firms. Outsourcing such IT activities is often more economical than to have similarly skilled employees on your payroll. The downsides of outsourcing are threefold. First, another firm's employees do the work; your firm cannot legitimately command and control them. No contractual detail can compensate for their allegiance to their own firm over yours. Second, you can only hold IT vendors accountable for meeting their contractual obligations (typically technical, budget, and schedule expectations), unlike your own IT unit that you can hold accountable for business results. The sort of intense iteration needed to discover latent needs and introduce business innovations is rarely possible with outsourcing.[10, 11, 12] Outsourced IT work can therefore become disconnected from your business needs. Third, outsiders rarely have the in-depth knowledge of your firm's existing IT assets as an in-house IT unit does.[13] No outsourced project is an island. Its integration with existing IT assets in your firm's IT portfolio is often necessary but is more challenging. Firms have increasingly found that such integration problems wipe out any potential cost savings from IT outsourcing. This has prompted large-scale insourcing of IT activities that were previously outsourced (called *backsourcing*).[14, 15]

IT insourcing and outsourcing are not mutually exclusive; you can simultaneously insource and outsource the same types of IT activities.[16] This approach of *concurrent sourcing* simultaneously exploits the advantages and safeguards against the disadvantages of both insourcing and outsourcing. We subsequently describe when this makes sense.

The IT Sourcing Decision Tree

Figure 7.1—the IT *sourcing decision tree*—summarizes the choices available to a firm for sourcing IT. On the left is insourcing, where a firm's in-house IT unit typically does the work. A firm can also choose to create a *captive center*, which is a dedicated IT development facility staffed by a firm's employees with all the upsides of insourcing. Captive centers are most commonly located in a *foreign* country, typically to access a talent pool unavailable at the same cost domestically or to localize its IT activities to a foreign market where it has a significant presence.[17] All major American firms such as Boeing, Microsoft, Apple, and Google have captive centers in India, Canada, and Europe for both reasons. A second type of captive center is located in a rural domestic area where IT talent is readily available and costs are lower (*rural sourcing*). For example, many American firms operate captive centers in university towns with major research universities throughout the Midwest, like in Iowa. Although the skills available through rural sourcing (largely part-time student workers) might be inferior to foreign captive centers, the commonalities in culture and accents make them attractive for IT work that requires interacting with customers.

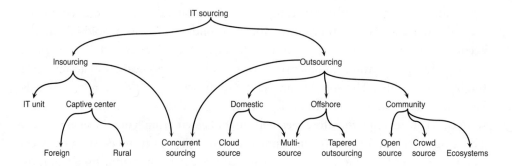

Figure 7.1
The IT sourcing decision tree.

On the right side of figure 7.1 is IT outsourcing, where a firm has three alternatives to insourcing: using (a) a *domestic* firm, (b) an *offshore* foreign firm, or (c) a *community* of individuals to do the work. When using another domestic or foreign firm, the outsourced services can sometimes be delivered entirely through the Internet (*cloud sourcing*) and also outsourced to multiple IT vendors (*multisourcing*). Cloudsourcing is widely used for specialized business apps that the firm rents but does not own, typically paying a subscription fee for each user.[18] Cloudsourcing does not require up-front capital, and service level agreements (SLAs) contractually guarantee operational reliability, but at no point does your firm own the software. Cloudsourcing allows a firm to stick to its knitting while letting specialists manage the necessary *but nonstrategic* parts of its IT portfolio. Cloudsourcing is usually cheaper than doing the same work in-house, but the fact that your archrivals and their uncles outsource to the same vendors guarantees that it will never provide your firm an enduring competitive advantage. Your firm can also divvy up the outsourced work among multiple contracted vendors (*multisourcing*[19]). This approach spreads the risk of one vendor underperforming and allows benchmarking them against each other. Its downside is an increased overhead of coordinating with all of them.

Offshoring is a special case of outsourcing to a vendor in another country. The motivations are identical to outsourcing to domestic firms, but offshoring entails three additional risks.[20, 21] First, language barriers can aggravate the already challenging IT-business communication barrier. Second, contracts can be difficult to enforce legally in developing countries, which are popular IT outsourcing destinations. Third, currency fluctuations can uncontrollably raise your costs unless you specify contracts in your own currency. Your firm can also use a *multisourcing* strategy for offshoring to speed IT development using a twenty-four-hour "follow-the-sun" model. (Picking three locations about eight hours apart in time zones—e.g., Paris, San Francisco, and India—lets each location hand off their work to the next location at the end of an eight-hour workday.) To reduce the challenges of outsourcing vis-à-vis in-house development, some firms—especially in Japan—delay the stage at which they hand off a project to a foreign vendor. We will subsequently describe how this *tapered outsourcing* strategy can reduce the challenges of outsourcing. Foreign captive centers can allow firms to realize most of the advantages of offshoring without the headaches of outsourcing. Many Japanese firms also follow an eclectic practice midway between offshoring and captive centers: buying a financial stake in a foreign vendor firm.[22] This dilutes the divergence of interests between the two firms, but its high cost and dependence on the contract-light Japanese corporate culture make it rarely feasible for firms in most other countries.

A third option for IT outsourcing is to rely on a community of individuals rather than a contracted firm to accomplish the outsourced IT activities. Your firm can tap into three types of communities: (a) open-source, (b) crowd, and (c) ecosystem communities. *Open-source* communities are online communities that freely share the software code that they develop.[23] You can freely modify most open-source code and use it for business with one stringent requirement: you must share any modified software code back with the community as open source. (For example, the popular open-source code repository Sourceforge.com had about half a million business apps in 2017 in every category imaginable.) Their quality can match commercial rivals. However, their free availability and share-back requirement wipes out any potential as a building block for competitive differentiation from your rivals. Most commercial-grade open-source software follows Gillette's free-razor-but-expensive-blades model. The software itself is free, but you pay an outside firm to integrate it with your firm's existing IT assets and to provide maintenance support.

A second more niche alternative is *crowdsourcing*, where a firm enlists a paid or unpaid group of customers. The scope of crowdsourcing IT work is limited to online customer support message boards, where they help each other with technical problems or with data cleansing (e.g., customers tagging photos on Google Maps), and beta testing of software before public release. Firms occasionally run tournaments inviting the crowd to compete in solving a particularly vexing technical problem. Netflix, for example, paid a "Netflix prize" bounty of $1 million to the winner out of two thousand teams who improved its movie-matching algorithm. It is difficult to scale this approach to consider it a mainstream outsourcing option.

The third approach—using *ecosystems* of smaller partner firms—is probably the most promising.[24] Here the firm lets outsiders build software extensions around its own IT systems with an agreement to split the revenue that they generate. The most visible examples are thousands of small applications that third-party developers build for mobile consumer platforms like iOS and Android. Less visible are their corporate parallels, where outsiders produce novel extensions built around "hooks" (APIs) into a firm's IT systems. These typically bring additional sales to the firm or create novel value by using sanitized data assets that a firm chooses to share. APIs have historically been a norm in technology firms but are now becoming increasingly common in nontechnology firms as well. Examples of nontechnology firms, nonprofits, and government organizations that have used this approach include Nike (see developer.nike.com), American drugstore Walgreens (developer.walgreens .com), genomics firm 23andMe (api.23andme.com), National Public Radio (dev.npr .org), and even the US federal government (api.data.gov). Community sourcing can complement insourcing or outsourcing but should never be considered a substitute for in-house IT.

Box 7.2
Not Lost in Translation: Mozilla's Software

Entry-level smartphones in many developing countries run on the FirefoxOS created by the American nonprofit Mozilla Foundation. FirefoxOS uses sixteen thousand words, many of which do not translate across cultures and more than two hundred languages spanned by its users. Technical terms such as cookies, file, crash, timeout, and mouse must be expressed in alternative culture-specific words tied to farm animals and fishing to communicate their intended meaning.[25] Their original coinage is steeped in American English. (For example, the word for "cookie" in British English is "biscuit.") The Firefox OS translation into the Fulah language spoken around Senegal in Africa therefore uses *hookii* for "crash," which means a cow falling over but not dying, and *honaama* for "timeout," which means your fish have gotten away. In the Chichewa language in Malawi in Africa, it uses *mfusto wa tsamba* for "cached content," which means food leftovers. In Zapotec, spoken by indigenous Mexicans, the word for "eyes" has to be used instead of "windows" because most houses in that region do not have windows. Humans speak more than five thousand languages; connecting them is literally more a language challenge than an economic one. Technological nonprofits such as Mozilla and Code for America alone—not firms—can dare invest in connecting the many non-English-speaking pockets of humanity left behind isolated from our connected world. Even for-profit firms must learn from Mozilla that sometimes sourcing to a foreign location is needed to localize your firm's offerings to the unique idiosyncrasies of the foreign markets in which you want to operate.

Business Challenges in Outsourced IT Projects

Two perpetual problems make it harder to realize *business* value from outsourced IT projects even when you have a competent IT vendor working with diligent staff from your IT unit. The first is integration problems—that is, the pieces do not fit. The second is ending up with the wrong system—technically fine but unable to serve its intended business purpose.

Challenge #1: Integration Costs

Integration problems arise when a delivered project works fine by itself but does not play well with other IT assets in your firm. An outsourced system often must use data produced by other apps or send data to them.[26] This requires a vendor to understand data sources and interfaces to other IT assets in your firm's IT portfolio with which the outsourced system must eventually interoperate. Among such assets, custom-built apps are especially harder for outsiders to comprehend. You can rarely transplant an app custom built outside your firm to plug and play with your patchwork of proprietary and custom-tweaked systems, which might span generations of technologies. Integrating a delivered system therefore adds considerable costs beyond the development costs paid to an outside vendor. Integration costs frequently exceed expectations and can wipe out any potential savings from outsourcing.[27] You must therefore compare outsourcing to insourcing using *total* costs—not just software development costs—to avoid sticker shock. Even these total costs cannot account for the undiscovered business innovation opportunities potentially forfeited by *not* insourcing.

Curbing Integration Costs Using Concurrent Sourcing and Vendor Screening
Firms can use two strategies to lower integration costs in IT outsourcing: (a) concurrent IT sourcing and (b) adopting a verify-then-trust approach instead of a trust-then-verify approach toward vendors. *Concurrent IT sourcing* is the practice of *simultaneously* insourcing and outsourcing the same sort of IT projects.[28] You need just a trace—as little as 10 percent by volume—of the work done in-house to benefit from concurrent IT sourcing.[29] Doing this retains mission-critical IT skills in-house, which excessive IT outsourcing can otherwise erode. If you are not careful, excessive outsourcing can hollow out your firm's in-house technical capabilities over time. There might not be enough in-house talent left to understand your own IT portfolio as well as a vendor does, potentially handcuffing your firm to your IT vendors. To paraphrase the Eagles' hit song "Hotel California," you can check out of IT outsourcing any time you like, but you can never leave.

Concurrent IT sourcing—by maintaining in-house IT skills—prevents IT outsourcing from becoming an irreversible decision. Doing the job in-house allows your IT unit to understand it well enough to communicate with an outside vendor, easing integration of outsourced IT work. It also helps write better outsourcing contracts and better specifications that lower integration costs.[30] In the long run, concurrent IT sourcing keeps alive the option to bring outsourced IT activities back in-house. Concurrent sourcing can also simultaneously improve the performance of both your in-house IT unit and outsourcing vendors by fostering healthy competition between them.

A second approach is to go an extra mile to screen for vendors with whom you are less likely to have higher integration costs. The norm in IT outsourcing is *trust-then-verify*: select vendors and then verify the quality of their work. Leading Japanese firms flip this approach to *verify-then-trust*. Toshiba, for example, injected ambiguities and integration problems into a *completed* project that it then simultaneously outsourced to three competing vendors. It did this just to verify how they dealt with integration problems, ambiguities, and how their finished code compared to their own engineers' code. Toshiba did all this just to decide who got the *real*, larger project that it wanted to outsource. It added the winner to its exclusive circle of trusted IT vendors to which it now extensively outsources.

Box 7.3
How Not to Make a Jet Plane: IT Outsourcing Lessons from Boeing's Dreamliner

Unlike cars that have a model lifespan of about six years, a typical passenger jet has a model lifespan of about thirty years. When Boeing began developing its 787 Dreamliner jet, it promised unprecedented fuel economy, longer range, and passenger comfort in a plane made largely using plastic-like carbon fiber and titanium instead of aluminum. The project involved about a hundred specialized firms in the United States, Japan, France, Germany, Italy, Sweden, Korea, and India. Each was responsible for a major part of the plane, which would be flown preassembled to Boeing's assembly plant in Everett, Washington. Japan's Yuasa supplied its lithium ion batteries, Iowan Rockwell Collins flight control systems, French Messier-Dowty its landing gear, Thales (also French) its electrical power converters, Germany's Diehl Luftfahrt Elektronik the cabin lighting, Italy's Alenia Aeronautica the fuselage, Sweden's Saab Aerostructures the access doors, and Japan's Jamco the toilets. The parts were designed to snap together in three days, down from the twelve days it took to assemble previous plane models. Boeing's rationale was that specialist firms could do a better job in their parts than one generalist firm could. It expected to cut development costs for the new plane by $4 billion and develop it two years faster. It developed its own custom software called Exostar to coordinate the work of all the firms involved in the project.

Box 7.3 (*continued*)

However, for the software to ensure coordination, all suppliers had to diligently use it. Several years into the project, Boeing realized that it had a big problem: the parts did not fit. It has severely underestimated the difficulty of integration among the parts. The project was 300 percent over budget and three years behind schedule by the time the first plane was ready. Even though major airlines had ordered 848 Dreamliners at about $300 million apiece, Boeing struggled to deliver even the first 50 on time. The integration problems persisted once the first set of planes entered service. Fuel leaks, brake failures, electrical fires, failing windshields, and emergency landings forced the US Federal Aviation Authority (FAA) to ground the entire fleet for three months. Boeing had to convince the FAA that it was an airworthy passenger jet. It eventually did, but after agonizingly costly rework. The Dreamliner project offers three lessons for IT outsourcing decisions.

a. *Do not underestimate integration costs.* Boeing based its decision to outsource 70 percent of the project based on a miscalculation of integration costs, which it severely underestimated. Such integration costs can wipe out the advantages of outsourcing when the outsourced parts must seamlessly work together. Boeing did not outsource to be cheap; it did so for expertise and speed. Neglecting integration costs meant that Boeing used the wrong metrics to decide what to outsource. Its 300 percent cost overruns also signal that Boeing failed to realize that it would actually cost far more to outsource than doing the same work in-house. The lesson for IT outsourcing is to evaluate sourcing decisions using total costs, including integration costs with your firm's other IT systems.

b. *Do not outsource design.* Boeing outsourced a lot of design responsibilities to its suppliers. Had Boeing done all the engineering design in-house and only outsourced production, the integration problems might have been less severe. Contrast the Dreamliner with a much simpler product: the iPhone. Although Apple outsources all manufacturing to outsiders, it first completely manufactures production-ready prototypes in-house. This reduces production problems when outsourced production ramps up. The equivalent to Apple's approach for IT outsourcing is tapered outsourcing and concurrent sourcing described in this chapter. Like Apple, Toyota outsources 70 percent of its car parts but maintains tight control over their design. Doing the entire design and continuing to maintain in-house IT capabilities on a smaller scale ensures that Boeing-like outsourcing fiascoes do not surface in your firm's IT outsourcing.

c. *Do not outsource what you have never done yourself.* It did not help that Boeing was building a plane with novel materials and technologies that no one had tried before. The risk of trying to outsource the production of a plane that involved too many untested ideas that interacted unpredictably aggravated Boeing's experiment with an untested way of organizing its production. The lesson for IT outsourcing is to stick with in-house development until your IT unit has first-hand experience doing the IT work that your firm is considering outsourcing. This is not always possible with new technologies where a vendor might have greater technical expertise. However, tapered outsourcing can still reduce risk by easing integration of the outsourced project with your firm's existing IT assets.

Challenge #2: Receiving the Wrong System

Outsourcing aggravates the problem of ending up with a technically sound system that fails to serve its intended business purpose. IT vendors often pinpoint volatile client requirements as the culprit.[31] However, volatile requirements do not necessarily mean that your IT unit or line functions are indecisive. A project's requirements might be latent and require intense interactions between business users and IT developers to iteratively flesh out. In an outsourced project, your IT unit is the go-between for your business users and the vendor's programmers. Adding this extra layer—absent in in-house projects—worsens the odds that your IT unit will fail to translate your latent business needs or the vendor to grasp them. An outsourced project therefore simultaneously faces a business-IT language chasm between the users and your geeks *and* a cultural barrier between your IT unit and an outside IT vendor.

Business apps also require a detailed understanding of your firm's business processes and ways of doing things, which an in-house IT unit is likely to grasp better than outsiders. The consequence is that you might end up with what your IT unit asked the vendor for but not what your firm needed. As this chapter later describes, projects with poorly specifiable requirements should not be outsourced at all. However, a lack of the relevant IT skills in-house can sometimes force you to.

Curbing Misdelivery by Tapering and Flexible Contracting

Firms can use two strategies to reduce the risk of ending up with an outsourced IT project that misdelivers: (a) tapered outsourcing and (b) structuring flexibility into contracts.

Tapered outsourcing is widely practiced in Japanese firms; figure 7.2 contrasts it to the conventional American model. Think of it as *control through design*. Your in-house IT unit completely owns the front-end of the development process (requirements and high-level design) and the handoff to a vendor occurs much later (at the coding stage ② in figure 7.2). In contrast, the handoff occurs at the earlier requirements stage (①) in the American model, which also dominates most countries outside Japan. The tapered outsourcing approach overcomes language barriers and cultural differences because the handoffs to the vendor are in language-independent, standardized design notations (such as the unified modeling language and screen mock-ups). This is like the blueprints that an architect would hand off to a contractor building a house; there is less room for misinterpretation. It allows a dictatorial level of control over the project's direction while also permitting *some* outsourcing to lower costs or access technical expertise. However, tapered outsourcing demands business-savvy software design skills in your firm's in-house IT unit.[32]

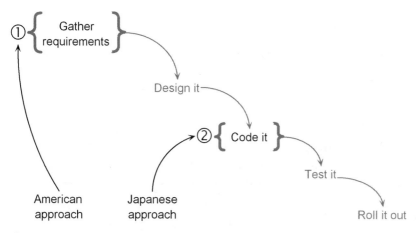

Figure 7.2
Tapered outsourcing delays (①→②) when the handoff to a vendor occurs.

The second strategy is to structure flexibility into project contracts when you cannot pin down project requirements.[33] You can structure IT outsourcing contracts as *fixed-price* contracts that pay the vendor a lump sum for completing a project or as *time-and-materials* contracts that pay the vendor for the hours of labor actually used to complete a project.[34] Fixed-price contracts are legally more complex, in contrast with simpler time-and-materials ones that expose your firm to greater cost variability.[35] Both types of contracts include provisions for a warranty period within which a vendor is obligated to fix bugs, pass acceptance tests performed by the client firm, and accommodate a limited number of no-fee changes in requirements while the project is under way.[36] (Testing of delivered software ought to be done in-house before accepting it.) Time-and-materials contracts have the advantage of greater flexibility to meet changing or newly discovered project requirements. Vendors are often receptive to them because they translate into a larger payout for them. A *hybrid* contract combines elements of fixed-price and time-and-materials contracts. The poorer the up-front specifiability of a project's requirements, the more your firm should lean toward time-and-materials contracts.

Recognizing What Can Be Outsourced

IT outsourcing decisions should be made one project at a time. In a turnaround from wholesale IT sourcing that was prevalent until the 2010s, IT outsourcing contracts have increasingly become shorter and narrower in scope.[37] Firms choose to outsource for two reasons: (a) to access IT skills that their in-house IT unit does not have or (b) a vendor can do the same job at a lower cost than your in-house IT unit can. Both of these motivations appear innocuous but can create vicious problems from which your firm can later struggle to extricate itself. The initial contribution of non-IT managers to their firm's IT sourcing decisions is recognizing IT projects that should *not* be outsourced. Figure 7.3 and figure 7.4 summarize the criteria for judging the outsourcability of an IT project.

Mission Criticality and Differentiation Potential
The first set of considerations—figure 7.3—are whether a project is for a mission-critical IT asset and potentially a competitive differentiator from your archrivals. An IT system is mission-critical if its failure would jeopardize a *primary* activity in your firm's value chain (e.g., sales, production, or operations). Mission-critical systems that also potentially differentiate your firm (cell ④; e.g., strategic apps) should be done in-house. The penalty of failure and the risk of intellectual property leakage is simply too high to not do it yourself. Embedded software—code that functions inside a piece of hardware such as a watch, TV, car, or laser printer—often meets this criterion. Embedded software is almost always central to the functioning, quality, and reliability of a firm's market offerings. It defines how your customers interact with what you sell and often differentiates the customer experience. Each flaw, minor imperfection, or user-unfriendliness in such software multiplies on a massive scale in every unit of the product you sell or customer that you serve. Think about how much the software inside your car, television, thermostat, or smartphone shapes your perception about the firm that makes it. Embedded software ought to be done in-house and preferably never outsourced. The only reason to ever outsource it is the lack of appropriate in-house technical skills; this should at best be a temporary stopgap measure until you can hire appropriate in-house expertise. If you must outsource, is it possible to separate the less strategic from the more strategic parts of the

Figure 7.3
A project's mission criticality and competitive versus operational nature.

project? To prevent leakage of intellectual property, Japanese firms often follow an unusual practice of decomposing such software into pieces outsourced to different vendors that only they can reassemble.

If a project is a potential competitive differentiator from your archrivals but is not mission-critical (cell ③), insourcing is still preferable for a different reason. Insourcing safeguards against imitation and is more conducive to intense in-house iterations required to uncover latent business needs. If a project is an operational necessity rather than a strategic differentiator, it can be outsourced if it is not mission-critical (cell ②). Most cloudsourced IT services fall into cell ②. If it is also mission-critical (cell ①), you can cautiously outsource it if (a) your firm also maintains in-house IT expertise in the project's technical domain (i.e., does concurrent IT sourcing) *and* (b) you can have contractually enforceable performance guarantees to keep it from becoming an operational liability. The candidates in cell ① often are IT systems that once created a competitive advantage but are now widespread in your industry. If they are now commoditized, it is plausible that a cottage sector of competent and competitive IT firms specializing in them has emerged. The concurrent mix of insourcing and outsourcing in this cell should skew toward the side that has better *technical* talent available. Concurrent IT sourcing can also strengthen in-house IT expertise in the project's domain by learning from specialist vendors.

If your firm lacks in-house expertise in any project's domain or the underlying technology is evolving too fast to keep up, it has little choice but to outsource even if a project demands in-house development.[38] We next describe how your firm can reduce—but never eliminate—risk in such sticky situations.

Interaction Intensity and Labor Intensity

The second set of considerations—summarized in figure 7.4—are a project's labor intensity and the need for intense interactions between business users in the line functions and IT staff. If the need for such interactions is low, you can readily specify a project's requirements in writing. Outsourcing is appropriate for such projects when they are also labor intensive (cell ④). This is *the* ideal profile of a project that can be outsourced to lower costs: precise, stable requirements and labor intense. If labor intensity is low (cell ③), outsource if you lack in-house IT skills to do the job.

Intense interactions are needed in projects where it is difficult to precisely specify business requirements up front and difficult to verify that a delivered project meets its business intent.[39] Projects with a high need for business-IT interaction—the right part of figure 7.4—signal that a project's needs are too latent to be articulated in a document that you can hand over to an outside vendor. If you cannot describe what

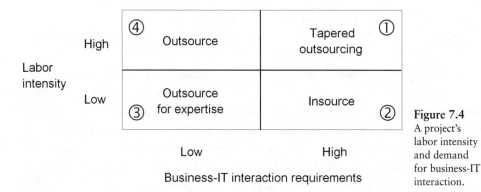

Figure 7.4
A project's labor intensity and demand for business-IT interaction.

your firm needs, you cannot successfully outsource it. Most IT-based business inno-vations that can create a competitive advantage are in cells ① or ②. Projects demand-ing intense business-IT interactions should be insourced if their labor intensity is low (cell ②). If they are labor intense (cell ①), tapered outsourcing controls their design without entirely forsaking the benefits of outsourcing.

The Chain of Responsibility in Outsourced IT Projects

Figure 7.5 shows the *chain of responsibility* for an outsourced IT project. It is your IT unit—not the vendor—that is accountable for meeting the project's intended *business* objectives. Your IT unit is the client of the vendor to which the project is outsourced. It is the IT unit's responsibility to ensure that the vendor meets the technical specifications specified by your IT unit. This includes features and func-tionality, as well as cost, schedule, and quality targets. Ensuring all this requires a rudimentary appreciation by non-IT managers of controls and vendor capability judgments.

   a. Controls. Vendor accountability to your IT unit requires *formal controls*. These are a combination of *output metrics* that reward or penalize a vendor for meeting pre-defined, objective targets in the delivered work (e.g., deadlines and cost constraints) and *process controls* that dictate the methods that a vendor should follow.[40, 41]

Figure 7.5
The chain of responsibility in an outsourced IT project.

Output metrics only work well if the vendor's outputs are measurable and the project's requirements precisely specifiable.[42, 43] Process control only works when your firm's technical expertise in the project domain is superior to the vendor's. In practice, the latter is rare.[44] The optimal control approach—as the historical examples in chapter 6 remind us—is to create accountability (i.e., use output metrics) without micromanagement (i.e., minimize process control).

b. Capability maturity. A competency in vendor selection and management is increasingly expected from corporate IT units. IT units frequently rely on vendors' capability maturity model (CMM) ratings on a one (worst) to five (best) scale based on a grueling evaluation by the US-based Software Engineering Institute.[45] CMM ratings are like eBay seller ratings—comparable across vendors and generally trustworthy. A vendor with a higher CMM rating is likely to charge more for the same project. (Only 7 percent of the CMM-rated IT organizations worldwide had a rating of five in 2016.) However, just as a well-rated eBay seller can fail to deliver, using a high CMM-rated vendor does not guarantee a successful project. Your IT unit should also triangulate such ratings with referral checks from other client firms in your own industry in your own home country.

Around the World in Eighty Seconds
IT outsourcing vendor firms exist in more than a hundred diverse countries. Figure 7.6 compares several countries with mature IT outsourcing industries on costs and quality of IT skill sets from the perspective of an American firm's business needs.[46]

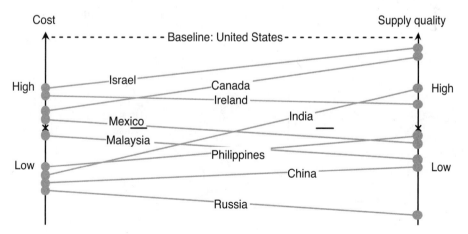

Figure 7.6
Cost and supply quality in global IT outsourcing destinations.

Five things merit attention in deciding where in the world to offshore an IT project:

1. *Time zone.* Is an overlapping time zone or a follow-the-sun spacing preferable? Figure 7.7 maps the time zones of the major outsourcing destinations relative to 8 a.m. in the United States' East Coast.

2. *Skill set.* Match the region's IT skills to your project's needs. For example, Israel and Russia are particularly strong in embedded programming; Canada, India, and Ireland in custom-developed business applications.

3. *Profile.* Who is already outsourcing there? How many vendors exist? Is it politically stable?

4. *Culture.* Are there language and cultural differences?

5. *Legal sophistication.* What is the country's track record for intellectual property rights and legal enforcement of contracts?

Key Takeaways

1. *IT sourcing is a strategic choice.* Obvious costs alone should never solely drive the decision about whether you will do your custom IT development in-house or outside. IT outsourcing usually fails because of challenges in integrating an outsourced project with your firm's existing IT assets or because the *wrong* system gets delivered.

2. *IT sourcing takes many forms.* In-house development can be done by your IT unit or in a foreign captive center and outsourcing by a domestic or foreign vendor or by an outside community.

3. *IT sourcing entails trade-offs.* Insourcing uses in-house employees who better appreciate your business and its customers, share their interests, and impede IT

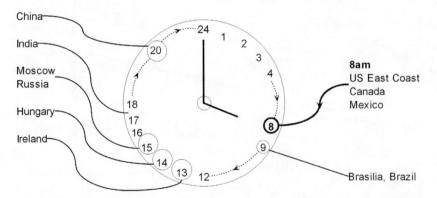

Figure 7.7
Time zones of outsourcing destinations relative to 8 a.m., US East Coast.

imitation by your rivals. Outsourcing sacrifices these advantages but gets you technical skills absent in-house and can be more economical for one-off tasks. Concurrent IT sourcing blends insourcing with outsourcing.

4. *Some IT projects should never be outsourced.* Projects that are mission-critical, are competitively differentiating, or require intense interaction between business users and IT specialists are better kept in-house. If your IT unit lacks the technical skills to do them, doing more of the up-front design in-house (*tapered* outsourcing) reduces risks.

5. *Outsourcing lengthens the chain of responsibility.* A vendor is accountable to your IT unit for meeting a project's technical specifications; your IT unit is accountable to non-IT managers for the project achieving its business objectives.

6. *Do not let outsourcing be a one-way street.* Excessive IT outsourcing can eventually hollow out your in-house IT capabilities. Concurrent IT sourcing prevents it from becoming an irreversible choice.

The Non-IT Managers' Checklist

For any major IT project that you are considering outsourcing:

☐ Is it mission-critical to the operations of your firm? What would be the *business* penalty if it failed to get done?

☐ Can it potentially differentiate your firm from its archrivals, or is it a competitive necessity?

☐ Would staving off copycat rivals increase its business payoff?

☐ Can its requirements be written down or does fleshing them out require lots of iteration between business users and IT?

☐ Does your IT unit have the technical chops to do it? If not, can you afford to create a foreign captive center where such skills are abundant?

☐ Can your IT unit do its entire detailed design in-house before handing it off to a vendor?

☐ How dependent is it on your existing IT assets (i.e., level of integration needed)?

☐ What would be the business cost of *not* doing it in-house?

Jargon Decoder

IT security breach	A malicious effort to either make an IT system inaccessible to its users or steal sensitive data or intellectual property.
Security trade-off	Increasing IT security usually inconveniences legitimate users.
Social engineering	Tricking a legitimate user into divulging information needed to access a secured IT system.
Security credentials	Something you know, have, or are; the more the better.
Continuity planning	A tactical plan to resume business operations if your entire IT portfolio were knocked out or destroyed.

8

Security and Business Continuity

IT is a vulnerable business engine. Imagine if you could not see a burglar inside your house while he stole your stuff, he remained undetected for months, and you could not tell what he stole even months later. That is precisely the problem with securing corporate IT systems. Unlike conventional attacks, an attack on digital assets is possible from miles away, it can go undetected for months, it's hard to figure out the aftermath, and it is often impossible to find the culprits because adept hackers cover their tracks.

This chapter delves into how firms can secure their IT assets against malice and disaster. This challenge is not strategic, but its failings can threaten your firm's survival. We explain why the strongest of security technology leaves firms vulnerable to security breaches and how non-IT managers can help protect their firms' IT assets in ways that IT managers cannot.

Sizing Up the Security Problem

On average, a single corporate IT security breach costs firms about $4 million.[1] It takes firms about five months to even *realize* that they have been hacked.[2] Hackers are able to roam around freely for almost eight months on average after breaking in before firms discover them.[3] Firms widely underreport such breaches because of liability, negative publicity, and the inability to prosecute across national borders. As figure 8.1 shows, the cost of *every stolen record* due to an IT security breach varies by industry, increasing in more regulated industries such as financial services, pharmaceuticals, and health care.[4]

The scale of industrial espionage, sabotage, and theft using IT pales legendary crimes that are the stuff of Hollywood thrillers. One of the biggest bank robberies *ever* was a digital one in 2016, where hackers broke into the SWIFT[5] network that eleven thousand banks use to move money among themselves. Why risk going after

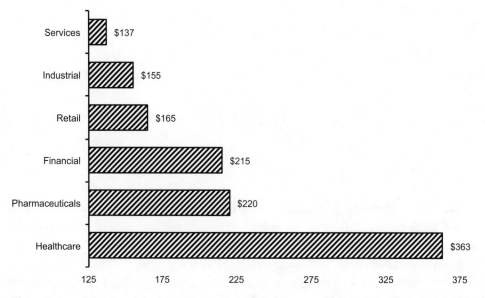

Figure 8.1
The cost of *each record* breached in US firms differs dramatically across industries.

individual banks at gunpoint when you could tap into the plumbing that connects banks to steal on a massive scale? Beyond theft, industrial espionage costs firms about half a trillion dollars annually—about the size of Austria's entire economy.[6]

Hostile spooks and terrorists can attack—and have attacked—power stations, electric grids, nuclear plants, and air traffic control systems from a keyboard thousands of miles away. It is not just industrial spies, terrorists, and spooks. A new breed of crooks have digitized their crookery: they encrypt unsuspecting smartphones using *ransomware* and then demand a ransom to unlock them,[7] contract killers promise hits by manipulating Internet-enabled pacemakers and insulin pumps, and online drug dealers obsess over feedback star ratings and the daily exchange rates of cryptocurrencies like Bitcoin.

Securing IT assets is hard because the Internet's original intent was connectivity, not security. IT security breaches can paralyze operations, compromise sensitive information and intellectual property, and do enormous reputational harm to firms.[8] Megabreaches involving more than ten million records are increasingly common. Examples include megabreaches of the US voter registry (191 million individuals; 2016), Athem's medical records (80 million; 2015), eBay (145 million; 2014), Evernote (50 million; 2013), Sony (77 million; 2012), Heartland payment systems (130 million; 2010), BNY Mellon (12.5 million; 2009), and TJ Maxx stores (94 million; 2007). If the staggering financial losses do not drive breached firms out of business, losing their customers' faith will.

The two broad IT security threats that firms face are compromises of availability and intrusion into internal corporate systems. Availability is most often compromised by *denial of service* attacks, where a malicious outsider overwhelms a corporate IT system with so much traffic that it renders it unresponsive to legitimate users. Intrusion—called hacking in popular culture—is usually in search of sensitive data and intellectual property. A whole eBay-like underground global community—called the dark net—exists to buy and sell stolen intellectual property and financial data such as credit card numbers.

Let us begin by discarding the myth of secure computing. The aspiration should be acceptable—not perfect—security and resilience to rapidly bounce back from breaches without excruciating losses.[9] For each of the three classes of IT assets, the IT unit should be responsible for implementing and solidly executing operational best practices for IT security. However, not every IT asset is equally important; judgments about what's more important to your business should come from non-IT managers. Here is an overview of where non-IT managers can contribute.

• *IT infrastructure* needs the least input from business since it is largely a technical challenge; the IT unit is best positioned to decide how to protect it.
• *IT apps*. Line functions—not IT units—are more knowledgeable about which IT apps need what level of protection. Apps' vulnerabilities are (a) the occasional *brute force* attacks to forcibly access them and (b) the more widespread approach of convincing a legitimate user inside your firm to willingly divulge information needed to access them (*social engineering*[10]).
• *Data*. Non-IT managers' primary contributions to their firms' IT security decisions are data related. Most security breaches are motivated to acquire confidential data that can be sold, exploited, or altered (e.g., customer financial information, trade secrets, and intellectual property). What data is more sensitive varies by industry: accounts data for banks, R&D data for drug firms, and customer financial data and pricing data for retailers. IT units often do not receive explicit guidance from non-IT managers about what data assets in their departments are the most critical.[11]

To appropriately secure corporate IT assets, the IT unit must know (a) what data and apps are more critical and (b) the trade-off between security and convenience acceptable to business users. Your IT unit can be more effective at its job—executing security policies and preventing breaches—when it knows what is *really* worth protecting for your business. Non-IT managers alone can make that judgment. They must take a lead in formulating their firms' security policies for both apps and data

Box 8.1
How Target Became the Target

One of the biggest retail hacks in US history was the American retailer Target during the 2013 Christmas season. The attack was unoriginal and sloppy yet successful.[12] Right before the holiday season, a hacker installed a little piece of malicious software in Target's payments processing system. The hackers designed it to steal every credit card that would be used in Target's 1,800 US stores. Any time a customer swiped a credit card to pay for a purchase, the malware would quietly make a copy of the credit card number and ferret it away on one of Target's own hijacked servers. It pillaged financial data with impunity for two weeks undetected. The hackers cleverly planned the data's escape route to cover their tracks; it would bounce around several locations throughout the United States and then to Russia. To make sure it escaped detection by blending in with legitimate data traffic, they siphoned it out of Target's own servers only during the busiest times of 10 a.m. to 6 p.m. This is like a Hollywood thriller where the bad guy runs into a crowded subway station to get lost in the crowd. It worked. Forty million credit cards and seventy million customer addresses were lost. Target's sales in the busy holiday season plummeted.

What went wrong were entirely human failings. Target had anticipated problems, which is why it purchased the same security software that the US Central Intelligence Agency (CIA) used. Its thinking was that if it is good enough for spooks, it should be good enough for a retailer. Nevertheless, if you try breaking into someone's home, you do not try knocking down a wall. Instead, you look for a weak spot—an open window or a flimsy back door. Target's weak spot was a vendor with which it did business. The hackers used the credentials of a small company in Pittsburgh that maintained Target's refrigeration systems to enter its corporate network. Any entry-level IT person will tell you that you should wall off IT systems with sensitive data from ones that your refrigeration vendor can access. However, there were holes in this wall (an architectural failing; see chapter 3). The hackers cloaked their stolen data using the name of widely used software used to *protect* credit card data. Target's security team thought they were seeing a legitimate program file as the stolen stash passed right in front of them. The CIA-grade malware detector did no good because Target's security turned off a critical part of it, thinking it was creating too many false alarms.[13] Target spent $500 million a year for the next two years mitigating the damage. (This appears as an "unusual expense" in its 2014 and 2015 annual reports.[14]) It is hard to estimate the cost of lost customer confidence and a tarnished image. The incident cost the CEO and CIO their jobs.

for the IT unit to implement. These inputs also lay the groundwork for business continuity planning.

Conventional Technical Approaches to IT Security
You must grasp how IT is secured technically to appreciate why it fails. You can use three things to secure any IT system: (a) something you *know* (e.g., a password or

access code), (b) something you *have* (e.g., an ATM card or smartcard), and (c) something you *are* (e.g., your unique fingerprint). The more of these three credentials you combine (called *multifactor authentication*), the more secure it is. Outside attacks rely primarily on getting hold of the first two.

Firms generally do two things to safeguard themselves against outside attacks. First, they use credit-card-industry-inspired *intrusion detection* tools that identify patterns of suspicious activity (e.g., numerous failed login attempts) and *intrusion prevention* tools that instantaneously block access if they detect such a pattern. (Such monitoring and anomaly detection are standard fare in the IT security arsenal, as should be routine *patching* of newly discovered vulnerabilities in purchased software.[15]) However, they provide no defense against a legitimate password—one that the user has been tricked into revealing or that is stolen using *key-logging* spyware that covertly captures her keystrokes.

Skilled hackers prefer social engineering over brute force since it is easier to fool a human than to fool a machine.[16] Biometric authentication technologies such as fingerprint or facial recognition, voiceprints, or retina scans prevent attacks from outsiders but not from rouge insiders (as the Snowden espionage case demonstrated). The conventional technical approaches to IT security overemphasize *identifiable* security risks, which can lull firms into complacency and a false sense of security. Even the most comprehensive IT security can fail for five nontechnical reasons.

Five Nontechnical Reasons for IT Security Failures
IT security failures occur in spite of technical safeguards for five reasons: (1) firms view IT security as a technical problem, (2) they overlook the insider threat, (3) the weakest link in a permeable boundary with other firms creates vulnerabilities, (4) non-IT managers don't explicitly make a trade-off between security and convenience, and (5) the Internet of Things (IoT) opens a new vista for hackers.

Viewing Security as the IT Unit's Job
Most firms erroneously treat IT security as solely the IT unit's responsibility. They view it as a technological problem calling for technological solutions. That is like treating your home's security as your lockmaker's responsibility. Even the strongest lock will not protect you if you do not follow basic security hygiene—such as properly locking your door, hiding your passport better than your coffee machine, not handing out keys to strangers, and being observant. For IT, this parallels using security tools properly, holding sensitive data to a higher security standard, preempting social engineering, and sensitizing business users.

Human blunders—not inadequate technology—open the door to the vast majority of successful data breaches. Your IT unit has little power to effect good behavior without a push from non-IT managers for good security hygiene within line functions. Avoiding human blunders requires fostering a firm-wide culture of responsibility and awareness among business users. You must reinforce it with training, irrespective of whether you incentivize it with carrots or sticks.[17]

Overlooking the Insider Threat

Although mastermind hackers from China and Russia get the most press, the real danger is from your own employees and connected business partners in your firm's value stream. The breaches can be accidental slipups or intentional actions by a malicious or disgruntled employee. Firms obsess over safeguarding against outside attacks but not against ones from inside. Insider attacks are the single largest IT security vulnerability. Insiders have easier access and more opportunities, and most widespread IT security policies and protections are defenseless against them. For example, mandating frequently changing passwords causes them to appear on sticky notes under people's keyboards, hardened perimeter defenses do not deter insiders with legitimate access, and simply requiring employees to read corporate security policies does not prevent slipups either.

To tackle insider threats, you must put yourself in the shoes of a disgruntled employee and a hacker.[18] The safeguards against insider threats are stronger internal controls and user awareness, both of which require non-IT managers' contributions. Non-IT managers—not the IT unit—must determine the appropriate access privileges for apps and data for individual users in their line functions. This involves decisions about who can access what data, what they can do with it, and when and where. This set of choices together represents your firm's *IT access policies*. The IT unit should not create such policies, only implement them.

Each line-function employee should be granted the most restrictive clearance level sufficient to do her job.[19] Non-IT managers must define what data is more sensitive and what apps are critical to their line function's activities. What are the *business* risks of having them compromised? You can help tailor IT security policies to your firm's priorities and ask the IT unit for differentiated protection based on the business importance of particular IT assets. The simplest way to secure data assets is by creating tiers of access privileges specific to *your* firm; generic security policies produce generic protection. As employees depart or change responsibilities, you must also regularly revise these lists.

Six other practices can strengthen the protection of data assets against insider threats.

• *Monitor* employees IT usage for patterns of suspicious activities, and be transparent about such monitoring. Knowing that they are being watched—like theft-deterrent cameras in a store—psychologically discourages undesirable behavior. (Such *audit logs* are harder to maintain for big data.)
• *Encrypt* sensitive data—both in transit and where it is stored—so that it is unreadable even if it does fall into the wrong hands. (Encrypted data is scrambled into gobbledygook and only its owner can help decrypt it.)
• *Wall off* systems with truly sensitive data from others.
• *Unlink* sensitive data from other data to minimize the damage if it is stolen (e.g., using a customer identification number instead of a social security number).
• *Anonymize* sensitive data if you only need aggregates for analytics initiatives.
• *Refrain* from collecting excessive data just because you can.

The Porous Boundary with Business Partners

Ironically, sharing data across interconnected supply chains makes data more valuable but also more vulnerable. Protecting the perimeter of your own firm is insufficient as firms interconnect their IT systems in the pursuit of efficiency and coordination. Increased connectivity of your firm's IT systems with your business partners' systems means that your own IT security depends on other firms' systems that you do not control. It is increasingly harder to define where your own firm's IT boundaries end and your partners' begin. The weakest link defines the vulnerability of an interconnected supply chain. Weak defenses in one partner firm with a higher appetite for risk makes your firm more vulnerable; a hacker can commandeer a device in their IT portfolio to cripple your firm.

Dealing with these problems demands industry-wide cooperation. Industry-specific consortia now exist specifically to share information about digital threats among member firms.[20] Firms must also regularly prune lists of access-privileged users in business partner firms and contractors. Snowden's pillaging of secret documents of the US National Security Administration (NSA) was possible because he had unfettered access to its systems even though he was an outside contractor and not an NSA employee.

Imbalance between Convenience and Security

Underprotection makes your firm's IT assets vulnerable and overprotection can inconvenience your employees and customers by forcing them to jump through too many hoops. If doing business with your firm is a constant inconvenience, they will take their business to a rival with better sensibilities. The delicate trade-off is balancing protection of sensitive data and the risk of irking users with excessive security. This is a business decision, not a technical one to be left to your IT unit. Walling off data too aggressively can also diminish its value in enhancing your firms operations. Yet one serious breach of sensitive data can be fatal for a firm. If your customers cannot trust your firm, the rest does not matter. Non-IT managers alone should decide—explicitly—the level of security risk that is acceptable to your firm.[21]

Internet of Things

The IoT escalates both vulnerability and consumers' expectations of security. Billions of objects, such as cars, appliances, and medical devices, joining the Internet open up many more deep interfaces into corporate IT systems for malicious hackers

Box 8.2
A Hacker's Guide to Halting the Global Economy

The global banking system is nothing more than a set of promises between governments, institutions, and individuals.[23] Currency has value because governments promise to back the paper bills that represent it, banks accounts have value because banks promise to stand behind account balances, we believe that our employers have made good on their promise to pay us each month because we believe the bank that notifies us of a direct deposit, stores believe that we have paid at the cash register for our shopping because they believe their bank's electronic confirmation, and banks have credibility because governments often insure them. If all these participants no longer believed each other, the entire system collapses. Yet the very things the banking industry has done to make these promises more credible have introduced massive vulnerabilities. These vulnerabilities are concentrated in industry-wide IT systems that handle transactions among banks. These financial market infrastructure (FMI) systems and clearinghouses are the plumbing of the global banking industry. The Society for Worldwide Interbank Financial Telecommunication (SWIFT; www.swift.com) system, for example, connects more than eleven thousand financial institutions to each other, moving billions of dollars in about twenty-six million transactions each day. Similarly in 2015, TARGET2 (Europe's interbank settlement system) handled more than $500 trillion in eighty-eight million transactions, and American Automated Clearinghouse (ACH) had twenty-four billion transactions worth $42 trillion. Hackers are increasingly breaking into banks' IT systems to access such interbank systems, often changing numbers such as bank balances stored in their computers (e.g., adding two extra zeros to a checking account with a hundred-dollar balance). FMI systems have therefore increasingly become the favored targets of not just petty criminals but spooks and terrorists as well. A serious attack on such interbank infrastructure can deem the entire interbank infrastructure unreliable, halting all flow of money via credit cards, electronic transfers, online purchases, and put into doubt the believability of account balances in any account in a bank linked to a compromised FMI system. Government regulators have come to accept that such attacks cannot be prevented, shifting their attention to how they will respond to and recover from them.

to exploit. The weaker computing power of such devices invariably limits their security software to being rudimentary, and the large volume of Internet traffic that they produce can make it harder to detect attacks. This escalates an inconvenience (e.g., smartphone being hacked) to a matter of personal safety (e.g., a hacker commandeering a car or using a home security camera to snoop). (The US Secret Service tweaked former US vice president Dick Cheney's wireless heart monitor to prevent remote assassination attempts.[22]) Consumers will expect your firm to fiercely protect their private IoT data, with no second chances.

The Role of Non-IT Managers in Preparing Their Line Functions for a Security Crisis

Moments of crisis require special skills rarely used in day-to-day activities. Non-IT managers can play an integral role in three important ways to prepare their own line functions for responding swiftly to an IT security breach:

1. *Advance preparation.* Even the best-laid plans can fail if their documentation is outdated or if they are too generic for individual employees to act on their intended responsibilities after a security breach.[24] Walk through a dress rehearsal of how you would handle a security incident—internally and externally—to minimize its damage. This is like reading the safety leaflet on a plane, hoping you will never need it, but also knowing that it would be foolhardy to miss the instructions.
2. *Fast reaction.* A sloppy—poor or slow—response can be far more damaging than the breach itself. The first few hours count the most in mitigating damage. Get outside help to objectively evaluate the situation, quickly notify affected users, and shut down operational IT systems if a data breach is ongoing.
3. *Focus on the long term.* How much long-term damage a security breach inflicts depends not only on its gravity but also on the quality of your firm's communication with inside and outside stakeholders. In the long term, it matters more *how* your firm handled the situation and assuring customers what you will do to prevent it from ever happening again. A good-faith effort counts in the long term. Be honest in communicating with your customers and employees because misinformation or inaccurate information eventually backfires.

Business Continuity Planning and Disaster Recovery

IT environments are replete with redundancies and backups that kick in if a specific piece of hardware fails. Business continuity planning is concerned with the disruption of the *entire environment* by unexpected disasters, such as hurricanes,

Box 8.3
How PayPal Fights Fraud Using Artificial Intelligence

In 2016, PayPal, founded in 1999, handled more than $200 billion in four billion small online money transfers among 170 million individuals in almost two hundred countries. It keeps fraud losses well below its industry average by teaching machines to play Sherlock Holmes.[25] This is one of the early large-scale uses of one branch of artificial intelligence (AI) called deep learning (described in chapter 9). PayPal's AI spots fraud without making humanlike mistakes. It mines data in real time from each user's history, whereas most rivals rely solely on fraud detection rules used by credit card companies. The advantage of AI is that it no longer relies on humans to specify rules that a programmer then codes into software. Instead, it teaches itself new rules simply by being shown examples of fraudulent transactions. For example, if a PayPal employee flags a sudden string of one-dollar to five-dollar purchases at gas stations by a few customers as fraud, the AI creates a new rule for itself to automatically apply to all other PayPal users. It then declines transactions that fit that pattern. The system created thousands of new rules by itself within three years after its introduction in 2013. The more data a deep learning AI can crunch through, the better it gets; this is a perfect match for a data-intensive PayPal. PayPal runs the custom-built system in-house, allowing it to vet every incoming transaction using thousands of such rules in less than a second. The result: PayPal's fraud rate is 0.32 percent of revenue, a figure more than four times lower than an industry average of 1.32 percent. That 1 percent difference might not seem like much until you put it in context. For a large firm like Walmart that had revenues of about $500 billion in 2016, it translates into $5 billion in annual savings.

blackouts, fires, floods, earthquakes, or other acts of God. Their effect can range from an outage to complete destruction. Just as you keep a spare tire in your car and a fire extinguisher at home, planning for them is insurance against the worst that you hope to never need.

Business continuity planning is the tactical plan for quickly resuming your firm's business operations after such a catastrophe. *Disaster recovery* is a subset focused on getting IT operations back up and running after a disaster. Checklists widely taught to IT managers codify much of disaster recovery planning, but business continuity planning must involve all vulnerable line functions. You have to boil business continuity planning down to core business risks that can derail your firm's revenue stream. It must cover every line function's activities, especially primary value chain activities.

Hot, Warm, and Cold Sites

Business continuity planning relies on a *backup site* to which your firm can switch if disaster strikes. As figure 8.2 shows, the faster you can switch over your firm's

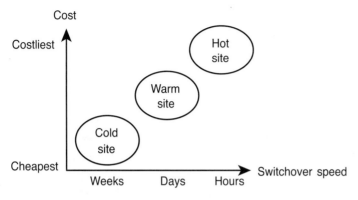

Figure 8.2
Hot, warm, and cold backup sites trade off switchover speeds against ongoing costs.

critical IT operations to a backup site, the costlier it is. A *hot site* is a fully operational, instantaneously usable replica of your firm's mission-critical IT assets. The data is an almost identical copy of the data in the operational systems before disaster hit, also making it the costliest choice. The more your firm uses custom-built, proprietary IT apps, the greater is the care needed in business continuity planning because such less-standardized IT assets can be harder to replicate in a hot backup site. A *cold site* is the opposite extreme, inexpensive and slow to start up. It requires setup when needed because it includes neither data nor hardware. It typically is a trailer with a power source, Internet connectivity, and workspace. *Warm sites* are cheaper to maintain than hot sites and more expensive than cold sites. They include mission-critical IT apps, hardware, and data. However, the data is not current, and their scale is smaller than hot sites. Non-IT managers' judgments should drive the option that makes most business sense.

Box 8.4
Why Airlines Tolerate IT Snafus

IT snafus routinely derail all major airlines because airlines' IT systems are a costly patchwork of epoch-spanning technologies and too costly to replace outright. For example, in 2016 alone, one malfunctioning power supply grounded four thousand Delta flights (employees could not access reservations data), one faulty Internet router grounded 2,300 Southwest flights, and similar glitches shut down United and American Airlines as well.[26] No single IT firm has the skills to build a new airline-wide IT portfolio even if an airline were willing and able to spend billions of dollars. So for many airlines, eliminating IT glitches that do not affect flight safety is simply not worth the cost and risk. Instead, the money is better invested in improving their business continuity so they can spring back from IT glitches.

Non-IT Managers' Contributions to Business Continuity Planning

Non-IT managers can contribute to business continuity planning in three areas, which help their firm decide what *ongoing* costs are worth bearing for the scope and responsiveness of their business continuity plans:

1. *Identification of critical IT assets.* What are the mission-critical IT assets—particularly apps and data—without which your line function's activities will stall? This must cover their dependencies on other IT assets, including those that stretch into partner firms. Non-IT managers—not IT—must define what constitutes critical. Critical refers to revenue-generating activities for firms and delivery of promised services for nonprofits and government organizations. Begin by identifying vulnerable business processes involving the primary activities in your value chain and the consequences if they went down for a few days or weeks.

2. *Recovery time objective.* How long can your firm withstand an interruption in *each* of them? How quickly must you restore each of them to prevent loss of revenues and public trust? What is the maximum tolerable downtime after which irreversible consequences arise? The key IT assets must individually be prioritized; some can wait longer than others to be restored.

3. *Recovery point objective.* How old can the recovered data be? How much data *loss* (not theft) a firm can survive depends on its industry. (A brokerage firm, for example, cannot survive any loss of financial transaction data.) Non-IT managers' answers to these questions determine whether the steep cost of a hot site is warranted. Remember that firms' IT systems also largely generate compliance data for government

Box 8.5
How Revlon Recovered from Its Burning Factory in an Hour

In June 2011, a major fire damaged cosmetics firm Revlon's factory and its data center in Venezuela. Its business continuity plan immediately kicked in to save the day. While the building was still ablaze, Revlon was able to switch over its Venezuelan operations to its cloud-based IT facility in New Jersey in little over an hour. It simply switched over the Internet addresses of its servers in the burning building to its servers in New Jersey 2,300 miles away. It then e-mailed its employees instructions for how to access a backup virtual image of their desktops as they were when the fire started. Revlon was jinxed; not too long after the Venezuela fire, it recovered just as rapidly from a flooding of its London offices and then devastation from a hurricane in New York. By that time, the value of good business continuity planning had fully sunk in. By 2016, Revlon operated more than five hundred of its corporate IT apps in a private, global cloud that not only made its IT more resilient but also reduced its IT costs by $70 million a year.

regulations (e.g., the Sarbanes-Oxley Act in the United States); destruction of its IT assets does not get it off the hook for compliance with reporting regulations.

Business continuity plans must also regularly be tested using simulations to ensure that your critical business activities do not crumble irrecoverably after a disaster. This is like occasionally checking your spare tire's pressure. Business continuity plans must also be updated regularly because employees, contractors, and business partners change.

Key Takeaways

1. *IT insecurity is unavoidable.* Connectivity that makes IT valuable also makes it vulnerable. Electronic espionage, sabotage, and theft do not need proximity and are hard to detect or persecute, and their aftermath can remain unknown. You secure IT using something that a legitimate user knows, has, or is—the more the better.
2. *IT breaches are almost always human failings.* Humans are more hackable (via social engineering) than are IT systems. Therefore, IT security is not just IT's responsibility nor solely a technical problem. The weakest link—including partner firms in your value stream—defines your own security. Overlooking insider threats and not explicitly making a convenience versus security trade-off increases your firm's vulnerability.
3. *Focus on the long term.* How you handle a breach is as important as its severity.
4. *Business continuity planning inoculates against a loss of your IT portfolio.* It is a tactical plan to resume business operations if your entire IT environment was knocked out or destroyed. Disaster planning is its IT-focused subset.

The Non-IT Managers' Checklist

☐ What apps used by your line function are mission-critical? Which way should the balance between security and user convenience tilt for *each* of them?

☐ What data is the most sensitive? What would be the consequence if it were (a) stolen or (b) destroyed?

☐ How long will your firm avoid permanent damage if your entire IT portfolio became unavailable? This justifies the ongoing costs of the type—cold, warm, or hot—of backup site.

Jargon Decoder

Emerging technology	A technology that is in the process of being developed.
Signal-to-noise ratio	The ratio of substance versus hype surrounding an emerging technology.
Artificial intelligence (AI)	A constellation of technologies that allows computers to mimic human reasoning and learning.
Timing misjudgment	Attempting to prematurely commercially use an emerging technology before the needed complements are available.
Transcending wave	Emerging technologies that transcend the existing boundary between the real world and the digital world.
Overlaying wave	Emerging technologies that overlay a digital thread on capital assets and humans.
Scale transforming wave	Emerging technologies that transform the familiar into gigantic or tiny versions.
The IT unicorn	The erroneous belief that corporate IT cannot simultaneously be cheap and strategic.

9

Fast-Forward

What will your industry look like if you fast-forward ten or twenty years? How can you position your firm to ride the industry-agnostic trifecta instead of being swept away by it? How must it reconceive its bread-and-butter business as the evolution of IT outpaces our capacity to domesticate it? These predicaments remind me of the old fable of the frog who fell into a boiling pot of water and survived because he immediately jumped out. The same frog in a pot of cold water on a stove would not notice the rising temperature until he is slowly cooked to death. Firms' predicaments about emerging technologies are like the unfortunate second frog. The impending technological ground shifts around us are *self-cloaking*: they occur so constantly and gradually that it is easy to entirely miss them.[1] By the time the need for change is obvious, it is often too late.

This chapter delves into how non-IT managers can become their firms' eyes and ears to make sense of the opportunities created by emerging technologies and to prepare them for nontraditional competitors unburdened by your industry's legacy costs and ingrained assumptions. Firms often stumble with emerging technologies because of their inherent noisiness, forgetting that their application begets value, and misjudging timing. To separate hyperbole from substance, you must watch out for three impending waves of IT innovations that transcend the physical-digital boundary, give the real world a digital coating, and transform scale of the familiar to gigantic or tiny.

Why Firms Stumble with Emerging Technologies

Predicting is easy; being right is hard. As new technologies proliferate, firms struggle with what to pay attention to and what to ignore. Four out of five firms cannot spot and act on weak signals about looming threats and opportunities.[2] Betting on the wrong horse can put you out to business. Not betting on the right one can also put you out of business. Every major industry disruption in the past five hundred years has come from industry outsiders, who share neither your assumptions nor your constraints. The death knell of firms is almost never an existing archrival who does it better but a newbie who does it differently. The music, publishing, and entertainment industries were transformed in recent memory by outsiders such as Apple, Amazon, and Netflix. You can expect the auto, health care, finance, and education industries to be disrupted by outsiders as well. Firms struggle against newbies with disruptive IT-enabled business models for three reasons: (1) they overinvest or underinvest in emerging technologies because they cannot separate signal from noise, (2) they forget that *solely* their application begets value, and (3) their timing is off.

Separating Signal from Noise

A low signal-to-noise ratio—useful versus irrelevant information—characterizes most emerging technologies.[3] Its actual business potential for your firm (the *signal*) is largely drowned out by assertions, beliefs, and hype (the *noise*) surrounding it. Think of any recent technology in the past ten years; it invariably went through a hype cycle in figure 9.1.[4] The initial hype unrealistically inflates expectations, which are bound to disillusion when the promised benefits do not materialize, until firms subsequently put it to productive use that delivers value somewhere between the optimistic and disillusioned extremes in figure 9.1. Such widespread bandwagon behavior of investing in a new IT innovation just because your rivals did epitomizes poor discipline in corporate IT investing.

Misclassifying signal and noise can lead to the sort of errors illustrated by figure 9.2.[5] If an emerging technology is all hype and you classify it as hype (cell 1) or one

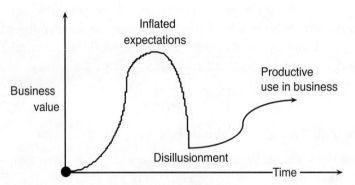

Figure 9.1
Emerging technologies progress through a hype cycle of inflated and deflated expectations before their actual potential is realized.

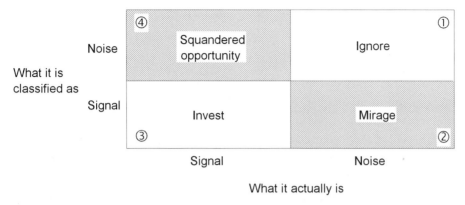

Figure 9.2
The shaded cells highlight errors of judgment in evaluating emerging technologies.

with clear business potential for your firm is correctly recognized (cell 3), both are good calls. Cell 3 is the proverbial needle in the haystack. Firms make mistakes in the other two shaded cells. Cell 2 is where the hype around an emerging technology leads you to mistakenly classify it as having potential, and your firm risks misinvesting in a technology that will not strategically pay off. It is hype without substance, a mirage. Cell 4 is the flip side of cell 2 where misclassifying a real opportunity as hype squanders an opportunity by underinvesting or not being timely.

Non-IT managers play an indispensable role in sensitizing their firms to weak signals and gathering early evidence of emerging technologies that will reshape your firm's place in its industry. You do not need a crystal ball. You already have the cognitive apparatus to cut through the noise. You can help your firm recognize cell 3 and steer clear of cells 2 and 4 by returning to the three enduring lenses in chapter 2 to ask whether and how a particular emerging technology will do the following:

1. *Alter some aspect of the digitization cube.* What opportunity spaces—not just the threats—will it create for *your* firm? Will it make viable an underserved market?
2. *Alter the balance of power among customers, suppliers, substitutes, and new entrants in your industry.* Who will your future rivals be, and what will be the basis of competition?
3. *Help create a new business model by altering your firm's value stream.* How (by altering a step or a connection between two steps)? However, improving today's business alone is a poor means of seeing the future. Watch your industry's newcomers but with skepticism. Can their novel business models that obviate your existing assets deliver sustainable margins?

4. *Create a sustainable competitive advantage or merely raise the floor for remaining in your industry.*

If an emerging technology will likely have any one of these effects, it is safer to assume that an industry disruption is coming even if you are unsure when. Use real options thinking from chapter 4 to proceed differently depending on whether the uncertainty is technological or about the market. If the uncertainty is market uncertainty, passively observe your customers, archrivals, and industry newbies. Remember than an emerging technology can take time to go mainstream; phones took fifty years, the Internet forty years; and digital music twenty years. There are no brownie points for first movers. If the uncertainty is technological, tiptoe into it with small experimental investments that allow your firm some control over an unpredictable future *before* it arrives. Use real options thinking as a low-cost, low-risk approach to reduce technological uncertainty without overinvesting on a bet-the-company scale.

New Technologies Are Solutions Waiting for Problems

New technologies often start out as solutions searching for problems to solve. They remain a curiosity until someone figures out a killer application for them.[6] Their *application* creates business value. The rewards go to firms that use them to rethink their business processes or business model to deliver more value than their archrivals. IT is just a tool whose use matters. What is in short supply in firms is imagination about how to use it. This requires managers who can envision possibilities at the intersection of technology and business. Such applications need deep insight into business problems, the sort of vantage point that can come only from non-IT managers deep in the trenches. It is too risky for you to be hands-off.

Many things we take for granted would have sounded impossible to our parents when they were our age: browsing a store five thousand miles away, having a letter delivered in a distant land in two seconds without paying a penny, showing up in a work meeting in our pajamas (video conferencing), or carrying the *Encyclopedia Britannica* and eight thousand music albums in our pockets. IT has already changed the world we knew in high school. And it has barely begun.

Technology innovations constantly erase the boundary between science fiction and reality. As *Star Trek*'s Captain Picard once said, things are only impossible until they are not. Many industry-rattling innovations are inspired by science fiction movies: tablets (*2001: A Space Odyssey*, 1968), driverless cars (*Total Recall*, 1990), robots (*Metropolis*, 1927), gesture interfaces (*Minority Report*, 2002), and online pizza ordering (*The Net*, 1995). The TV series *Star Trek* (1966–) inspired ideas such as Skype, cell phones (communicator), 3-D printers (replicator), augmented reality (holodeck), and collective intelligence such as Wikipedia and Kickstarter (the Borg). (For a living list of fiction turned reality, see technovelgy.com.) A looming new blueprint for your industry does not yet exist. It must first be imagined. Science fiction is a treasure trove to mine not-yet-practical ideas, waiting for technology to catch up. To connect the dots, you have to know what the dots are. Awareness is your weapon against surprise.

In the possibility factory of IT, emerging technologies constantly enlarge what is feasible (the shaded part of figure 9.3, modified from chapter 1).

Effective non-IT managers do what no one else can. They scan the external environment and, in all the noise, are able to spot patterns and trends that can alter their industry's landscape and their firm's place within it. Contributing as a curator of new business technologies also has a professional employability payoff: you sharpen your own value to employers by contributing something that cannot be automated and the IT folks creating the automation technologies cannot do. In a grim future, if you are not the automator, you will become the automated. In a bright future, your technology-augmented future self will do the job of ten colleagues. Either way, you do not want to be one of the other nine.

Timing Matters

Some early IT investments fail because the complementary technologies that would make them worthwhile have not yet arrived. If they are too early to market, they never move past niche appeal. Early movers such as Apple Pay and Google Wallet failed to live up to their expectations because so few stores accepted them. (Stores did not yet have compatible readers.) They also misjudged who their competition was. Their competition was not other electronic payment systems but rather the combination of credit cards and ubiquitous credit card readers. Similarly, early smartphones by Palm

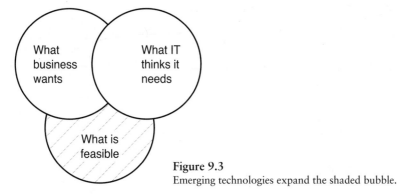

Figure 9.3
Emerging technologies expand the shaded bubble.

and digital music players by Creative arrived before inexpensive data networks and legal music content were widely available. Yet iPhones and Android phones (a billion of each had sold by 2016) and iPods (about four hundred million were sold by 2016) that came years later succeeded phenomenally. You cannot look at an emerging technology in isolation from its complements and, more important, from how it fits into your IT portfolio to move your firm toward its strategic aspiration.

Three Upcoming Waves of IT Innovation

Something much bigger is lurking beneath the glut of emerging technologies. Think of these as three big waves of impending change (figure 9.4): (1) transcending the boundary between the physical world and the digital world, (2) overlaying a digital mask on the existing physical world, and (3) transforming the scale of familiar things into gigantic or tiny. They will impact firms of all stripes but will be concentrated in the three IT laggards—government, health care, and education—that account for a third of global GDP.

Overall, they will enhance the productivity of both the capital assets that firms already own and the people that they employ. The definition of productivity is doing more with less, which means that they will create new losers and winners. The history of technological innovation is that it closes one door but opens another.

Wave 1: Transcending the Physical-Digital Boundary

The first wave is IT innovations—such as 3-D printing and robotics—that will transcend the boundaries between where the physical world ends and the digital world begins. Unlike conventional manufacturing where you chisel away a block

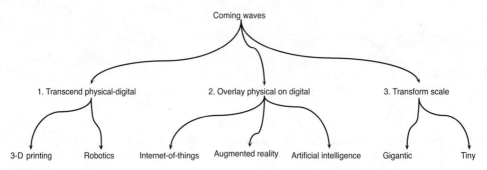

Figure 9.4
Three coming waves of IT innovation.

of material to create an object, 3-D printing (a.k.a. additive manufacturing) prints layer upon layer of diverse material fused by laser to create an object. Its significance is completing an unfinished transformation cycle: unlike digitization that converts atoms to electronic bits, 3-D printing converts electronic bits to atoms.[7] Its significance: zero transportation costs (products are "shipped" over the Internet and materialize where needed), economical production of one customized unit instead of mass production of clones, reduced need to hold inventories of parts or products, and further erosion of geography (a product can be delivered from anywhere to anywhere). It is weakening the constraint of the physical form.

We are in the infancy of 3-D printing, awaiting development of new materials and matching business uses. However, some initial applications have surfaced.[8] Endodontists have used digital scans of patients' teeth to produce tens of millions of dental implants; otolaryngologists have fitted a hundred million custom-shaped hearing aid molds. General Electric (GE) uses it to produce fuel nozzles for its jet engines; Airbus for airliner cabin fittings; and contract manufacturer Lite-On for printing 1/2,500-inch (10-micron) sensors and antennas directly onto circuits.

The auto industry is using it to prototype cars in the physical and digital world at the *same* time.[9] As a designer reshapes a 3-D printed car model by hand, a scanner detects changes and updates the digital model that optimizes for weight reduction and varying tensile strength in different parts of a single component. It even adds an "undo" button in the physical world; the 3-D printer can reverse any human misstep directly in the physical model. In the long term, future products such as cars could get physical upgrades just as smartphones now get software updates.

Another related emerging technology is robotics, which is automating repetitive human jobs—factory work, driving trucks, and serving food. The IT that runs them holds *all* of their intelligence. Robotic automation increases productivity by substituting human physical labor. This is making labor costs are less and less important; the first generation iPad, for example, included only eight dollars of labor for its final assembly in China.[10] Amazon already uses robots alongside humans in its warehouses; a new generation of *dark factories* will allow one human to do the job previously done by six.[11] Robots can also be software (e.g., Siri), not just the humanoid sort portrayed in the popular media. In combination with artificial intelligence (AI) and natural language processing, they will substitute human cognitive labor to do customer service jobs, perform bookkeeping, and control self-driving cars.[12] Self-driving cars are closer than they appear because you might have unknowingly already trusted your life to the underlying technology if you have flown in Boeing's 787 Dreamliner jet. A Dreamliner needs a human pilot only for

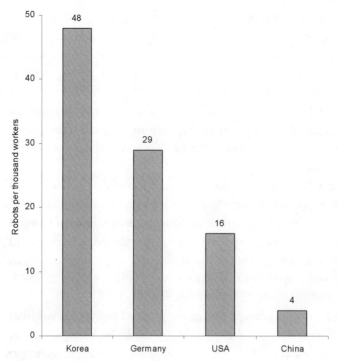

Figure 9.5
Robots per thousand workers in the four largest manufacturing economies circa 2016.

seven minutes of its fifteen-hour flight from Atlanta to Seoul.[13] Figure 9.5 shows how starkly the ratio of robots to human workers differed in the four largest manufacturing economies.[14]

Wave 2: Overlaying Digital on the Physical

The second wave is overlaying a digital thread on physical assets and humans to wring more productivity out of them. Physical objects acquiring a digital essence is creating entirely new ways for firms to interact with customers. This wave—beginning with the Internet of Things (IoT), augmented reality, and AI—is morphing staid, old-school industries into information businesses.

Internet of Things

The IoT is displacing the Internet of people. Inexpensive, Internet-connected sensors embedded in ordinary physical objects provide context—location, temperature, movement, and brightness—that has historically been unavailable to firms. The open

Box 9.1
Why an American Robot—and Not a Bangladeshi Worker—
Might Make Your Next Pair of Khakis

Sewing garments has always been a labor-intensive task. It has provided a livelihood to millions of sweatshop workers in China, Bangladesh, India, and Myanmar. The trickiest part that needs the dexterity of human hands is stitching two pieces of cloth together—constantly aligning the pieces as they pass under a sewing machine's needle without allowing unseemly buckling of cloth, clumping of fabric, or pulling of the thread. Firms have successfully automated cutting, weaving, dyeing, and just about everything else except for stitching, which has resisted every automation attempt. A robotic sewing machine intended to automate this step might soon replace human workers.[15] It uses a high-resolution camera linked to a computer to capture a thousand images a second to track individual threads passing under a sewing needle. Instead of measuring fabric like humans do, the robotic version counts the number of threads to decide where the next stitch goes. Software coordinates robotic arms that pick every piece of cut fabric such as a pocket in the correct order. (Nike has been using similar technology to produce the fabric uppers of its customized sneakers since 2015.) The robotic tailor is far from perfect, but if the history of the now automated car-manufacturing business is a guide, it is only a matter of time before the kinks will be worked out well enough to replace their human predecessors.

opportunity is for firms to figure out creative business uses for such contextual data, as a few firms have begun to. For example, a modern GE jet engine has hundreds of sensors that continuously capture data on engine heat, fuel consumption, blade wear, and its operating environment. A GE engine powering a single New York-Chicago flight generates more than sixty iPhones' worth of data (one terabyte), which GE uses for preventive maintenance.[16] Elsewhere, FedEx places a device about the size of a smartphone in sensitive packages to remotely monitor their location, temperature, and light exposure. Similarly, Norfolk Southern is embedding IT throughout its railroad network to increase its average speed and to reduce downtime. A one-mile-per-hour bump in the average speed for its freight trains makes a $250 million difference in annual profitability.

On the social front, infusion of IT in *precision farming* is ensuring in several ways that our farms will produce enough food to feed the billions not yet born.[17] (The human population will reach ten billion by 2050.)

• Connected sensors throughout a farm generate precise data about things that drive crop yield (weather, soil moisture, nutrient levels, and weeds). This year's yield data drives next year's seeding depth, which is then done by Internet-connected machines precise to an inch.

• Software-guided GPS connections prevent tractors from ploughing the same ground twice or missing a patch, lowering fuel costs and improving crop yield.
• Drones coupled with inexpensive miniature three-inch satellites map farm conditions to optimize the size of each harvest.

By removing guesswork about how capital assets are being used, the IoT is leading to a convergence of IT with operations management. Beyond these fledgling uses, the untapped potential for improving the productivity of existing assets worldwide is estimated at about $10 trillion by 2025.[18] Businesses have stronger incentives to embrace the IoT because their data can potentially reduce costs and increase asset productivity. Other personal uses are interesting but not game changing.

Augmented Reality

Augmented reality electronically superimposes visible information on physical objects to aid human decisions. Boeing aircraft assemblers use virtual reality glasses (similar to Google Glass) that show them annotated pointers to proper drilling locations on airplane parts, heads-up displays project directions on car windshields, online eyeglass sellers such as Warby Parker let buyers try on glasses using their own headshots, and smartphones that instantaneously translate street signs from one language to another give users language skills that they do not have.

The $200 billion online clothing retail industry is using such digital-physical overlays to fix a pesky problem: it is plagued by 30 percent return rates.[19] (Customers order multiple sizes since they do not know how they will fit.) They use "selfies" to show you how a shirt you are seeing online will look on you based on one that you own. Such visual overlays figure out height, weight, body shape—not tailors' measurements—from selfies to do such matching and to show how the cut of an online item differs from one that you are wearing. All of this raises ethical and privacy issues with which firms have never had to contend.

Artificial Intelligence

AI broadly refers to the constellation of technologies that allow computers to mimic human reasoning and learning, primarily in recognizing patterns. AI has made strides in one branch called *deep learning*, which is modeled on neural networks in the human brain. It feeds on huge volumes of data to teach itself to do *specialized* tasks. Unlike programmed software where a human expert must specify rules that programmers then implement in software code, AI does it the other way around. By analyzing troves of examples (e.g., tagged photos in Facebook, product clicks on

Amazon, or cancer cells in medical images), it discovers complex rules that humans cannot articulate. The system learns directly by chewing through lots of examples.

For example, billions of queries each day tutor Google's deep learning AI, making it better each day.[20] If you Google "Red Queen" and click on one image that most looks like her from the picture in chapter 1 in this book or at the end of this chapter, you have just shown Google's AI an example. A few thousand similar searches later, it will no longer need your help to recognize the Red Queen.

Although AI has existed since the 1950s, the deluge of big data and powerful processors—originally developed for video gaming—has suddenly supercharged its progress. Its value lies primarily in doing rote tasks so menial for humans that they would otherwise have not been done and tasks for which humans are simply too slow. For example, it can identify patterns in massive data streams to instantaneously detect subtle trends that are beyond human capacity. This enables more business experimentation and real-time testing of business ideas than has previously been possible.[21] A side benefit is making computer interfaces conversational—through natural language processing—to make them accessible to the billions who cannot read or write.

Unlike mechanization that replaced physical labor or IT that has replaced rote blue-collar labor so far, AI will replace rote white-collar labor. The human jobs that AI makes vulnerable are ones that can be broken down into a series of rote steps. Non-IT industries where AI has the most promise are data-intensive ones such as insurance, finance, accounting, manufacturing, and health care. It is already replacing laboratory technicians analyzing X-ray and MRI scans, paralegals gathering pre-trial evidence, and customer service representatives.[22] In medical imaging analyses, it can detect problems that even skilled doctors might miss. It is helping predict heart attacks 50 percent more accurately than doctors can, predicting prisoners most likely to skip bail better than judges, and finding the best time to sow seeds better than seasoned farmers.[23] Industry pundits anticipate that up to 70 percent of all existing occupations will be automated by IT-based AI and robotics by 2100 AD.[24] New occupations replacing disappearing ones will require different skills: things that machines cannot do. What got you here will not get you there.

AI will redefine white-collar jobs and the skills needed to do them, effectively raising the value of tasks that only humans can do. With such upgraded skills, humans and machines can be equal partners playing to their unique strengths. AI therefore amplifies humans' cognitive capacity in white-collar work, allowing one individual to do the work that previously required many. Just as most IT increases the productivity of capital assets, AI better utilizes human workers for tasks that *truly* use their skills. Human judgment and feedback nevertheless remain integral to improving AI.

Wave 3: Transforming Scale

The third wave of emerging IT innovations transforms the scale of activities to either a gigantic or a tiny version of the familiar. The gigantic version harnesses a collective to create vast assemblages of humans or machines. Imagine the iOS ecosystem of more than two hundred thousand firms and a billion users but outside the technology industry. *Star Trek*'s Borg, but real. Such IT facilitated conglomerations—built around a hub firm—are called *business ecosystems* when they involve other firms and *crowdsourcing* when they involve other individuals such as your customers. They are shifting firm-against-firm competition to ecosystem-against-ecosystem, which means that stand-alone firms (e.g., Walmart) will struggle to compete with a rival ecosystem (e.g., Amazon). They are increasingly becoming the engines of innovation in diverse industries such as consumer goods, manufacturing, services, retail, publishing, automobiles, and health care. Gigantic technology-based human aggregations and machine aggregations both exist separately, and their crossing over is only a matter of time.

Rudimentary examples of gigantic human aggregations using crowdsourcing abound in venture funding (e.g., Kickstarter), banking (Kiva.org), artisan markets (Etsy), cartography (Open Street Map), product development (Quirky), human-powered encyclopedias (Quora), research and development (Innocentive), genetics (Merck Gene Index), and even social innovation (Open IDEO). For a firm like Starbucks, customers are now both the primary source of product ideas and their vetters (see its crowdsourcing platform at mystarbucksidea.com). Similarly, American retailer Macy's uses Facebook "likes" to choose colors for upcoming apparel. Uber increases utilization of idle vehicles by matching them with someone needing transportation. The business opportunity beneath this iceberg is for non-IT managers to reimagine how the trifecta might enable them to piece together some part of their firms' offerings from a globally dispersed set of specialized firms and instantaneously deliver them anywhere digitally. Ecosystems repel command and control and thrive on coordination. Successfully organizing them requires enabling IT *and* incentives for participants.

IT is also making it possible for gigantic aggregations of previously autonomous machines to become what appears to be synchronized metamachines. For example, several dozen cars on the highway can self-assemble into a synced convoy using car-to-car networks. Each car wirelessly broadcasts its speed, location, steering wheel position, and brake status several times a second so other cars have a sense of their surroundings (using a dedicated wireless standard, 802.11p).[25] Such machine-to-machine networks can increase traffic throughput on existing highways while also reducing accidents that annually kill a million people worldwide. Similar ideas of machine-to-machine networks devoid of humans will also become possible in factories and homes as connected devices proliferate. The business potential of machines' growing ability to talk to each other—rather than with humans—is limited only by the ingenuity of non-IT managers.

The opposite end is scale transformation to *tiny*, which has a shorter history than gigantic. The most visible are short-range wireless networks (e.g., such as the Bluetooth used in wearable technologies such as smart watches) that serve a purpose but are not game-changing like ones in the pipeline. One physical example is tiny medical drones enclosed in ingestible dissolving capsules that can obviate surgery for some procedures.[26] On the nonphysical side is *blockchain* technology: elaborate decentralized records stored on thousands of different computers worldwide that can make financial records and medical data more tamper-proof and fraud-proof. Microscopic IoT devices that power themselves using solar, static electricity, or even ambient electricity (extracted from Wi-Fi signals) will open up other business possibilities limited only by our imagination.

A Recap of the Book

Corporate IT lacks strategic prowess and is costlier than it needs to be primarily because most firms' IT strategy lacks the business acumen that only engaged non-IT managers' can contribute. IT is a possibility factory where in short supply are non-IT managers who can envision business possibilities before they become obvious. A firm can have many flaws, but an inability to grasp corporate vulnerability should not be one of them. Grasping the industry transformation wrought by the digitization-infusion-ubiquity trifecta requires understanding how IT is reshaping your entire industry, how your firm can harness IT to deliver more value than its archrivals, and whether an IT asset is a sustainable advantage (the three lenses in chapter 2).

Syncing IT and business strategy propels firms ahead in Red Queen competition. It demands obsessing over how your IT infrastructure, apps, and data collectively inch your firm toward its strategic aspiration (chapters 1 and 3). IT governance ensures that you invest in just the strategically appropriate places and spend less everywhere else (chapter 5). Governing IT well includes successfully accomplishing IT projects (chapter 6), avoiding regrettable IT sourcing decisions (chapter 7), keeping your IT assets safe (chapter 8), and holding IT accountable for business impact (chapter 4).

Corporate IT that is cheap yet strategic is a unicorn only until non-IT managers meet IT strategy.

"Well, now that we have seen each other," said the unicorn, *"if you'll believe in me, I'll believe in you."*

Source: Carroll, L. *Through the Looking Glass.* Chicago: Rand McNally, 1871.

Key Takeaways

1. *Firms stumble with emerging technologies for three reasons.* They misjudge hyperbole for substance, forget that their business application alone creates value, and are off in their timing, often before complementary technologies have arrived.

2. *Signal-to-noise ratio clouds judgment.* The low ratio of substance versus hype for emerging technologies makes judging their business potential challenging. Using the three lenses in chapter 2 helps cut through the noise.

3. *Three waves describe the business implications of emerging technologies.* Three patterns lurking beneath the glut of emerging technologies can help grasp their business implications. These waves are emerging technologies that transcend the physical-digital boundary, overlay a digital coat on the real world, and create gigantic or tiny versions of familiar activities.

4. *Transcending the physical-digital boundary (wave 1).* Emerging technologies that lower physical constraints by transcending the boundaries between the physical world and the digital world (e.g., 3-D printing and robotics).

5. *Overlaying digital on the physical (wave 2).* Emerging technologies that overlay a digital thread on physical assets and humans (e.g., IoT, augmented reality, and AI). They squeeze more productivity out of them and transform old-school industries into information businesses.

6. *Scale transforming innovations (wave 3).* Emerging technologies that transform the scale of familiar activities to either gigantic or tiny versions. The former creates vast, coordinated assemblages of humans and machines to harnesses a collective (e.g., ecosystems, crowdsourcing, and machine-to-machine networks)—the latter on a much smaller scale than previously possible.

7. *The IT unicorn connection.* Corporate IT that is cheap yet strategic—often presumed to be a fiction—can become reality when non-IT managers become engaged contributors to their firm's IT strategy.

The Non-IT Managers' Checklist

☐ Identify three emerging technologies that alter any one dimension of the digitization cube for your firm. Which one?

☐ What opportunities and threats does each create for your firm? Do they enable rookie firms with novel business models to enter your industry unburdened by its assumptions and assets? Are their margins sustainable?

☐ How do they alter the power of your customers, your suppliers, or your firm?

☐ In which bucket of the three waves would you put each of them? How can they strengthen the value that your firm delivers to its existing customers and prospective customers that are unviable to serve today? Think of specific steps in your existing value chain, especially ones decomposable into automatable rote steps.

☐ How will each alter the basis of competition in your industry and who your new archrivals will be?

☐ Which of these deserve a wait-and-watch approach (market uncertainty), and which ones must you tiptoe into with real options (technical uncertainty)?

☐ What complementary technologies make their exploitation viable? When will they arrive?

☐ Are your archrivals using IT to nurture formidable business ecosystems that a stand-alone firm will struggle to match?

Notes

Introduction

1. These numbers are for 2017. There were only 19,000 US firms with more than five hundred employees.

2. The Economist. "Shedding Light on the Dark Web." *The Economist* (2016) http://www.economist.com/news/international/21702176-drug-trade-moving-street-online-cryptomarkets-forced-compete (accessed July 28, 2016).

3. The Economist. "More Bang for Your Buck." *The Economist* (August 9, 2014) http://www.economist.com/news/briefing/21611074-how-new-technology-shaking-up-oldest-business-more-bang-your-buck (accessed August 17, 2014).

Chapter 1

1. Carroll, L. *Through the Looking Glass*. Chicago: Rand McNally, 1871.

2. Barnett, W., and M. Hansen. "The Red Queen in Organizational Evolution." *Strategic Management Journal* 17, no. 1 (1996): 139–157.

3. Heller, M. *The CIO Paradox: Battling the Contradictions of IT Leadership*. Brookline, MA: Bibliomotion, 2012. Page 75.

4. Agarwal, R., and A. Tiwana. "Evolvable Systems: Through the Looking Glass of IS." *Information Systems Research* 26, no. 3 (2015): 473–479.

5. Carr, N. "IT Doesn't Matter." *Harvard Business Review* 38 (2003): 24–38.

6. Public domain sketch by L. Yaggy and T. Haines, Museum of Antiquity, Standard Publishing House, New York, 1882. Page 709.

7. Weill, P., and J. Ross. *IT Governance: How Top Performers Manage IT Decision Rights for Superior Results*. Boston: Harvard Business School Press, 2004. Page 22.

8. Yoo, Y., O. Henfridsson, and K. Lyytinen. "The New Organizing Logic of Digital Innovation: An Agenda for Information Systems Research." *Information Systems Research* 21, no. 4 (2010): 724–735.

9. El Sawy, O., A. Malhotra, Y. Park, and P. Pavlou. "Seeking the Configurations of Digital Ecodynamics: It Takes Three to Tango." *Information Systems Research* 21, no. 4 (2010): 835–848.

10. Brynjolfsson, E., and M. Schrage. "The New, Faster Face of Innovation." *Wall Street Journal* (August 17, 2009).

11. Weill and Ross. *IT Governance*. Page 34.

12. Tiwana, A., and S. Kim. "Discriminating IT Governance." *Information Systems Research* 26, no. 4 (2015): 656–674.

13. Ibid.

14. Agarwal, R., and V. Sambamurthy. "Principles and Models for Organizing the IT Function." *MISQ Executive* 1, no. 1 (2002): 1–16.

15. Xue, L., G. Ray, and B. Gu. "Environmental Uncertainty and IT Infrastructure Governance: A Curvilinear Relationship." *Information Systems Research* 22, no. 2 (2011): 389–399.

16. Weill, P., and J. Ross. "A Matrixed Approach to Designing IT Governance." *Sloan Management Review* 46, no. 2 (2005): 26–34.

17. Shpilberg, D., S. Berez, R. Puryear, and S. Shah. "Avoiding the Alignment Trap in IT." *Sloan Management Review* 49, no. 1 (2007): 51–55.

18. Tiwana and Kim. "Discriminating IT Governance."

19. Baschab, J., and J. Piot. *The Executive's Guide to Information Technology*. New York: Wiley, 2003.

20. Ross, J., P. Weill, and D. Robertson. *Enterprise Architecture as Strategy: Creating a Foundation for Business Execution*. Boston: Harvard Business School Press, 2006. Chapter 1. Some experts count operational apps as part of IT infrastructure. See, for example, Weill and Ross. *IT Governance*, and Byrd, T. A., and D. E. Turner. "Measuring the Flexibility of Information Technology Infrastructure: Exploratory Analysis of a Construct." *Journal of Management Information Systems* 17, no. 1 (2000): 167–208.

21. Porter, M. "Strategy and the Internet." *Harvard Business Review* March (2001): 62–78.

22. Jiang, Z., and D. Jain. "A Generalized Norton–Bass Model for Multigeneration Diffusion." *Management Science* 58, no. 10 (2012): 1887–1897.

23. A basic IBM mainframe computer in 1970 cost $29 million in 2016 dollars.

24. Knight, W. "Inside Amazon's Warehouse, Human-Robot Symbiosis." *MIT Technology Review* (2015) http://www.technologyreview.com/s/538601/inside-amazons-warehouse-human-robot-symbiosis (accessed July 11, 2015).

25. Kelly, K. *The Inevitable: Understanding the 12 Technological Forces That Will Shape Our Future*. New York: Viking, 2016. Page 283.

26. The Economist. "On and Offline." *The Economist* (September 24, 2016). Page 85.

27. Wells, H. G. *World Brain*. London: Methuen, 1938.

28. Brynjolfsson, E., and A. McAfee. *The Second Machine Age: Work, Progress, and Prosperity in a Time of Brilliant Technologies*. New York: W. W. Norton, 2014.

29. BBC. "US Nuclear Force Still Uses Floppy Disks" (May 26, 2016) http://www.bbc.com/news/world-us-canada-36385839 (accessed May 26, 2016).

30. BBC. "The Long Legacy of the Floppy Disk" (2016) http://www.bbc.com/news/technology-36389711 (accessed May 26, 2016).

31. Kevin Kelly calls this dematerialization. See page 83 in Kelly. *The Inevitable*.

32. Bhattacharjee, S., R. Gopal, K. Lertwachara, J. Marsden, and R. Telang. "The Effect of Digital Sharing Technologies on Music Markets: A Survival Analysis of Albums on Ranking Charts." *Management Science* 53, no. 9 (2007): 1359–1374.

33. Asvanund, A., K. Clay, R. Krishnan, and M. Smith. "An Empirical Analysis of Network Externalities in Peer-to-Peer Music-Sharing Networks." *Information Systems Research* 15, no. 2 (2004): 155–174.

34. The use of IT to deliver financial services is called *fintech* in the finance industry.

35. Hitt, L. "Information Technology and Firm Boundaries: Evidence from Panel Data." *Information Systems Research* 10, no. 2 (1999): 134–149.

36. For example, the first copy of this $35 book might cost the publisher $200,000 to produce, but subsequent copies might cost about $10.

37. Kelly. *The Inevitable.*

38. Hitt. "Information Technology and Firm Boundaries."

39. Shirky, C. *Cognitive Surplus: How Technology Makes Consumers into Collaborators.* London: Penguin, 2011. Page 85.

40. Brian-Arthur, W. "The Second Economy." *McKinsey Quarterly* October (2011): 1–9.

41. Andreessen, M. "Why Software Is Eating the World." *Wall Street Journal* (August 20, 2011).

42. Porter, M., and J. Heppelmann. "How Smart, Connected Products Are Transforming Competition." *Harvard Business Review* November (2014): 64–88.

43. Examples are Apple Watch, August locks, Toto toilets, Nest thermostats, Nike+ sneakers, Samsung refrigerators, Brew Genie coffee machines, and Philips Hue lightbulbs.

44. Raw data sourced from Codebases: Millions of Lines of Code, http://www.informationisbeautiful.net/visualizations/million-lines-of-code/ (accessed March 21, 2016). The equivalent lines of code in a living mouse is 120 million, and in a human, it is 3.3 trillion.

45. Regalado, M. "Business Adapts to a New Style of Computer." *MIT Technology Review* May 20 (2014) http://www.technologyreview.com/s/527356/business-adapts-to-a-new-style-of-computer (accessed June 3, 2015).

46. Intel. "Internet of Things" (2015) http://www.intel.com/content/www/us/en/internet-of-things/infographics/guide-to-iot.html (accessed August 12, 2015).

47. The Economist. "The Third Industrial Revolution." *The Economist* (April 19, 2012) http://www.economist.com/node/21553017 (accessed May 2013).

48. The text of the Bible is about 5 megabytes. A 100-megabit-per-second connection transmits about 9.7 megabytes of data per second, approximating two copies of the Bible.

49. The Economist. "The Future of Computing." *The Economist* (March 10, 2016) http://www.economist.com/news/leaders/21694528-era-predictable-improvement-computer-hardware-ending-what-comes-next-future (accessed April 2016).

50. Greenstone, M., and A. Looney. "A Dozen Economic Facts about Innovation" (2011) http://www.hamiltonproject.org/papers/a_dozen_economic_facts_about_innovation (accessed February 19, 2016).

51. AI Impacts. "Trends in the Cost of Computing" (2015) http://www.aiimpacts.org/trends-in-the-cost-of-computing (accessed November 2, 2015).

52. Richtel, M. "The Long-Distance Journey of a Fast-Food Order." *New York Times* (April 11, 2006).

53. While IT is automating rote transactional tasks, it is simultaneously creating opportunities to use displaced workers in novel new ways.

54. The Economist. "Shedding Light on the Dark Web." *The Economist* (2016) http://www.economist.com/news/international/21702176-drug-trade-moving-street-online-cryptomarkets-forced-compete (accessed July 28, 2016).

55. The Economist. "The Amazons of the Dark Net." *The Economist* (2014) http://www.economist.com/news/international/21629417-business-thriving-anonymous-internet-despite-efforts-law-enforcers (accessed April 10, 2015).

56. The Economist. "The Net Closes." *The Economist* (2015) http://www.economist.com/news/business/21647977-webs-two-largest-drug-markets-go-down-panicking-dealers-and-buyers-net-closes (accessed June 11, 2016).

57. Kirsch, L. "Deploying Common Systems Globally: The Dynamics of Control." *Information Systems Research* 15, no. 4 (2004): 374–395.

58. Sambamurthy, V., A. Bharadwaj, and V. Grover. "Shaping Agility through Digital Options: Reconceptualizing the Role of IT in Contemporary Firms." *MIS Quarterly* 27, no. 2 (2003): 237–256.

59. Lu, Y., and K. Ramamurthy. "Understanding the Link between Information Technology Capability and Organizational Agility: An Empirical Examination." *MIS Quarterly* 35, no. 4 (2011): 931–954.

60. Carr himself noted that in the early 1900s, electrification did not realize its potential when industrial firms tried to snap in electric motors where steam engines used to be. It instead required rethinking the original way firms had always set up factories, using electric motors to reimagine how they could concurrently redesign factory layouts with pulleys. See Carr. "IT Doesn't Matter."

61. Software averages ten to fifteen errors in every hundred lines of code; even the most rigorous testing cannot catch more than 50 percent of such bugs. See Mann, C. "Why Software Is So Bad." *MIT Technology Review* July/August (2002): 33–38.

62. Koopman, P. "Better Embedded System Software" (2010) https://betterembsw.blogspot.com/2010/10/embedded-software-costs-15-40-per-line.html (accessed March 10, 2016). These numbers of fifteen to forty dollars per line of software code are conservative as newer estimates put them at twenty-five to fifty dollars.

63. For a book-length discussion of the broader ideas unrelated to IT, see Lewis, A., and D. McKone. *Edge Strategy: A New Mindset for Profitable Growth*. Cambridge, MA: Harvard Business Review Press, 2016.

64. Wagner, H.-T., D. Beimborn, and T. Weitzel. "How Social Capital among Information Technology and Business Units Drives Operational Alignment and IT Business Value." *Journal of Management Information Systems* 31, no. 1 (2014): 241–272.

65. Reich, B., and I. Benbasat. "Factors That Influence the Social Dimension of Alignment between Business and Information Technology Objectives." *MIS Quarterly* 24, no. 1 (2000): 81–111.

66. Bassellier, G., I. Benbasat, and B. Reich. "The Influence of Business Managers' IT Competence on Championing IT." *Information Systems Research* 14, no. 4 (2003): 317–336.

67. McDonald, K. "Sorry, College Grads, I Probably Won't Hire You." *Wall Street Journal* (May 9, 2013) http://www.wsj.com/articles/SB100014241278873237446045784709008 44821388.

68. Weill, P., and S. Aral. "Generating Premium Returns on Your IT Investments." *Sloan Management Review* 47, no. 2 (2006): 39–48.

69. Porter, M. "The Five Competitive Forces That Shape Strategy." *Harvard Business Review* January (2008): 2–17.

70. A firm can have a diversity of products and a diversity of markets; they just must not span widely different cells in the same firm. This is often why large firms create independent divisions or subsidiaries (Walmart versus Sam's Club and Old Navy versus Banana Republic). Even when you have multiple lines of business, you can generate scale economies by sharing activities across them and also leveraging skills from one to another.

71. Here are a few additional examples in other industries: Among airlines, cells 1 through 4 would be Emirates, Delta, Southwest (and Ryanair in Europe), and Air Nippon Airways. Among American general merchandise stores, cells 1 through 4 would be Target, Walmart, Big Lots, and 7-Eleven.

72. A differentiation strategy does not make operational effectiveness irrelevant; it must not put you at a competitive disadvantage relative to your archrivals. Neglecting it can hurt you.

73. Porter, M. "From Competitive Advantage to Corporate Strategy." *Harvard Business Review* May (1987).

74. Little consensus exists in research on what IT strategy is, much less about how a firm should formulate it.

75. Preston, D., and E. Karahanna. "Antecedents of IS Strategic Alignment: A Nomological Network." *Information Systems Research* 20, no. 2 (2009): 159–179.

76. Brown, C., and S. Magill. "Alignment of the IS Function with the Enterprise: Toward a Model of Antecedents." *MIS Quarterly* 18, no. 4 (December 1994): 371–403.

77. Tallon, P. P. "A Process-Oriented Perspective on the Alignment of Information Technology and Business Strategy." *Journal of Management Information Systems* 24, no. 3 (2008): 227–268.

78. Sabherwal, R., R. Hirschheim, and T. Goles. "The Dynamics of Alignment: Insights from a Punctuated Equilibrium Model." *Organization Science* 12, no. 2 (2001): 179–197.

79. The classic business model template throughout the 1900s was to find a good niche, then develop a timeless product and execute a plan to dominate it. Mars, a candy maker, has done this with its Milky Way bar that's remained unchanged since 1923; Proctor and Gamble has done it with its Tide detergent since 1946; Crane and Company has supplied paper for printing US currency since 1879; and Church & Dwight has made its Arm & Hammer baking soda products since 1967. This niche domination strategy no longer works because it requires minimizing variation to squeeze out costs. This works only when markets are stable.

80. Sabherwal, R., and Y. Chan. "Alignment between Business and IS Strategies: A Study of Prospectors, Analyzers, and Defenders." *Information Systems Research* 12, no. 1 (March 2001): 11–33.

81. Tiwana, A., and B. Konsynski. "Complementarities between Organizational IT Architecture and Governance Structure." *Information Systems Research* 21, no. 2 (2010): 288–304.

82. Chan, Y., and B. Reich. "IT Alignment—What Have We Learned?" *Journal of Information Technology* 22, no. 4 (2007): 297–315.

83. Feld, C., and D. Stoddard. "Getting IT Right." *Harvard Business Review* February (2004): 72–81.

84. Biddle, S. *Military Power: Explaining Victory and Defeat in Modern Battle*. Princeton, NJ: Princeton University Press, 2006.

85. These numbers are the product of the IT and operational likelihoods. Consider other examples. If you're 80 percent likely to be able to pull off your operational strategy and your IT strategy, the likelihood of progressing toward your strategic aspiration is a depressingly low 64 percent (80 percent × 80 percent). If you have 80 percent confidence in your operational strategy but 50 percent in your IT strategy, you're almost guaranteed to fail to execute your operational strategy because the likelihood is 40 percent (80 percent × 50 percent).

86. Ross, J. "Six IT Decisions Your IT People Shouldn't Make." *Harvard Business Review* November (2002): 84–95.

87. Thrasher, H. *Boiling the IT Frog*. North Charleston, SC: BookSurge, 2007. Page 212.

Chapter 2

1.   Simon, H., ed. "Designing Organizations for an Information-Rich World." In *Computers, Communication, and the Public Interest*, ed. M. Greenberger. Baltimore: Johns Hopkins University Press, 1971.

2.   Schlenoff, D. "The Future: A History of Prediction from the Archives of Scientific American." *Scientific American* (January 3, 2013) http://www.scientificamerican.com/article/50 -100-the-future-history-prediction-from-archives-scientific-american.

3.   The Economist. "They Also Served." *The Economist* (December 20, 2014) http://www .economist.com/news/christmas-specials/21636589-how-statisticians-changed-war-and-war -changed-statistics-they-also-served (accessed December 27, 2014).

4.   Experience and gut feel are forms of knowledge.

5.   Kelly, K. *The Inevitable: Understanding the 12 Technological Forces That Will Shape Our Future*. New York: Viking, 2016. Page 270.

6.   Agarwal, R., and V. Dhar. "Big Data, Data Science, and Analytics: The Opportunity and Challenge for IS Research." *Information Systems Research* 25, no. 3 (2014): 443–448.

7.   Agarwal, R., and A. Tiwana. "Evolvable Systems: Through the Looking Glass of IS." *Information Systems Research* 26, no. 3 (2015): 473–479.

8.   Three hundred terabytes versus fifteen terabytes.

9.   By 2014, more than half of all American exports were digitally deliverable. See The Economist. "Priceless." *The Economist* (June 8, 2016). Pages 76–77.

10. Brynjolfsson, E., and A. McAfee. *The Second Machine Age: Work, Progress, and Prosperity in a Time of Brilliant Technologies*. New York: W. W. Norton, 2014.

11. Shirky, C. *Cognitive Surplus: How Technology Makes Consumers into Collaborators*. London: Penguin, 2011. Page 49.

12. The idea is identical to the perception of motion in the old Disney cartoons; the more rapidly the frames change, the more they *appear* to be in fluid motion.

13. D'Aveni, R., G. Dagnino, and K. Smith. "The Age of Temporary Advantage." *Strategic Management Journal* 31, no. 13 (2010): 1371–1385.

14. Porter, M. "How Information Gives You Competitive Advantage." *Harvard Business Review* July (1985).

15. There is no one answer for how IT affects an industry. Some technologies hurt margins by raising costs and lowering prices; others do the opposite.

16. For example, firms such as HP in the PC industry are squeezed between powerful suppliers (e.g., Intel, Microsoft, and Seagate) and powerful buyers who can easily switch to Dell or Lenovo, leaving little margins for HP.

17. Porter, M. "The Five Competitive Forces That Shape Strategy." *Harvard Business Review* January (2008): 2–17.

18. Magretta, J. *Understanding Michael Porter*. Boston: Harvard Business Review Press, 2011. Page 6.

19. Ibid. Page 90.

20. Return-on-sales, net margins, bottom line, and profits refer to the same underlying idea.

21. Cashin, P., and J. McDermott. "The Long-Run Behavior of Commodity Prices: Small Trends and Big Variability." *IMF Staff Papers* 49, no. 2 (2002): 175–199.

22. Charan, R. *What the CEO Wants You to Know: How Your Company Really Works.* New York: Crown Business, 2001. Page 31.

23. Magretta. *Understanding Michael Porter*. Page 37.

24. Ibid. Page 212.

25. Ibid. Page 20.

26. The Economist. "Look, No Claims!" *The Economist* (September 24, 2016). Page 63.

27. Magretta. *Understanding Michael Porter*. Page 21.

28. Bustillo, M., and A. Zimmerman. "Phone-Wielding Shoppers Strike Fear into Retailers." *Wall Street Journal* (December 15, 2010).

29. Wu, D., G. Ray, and A. B. Whinston. "Manufacturers' Distribution Strategy in the Presence of the Electronic Channel." *Journal of Management Information Systems* 25, no. 1 (2008): 167–198.

30. Clemons, E. K., R. M. Dewan, and R. J. Kauffman. "Competitive Strategy, Economics, and Information Systems." *Journal of Management Information Systems* 21, no. 2 (2004): 5–9.

31. This being an industry-level model, the threat of substitutes is not for a particular firm's products but for the *industry's* products.

32. Porter, M., and J. Heppelmann. "How Smart, Connected Products Are Transforming Competition." *Harvard Business Review* November (2014): 64–88.

33. Parker, G., and M. Van Alstyne. "Two-Sided Network Effects: A Theory of Information Product Design." *Management Science* 51, no. 10 (2005): 1494–1504.

34. Porter, M. "Strategy and the Internet." *Harvard Business Review* March (2001): 62–78.

35. Kelly. *The Inevitable*. Page 169. The numbers are for 2015.

36. Sundarajan, A. *The Sharing Economy*. Cambridge, MA: MIT Press, 2016.

37. The Economist. "Driving Hard." *The Economist* (2015) http://www.economist.com/news/business/21654068-taxi-hailing-company-likely-disrupt-delivery-business-driving-hard (accessed July 3, 2015).

38. The Economist. "A Fare Shake." *The Economist* (2016) http://www.economist.com/news/finance-and-economics/21698656-jacking-up-prices-may-not-be-only-way-balance-supply-and-demand-taxis (accessed May 22, 2016).

39. To avoid losing sight of whom you must deliver value to, you must first *explicitly* define your customers. For example, for the major American public universities, the customers who are the ultimate arbiters of value are employers, not the students (who are the product), not the taxpayers (who contribute only 20–30 percent of university funding), and not the government. The latter set are stakeholders with a vested interest but are *not* the customer.

40. Tiwana, A. "Evolutionary Competition in Platform Ecosystems." *Information Systems Research* 26, no. 2 (2015): 266–281.

41. Adner, R., and R. Kapoor. "Value Creation in Innovation Ecosystems: How the Structure of Technological Interdependence Affects Firm Performance in New Technology Generations." *Strategic Management Journal* 31, no. 3 (2010): 306–333.

42. Cennamo, C., and J. Santalo. "Platform Competition: Strategic Trade-Offs in Platform Markets." *Strategic Management Journal* 34 (2013): 1331–1350.

43. Service firms such as consulting, financial services, and banking are called "value shops" in Stabell, C., and Ø. Fjeldstad. "Configuring Value for Competitive Advantage: On Chains, Shops, and Networks." *Strategic Management Journal* 19, no. 5 (1998): 413–437.

44. Porter, M. "From Competitive Advantage to Corporate Strategy." *Harvard Business Review* May (1987).

45. Sambamurthy, V., A. Bharadwaj, and V. Grover. "Shaping Agility through Digital Options: Reconceptualizing the Role of IT in Contemporary Firms." *MIS Quarterly* 27, no. 2 (2003): 237–256.

46. See Davenport, T. "Competing on Analytics." *Harvard Business Review* February (2006): 98.

47. Schuetze, C. "Dutch Flower Auction, Long Industry's Heart, Is Facing Competition." *New York Times* (December 16, 2014) http://www.nytimes.com/2014/12/17/world/europe/dutch-flower-auction-long-industrys-heart-is-facing-competition-.html (accessed October 11, 2015).

48. The Economist. "Stamping It Out." *The Economist* (April 23, 2016) http://www.economist.com/news/international/21697218-china-grew-richer-and-more-innovative-people-assumed-it-would-counterfeit-less-think (accessed May 2, 2016).

49. Nickell, J. "Welcome to Harrah's." *Business 2.0* April (2003): 48–54.

50. Kambil, A., and E. van Heck. "Reengineering the Dutch Flower Auctions: A Framework for Analyzing Exchange Organizations." *Information Systems Research* 9, no. 1 (1998): 1–19.

51. Amit, R., and C. Zott. "Value Creation in E-Business." *Strategic Management Journal* 22 (2001): 493–520.

52. Slaughter, S., L. Levine, B. Ramesh, J. Pries-Heje, and R. Baskerville. "Aligning Software Processes with Strategy." *Management Information Systems Quarterly* 30, no. 4 (2006): 891–918.

53. Chircu, A. M., and R. J. Kauffman. "Competitive Strategy, Economics, and the Internet." *Journal of Management Information Systems* 19, no. 3 (2003): 11–16.

54. Rai, A., R. Patnayakuni, and N. Seth. "Firm Performance Impacts of Digitally-Enabled Supply Chain Integration Capabilities." *MIS Quarterly* 30, no. 2 (2006): 225–246.

55. For example, General Electric's washing machines can shop for detergent online; more than half of all Amazon orders for Maxwell House coffee in the United States in 2016 were triggered through Amazon's Dash Button. See The Economist. "Push My Buttons." *The Economist* (October 22, 2016). Page 58.

56. Goodwin, T. "The Battle Is for the Customer Interface." *TechCrunch* (March 3, 2015) http://www.techcrunch.com/2015/03/03/in-the-age-of-disintermediation-the-battle-is-all-for-the-customer-interface (accessed April 11, 2015).

57. Wong, V. "Everyday Peeps Break out of the Easter Basket." *BusinessWeek* (April 8, 2014) http://www.bloomberg.com/news/articles/2014-04-08/peeps-candies-look-to-break-out-of-easter-season-and-sell-all-year (accessed March 14, 2015).

58. Kaplan, S. "Easter in November Christmas in July." *CIO* November (2001): 95–104.

59. Tiwana, A., and S. Kim. "Discriminating IT Governance." *Information Systems Research* 26, no. 4 (2015): 656–674.

60. Remember that apps extract business insight from a firm's data assets; this approach is simply manipulating raw data into actionable information that your archrivals do not have.

61. Davenport, T., and J. Harris. "The Prediction Lover's Handbook." *Sloan Management Review* 50, no. 2 (2009): 32–34.

62. A predictive model is a regression equation, all statistical and econometric variants of which are adaptations to different types of data and assumptions.

Chapter 3

1.   Agarwal, R., and A. Tiwana. "Evolvable Systems: Through the Looking Glass of IS." *Information Systems Research* 26, no. 3 (2015): 473–479.

2.   Cortada, J. *Information and the Modern Corporation.* Boston: MIT Press, 2011. Page 95.

3.   Breselor, S. "Why 40-Year-Old Tech Is Still Running America's Air Traffic Control." *Wired* (2015) http://www.wired.com/2015/02/air-traffic-control (accessed August 14, 2015).

4.   Tyre, M. J., and W. J. Orlikowski. "Windows of Opportunity—Temporal Patterns of Technological Adaptation in Organizations." *Organization Science* 5, no. 1 (1994): 98–118.

5.   Roberts, N., and V. Grover. "Leveraging Information Technology Infrastructure to Facilitate a Firm's Customer Agility and Competitive Activity: An Empirical Investigation." *Journal of Management Information Systems* 28, no. 4 (2012): 231–270.

6.   Estimated by the author using regulatory reported data on Facebook's capital expenditures and user growth counts.

7.   Feld, C., and D. Stoddard. "Getting IT Right." *Harvard Business Review* February (2004): 72–81.

8.   Ross, J., P. Weill, and D. Robertson. *Enterprise Architecture as Strategy.* Boston: Harvard Business School Press, 2006.

9.   These estimates are only for Google's search and do not include other services such as Gmail, which alone had five hundred million users in 2016.

10. These are 2011 estimates. Dillow, C. "Google Releases Its Energy Consumption Numbers, Revealing a 260 Million Watt Continuous Suck." *Popular Science*, September 8, 2011.

11. Pearlson, K., and C. Saunders. *Managing and Using Information Systems (4/E)*. New York: Wiley, 2010. Page 163.

12. Ibid. Chapter 6.

13. Weill, P., and J. Ross. *IT Governance: How Top Performers Manage IT Decision Rights for Superior Results*. Boston: Harvard Business School Press, 2004. Page 33.

14. Richard, M. *97 Things Every Software Architect Should Know: Collective Wisdom from the Experts*. Sebastopol, CA: O'Reilly, 2009. Page 60.

15. Weill, P., and J. Ross. *IT Savvy*. Boston: Harvard Business School Press, 2009. Page 34.

16. Ross, Weill, and Robertson. *Enterprise Architecture as Strategy*. Page 13.

17. Ramasubbu, N., and C. Kemerer. "Technical Debt and the Reliability of Enterprise Software Systems." *Management Science* 62, no. 5 (2015): 1487–1510.

18. Iansiti, M., and R. Levien. *Keystone Advantage: What the New Dynamics of Business Ecosystems Mean for Strategy, Innovation, and Sustainability*. Boston: Harvard Business School Press, 2004. Page 152.

19. Tiwana, A. "Evolutionary Competition in Platform Ecosystems." *Information Systems Research* 26, no. 2 (2015): 266–281.

20. Gokpinar, B., W. Hopp, and S. Iravani. "The Impact of Misalignment of Organizational Structure and Product Architecture on Quality in Complex Product Development." *Management Science* 56, no. 3 (2010): 468–484. See also Mendelson, H. "Organizational Architecture and Success in the Information Technology Industry." *Management Science* 46, no. 4 (2000): 513–529.

21. Sterling, C. *Managing Software Debt: Building for Inevitable Change*. Boston: Addison-Wesley, 2010. Page 135.

22. Thrasher, H. *Boiling the IT Frog*. North Charleston, SC: BookSurge, 2007. Page 70.

23. When usage outstrips capacity, a system should be designed to degrade gracefully rather than fail abruptly.

24. Lu, Y., and K. Ramamurthy. "Understanding the Link between Information Technology Capability and Organizational Agility: An Empirical Examination." *MIS Quarterly* 35, no. 4 (2011): 931–954.

25. Wang, K. "Creating Competitive Advantage with IT Architecture: An Interview with Shanghai Mobile's CIO." *McKinsey Quarterly* (2009) http://www.mckinsey.com/business-functions/business-technology/our-insights/creating-competitive-advantage-with-it-architecture-an-interview-with-shanghai-mobiles-cio (accessed January 8, 2016).

26. Tiwana, A., and B. Konsynski. "Complementarities between Organizational IT Architecture and Governance Structure." *Information Systems Research* 21, no. 2 (2010): 288–304.

27. Ross, Weill, and Robertson. *Enterprise Architecture as Strategy*.

28. Sambamurthy, V., A. Bharadwaj, and V. Grover. "Shaping Agility through Digital Options: Reconceptualizing the Role of IT in Contemporary Firms." *MIS Quarterly* 27, no. 2 (2003): 237–256.

29. Thrasher. *Boiling the IT Frog*. Page 43.

30. Shpilberg, D., S. Berez, R. Puryear, and S. Shah. "Avoiding the Alignment Trap in IT." *Sloan Management Review* 49, no. 1 (2007): 51–55.

31. It is okay to make apps internally monolithic (nonmodular) as long as the connections among them follow documented standards. This still allows you to change one app without disturbing its neighbors, permitting them to evolve in parallel without affecting each other. All technological products have an underlying architecture. See, for example, Sosa, M., S. Eppinger, and C. Rowles. "The Misalignment of Product Architecture and Organizational Structure in Complex Product Development." *Management Science* 50, no. 12 (2004): 1674–1689. This is distinct from organizational architecture as illustrated in Ethiraj, S., and D. Levinthal. "Bounded Rationality and the Search for Organizational Architecture: An Evolutionary Perspective on the Design of Organizations and Their Evolvability." *Administrative Science Quarterly* 49, no. 3 (2004): 404–437.

32. Ostrovsky, M., and M. Schwarz. "Adoption of Standards under Uncertainty." *RAND Journal of Economics* 36, no. 4 (2005): 816–832.

33. Baldwin, C., and K. Clark. "The Architecture of Participation: Does Code Architecture Mitigate Free Riding in the Open Source Development Model?" *Management Science* 52, no. 7 (2006): 1116–1127.

34. The opposite of a modular design is a monolithic design that tightly couples many apps into one larger system. Enterprise resource planning (ERP) systems commonly combine many operational apps into one big monolithic system. The price of such tight integration is structural inflexibility; changes in one part of the system can simultaneously require changes in other parts as well.

35. Tiwana, A. "Does Interfirm Modularity Complement Ignorance? A Field Study of Software Outsourcing Alliances." *Strategic Management Journal* 29, no. 11 (2008): 1241–1252.

36. Sanchez, R., and J. Mahoney. "Modularity, Flexibility, and Knowledge Management in Product Organization and Design." *Strategic Management Journal* 17, no. 1 (1996): 63–76.

37. de Weck, O., D. Roos, and C. Magee. *Engineering Systems*. Cambridge, MA: MIT Press, 2011. Page 188.

38. Tiwana. "Does Interfirm Modularity Complement Ignorance?" See also Tiwana. "Evolutionary Competition in Platform Ecosystems."

39. Frenken, K., and S. Mendritzki. "Optimal Modularity: A Demonstration of the Evolutionary Advantage of Modular Architectures." *Journal of Evolutionary Economics* 22, no. 5 (2012): 935–956.

40. Iansiti and Levien. *Keystone Advantage*. Page 54.

41. Examples of popular API standards include pragmatic representational state transfer, JavaScript Object Notation, and the OAuth protocol.

42. Laartz, J., E. Sonderegger, and J. Vinckier. "The Paris Guide to IT Architecture." *McKinsey Quarterly* (September 2000): 118.

43. Cortada. *Information and the Modern Corporation*.

44. Heller, M. *The CIO Paradox: Battling the Contradictions of IT Leadership*. Brookline, MA: Bibliomotion, 2012. Page 35.

45. The Economist. "Priceless." *The Economist* (June 8, 2016). Pages 76–77. These are 2016 cost estimates. Almost three hundred undersea cables were in active use in 2016.

See Telegeography Submarine Cable Map, http://www.submarinecablemap.com, for an interactive list.

46. Hybrid architectures are also called federated architectures.

47. McCormick, J. *Baseline*, http://www.baselinemag.com/c/a/Projects-Management/Deltas -Last-Stand/6 (accessed June 23, 2016).

48. Nicas, J., and S. Carey. "The World's Oddest Air Routes." *Wall Street Journal* (October 16, 2012).

49. Mouawad, J. "Delta Buys Refinery to Get Control of Fuel Costs." *New York Times* (April 30, 2012) http://www.nytimes.com/2012/05/01/business/delta-air-lines-to-buy -refinery.html (accessed October 14, 2016).

50. See Delta's filings with the US Security and Exchange Commission at http://ir.delta.com/ stock-and-financial/sec-filings (accessed July 9, 2016).

51. This includes how it accesses data.

52. This divvying is not black or white; some elements of a building block can be located on either side, but we focus on where the majority are.

53. Although apps historically required considerable up-front capital to build or purchase and install, many can now be "rented" in their cloud architecture reincarnations as a service. For example, many firms have replaced marketing and sales prospecting apps with online services (e.g., Salesforce.com), replacing steep up-front purchase costs with usage-based pricing.

54. Koopman, P. "Better Embedded System Software" (2010) http://www.betterembsw .blogspot.co.uk/2010/10/embedded-software-costs-15-40-per-line.html (accessed March 10, 2016). The author updated these original 2010 estimates in 2015 to twenty-five to fifty dollars per line of code, making our own numbers conservative.

55. Charan, R. *What the CEO Wants You to Know: How Your Company Really Works.* New York: Crown Business, 2001. Page 51.

56. Firms often blend peer-to-peer architecture with a client-server-inspired central server to give the app *some* central control.

57. For a detailed discussion of how IT architecture influences firms' ability to outsource IT, see chapter 7 in Ross, Weill, and Robertson. *Enterprise Architecture as Strategy*.

58. An alternative approach is to share the same central database for multiple apps. The technical constraints of this approach render it viable only in some niche applications.

59. Partitioning can also be used to reduce the size and to speed up very large databases such as online click-stream data with trillions of records.

60. See Netflix's technical blog at http://www.techblog.netflix.com and also Vance, A. "Netflix's Ken Florance: The Man Who Keeps the Video Streaming." *Bloomberg*, http:// www.bloomberg.com/news/articles/2014-07-24/netflixs-content-delivery-chief-endures-isp -streaming-fees.

Chapter 4

1. Jeffery, M., and I. Leliveld. "Best Practices in IT Portfolio Management." *MIT Sloan Management Review* 45, no. 3 (2004): 41–49.

2.   Kohli, R., and S. Devaraj. "Measuring Information Technology Payoff: A Meta-analysis of Structural Variables in Firm-Level Empirical Research." *Information Systems Research* 14, no. 2 (2003): 127–145.

3.   Barua, A., C. H. Kriebel, and T. Mukhopadhyay. "Information Technologies and Business Value: An Analytic and Empirical Investigation." *Information Systems Research* 6, no. 1 (1995): 3–23.

4.   Menon, N. M., B. Lee, and L. Eldenburg. "Productivity of Information Systems in the Healthcare Industry." *Information Systems Research* 11, no. 1 (2000): 83–92.

5.   Kelley, M. R. "Productivity and Information Technology—the Elusive Connection." *Management Science* 40, no. 11 (1994): 1406–1425.

6.   Devaraj, S., and R. Kohli. "Performance Impacts of Information Technology: Is Actual Usage the Missing Link?" *Management Science* 49, no. 3 (2003): 273–289.

7.   Karahanna, E., and D. Straub. "Information Technology Adoption across Time: A Cross-sectional Comparison of Pre-adoption and Post-adoption Beliefs." *MIS Quarterly* 23, no. 2 (1999): 183–213.

8.   Fichman, R., and C. Kemerer. "The Illusory Diffusion of Innovation: An Examination of Assimilation Gaps." *Information Systems Research* 10, no. 3 (1999): 255–275.

9.   Thrasher, H. *Boiling the IT Frog*. North Charleston, SC: BookSurge, 2007. Page 60.

10. Srinivasan, K., S. Kekre, and T. Mukhopadhyay. "Impact of Electronic Data Interchange Technology on JIT Shipments." *Management Science* 40, no. 10 (1994): 1291–1304.

11. Rai, A., R. Patnayakuni, and N. Seth. "Firm Performance Impacts of Digitally-Enabled Supply Chain Integration Capabilities." *MIS Quarterly* 30, no. 2 (2006): 225–246.

12. Ross, J. "Six IT Decisions Your IT People Shouldn't Make." *Harvard Business Review* November (2002): 84–95.

13. Ibid. Page 124.

14. Devaraj, S. *The IT Payoff: Measuring the Business Value of Information Technology Investments*. Upper Saddle River, NJ: Financial Times Press, 2002.

15. Nambisan, S. "Complementary Product Integration by High Technology New Ventures: The Role of Initial Technology Strategy." *Management Science* 48, no. 3 (2002): 382–398.

16. Krishnan, V., and S. Bhattacharya. "Technology Selection and Commitment in New Product Development: The Role of Uncertainty and Design Flexibility." *Management Science* 48, no. 3 (2002): 313–327.

17. For example, satisfied customers should increase revenue, faster decision making should lead to better market performance, and increased brand awareness should lead to measurable market value.

18. Han, K., and S. Mithas. "Information Technology Outsourcing and Non-IT Operating Costs." *MIS Quarterly* 37, no. 1 (2013): 315–331.

19. The cost of an IT investment must be *amortized* through the process of spreading the cost of an IT investment over its hard-to-correctly-guess estimated lifespan.

20. Boehm, B. *Software Cost Estimation with COCOMO II*. Upper Saddle River, NJ: Prentice Hall, 2000.

21. Benaroch, M., Y. Lichtenstein, and L. Fink. "Contract Design Choices and the Balance of Ex Ante and Ex Post Transaction Costs in Software Development Outsourcing." *MIS Quarterly* 40, no. 1 (2016): 57–82.

22. To minimize this error, focus on the project's future cash flows, not profits.

23. The project's *opportunity costs* are things that your firm could not do because you decided to spend the money on the project. Instead of spending the money on an IT project, you could have spent it on advertising, opened a store, developed a new product, bought everyone shiny new laptops, or simply left it in the bank. If opening a store using that money would have yielded a 30 percent return, an IT project with a 20 percent return might be a poorer investment.

24. If actual costs turn out to be lower than billed, an end-of-year reconciliation process reduces the simplicity of the allocation method.

25. These costs include administration, support, software licensing, and hardware.

26. Davenport, T. "Analytics 3.0." *Harvard Business Review* July (2013): 64.

27. The Economist. "Little Things That Mean a Lot." *The Economist* (July 17, 2014) http://www.economist.com/node/21621704/print (accessed September 21, 2014).

28. Murphy, C. "UPS Positioned for the Long Haul." *InformationWeek* (2009) http://www.informationweek.com/applications/ups-positioned-for-the-long-haul/d/d-id/1075661 (accessed August 3, 2014).

29. Inventory turns is the number of times you sold out your stock and had to replenish it. It reflects how efficiently you use your inventory, which is frequently driven by IT-based inventory management software. Devaraj. *The IT Payoff.*

30. Davis, J. *The Logic of Causal Order*. Thousand Oaks, CA: Sage, 1985.

31. Dewan, S., and C. Min. "The Substitution of Information Technology for Other Factors of Production: A Firm Level Analysis." *Management Science* 43, no. 12 (1997): 1660–1675.

32. Brynjolfsson, E., and A. McAfee. *The Second Machine Age: Work, Progress, and Prosperity in a Time of Brilliant Technologies*. New York: W. W. Norton, 2014.

33. Focusing entirely on *changes* in these firm-level performance metrics is important because they have no distinct IT component. See Devaraj. *The IT Payoff.*

34. EVA is your firm's after-tax operating profit minus the costs of inputs (which accountants call "annual rental charge for total capital deployed"). All aspects of the EVA equation—revenues, costs, debt, and capital expenses—are under managers' control, so when EVA goes up or down, it can largely be attributed to managers' decisions. We do not explore EVA in detail here because it does not account for research and development expenses, which experimental uses of IT represent.

35. Brynjolfsson, E. "The Contribution of Information Technology to Consumer Welfare." *Information Systems Research* 7, no. 3 (1996): 281–300. Net operating margins subtract from revenue all costs and expenses including the cost of goods sold, expenses, and taxes.

36. Magretta, J. *Understanding Michael Porter*. Boston: Harvard Business Review Press, 2011. Page 90.

37. Brynjolfsson, E., and L. Hitt. "Paradox Lost? Firm-Level Evidence on the Returns to Information Systems Spending." *Management Science* 42, no. 4 (1996): 541–558.

38. Brynjolfsson, E., and A. Seidmann. "A Call for Exploration: Introduction to Special Issue on Frontier Research on Information Systems and Economics." *Management Science* 43, no. 12 (1997): 1–3.

39. Bharadwaj, A., S. Bharadwaj, and B. Konsynski. "Information Technology Effects on Firm Performance as Measured by Tobin's Q." *Management Science* 45, no. 6 (1999): 1008–1024.

40. Chung, K. H., and S. W. Pruitt. "A Simple Approximation of Tobins-Q." *Financial Management* 23, no. 3 (1994): 70–74.

41. Charan, R. *What the CEO Wants You to Know: How Your Company Really Works.* New York: Crown Business, 2001. Page 78.

42. The data source is Aral, S., and P. Weill. "IT Assets, Organizational Capabilities, and Firm Performance: How Resource Allocations and Organizational Differences Explain Performance Variation." *Organization Science* 18, no. 5 (2007): 763–780. See also MIT Center for Information Systems Research briefing IV-1A for a detailed breakdown. Services focus on finance and insurance; retail includes wholesale and transport. Our categories and their categories match up as follows: infrastructure (infrastructure + transactional IT), operational IT apps (informational IT assets), and strategic apps (strategic IT assets). Two cautionary notes: (1) the data is from 2002, thus dated, and (2) the sample size is small (147 firms). If you count only what they classify as IT infrastructure, the percentage ranges from 51 percent to 58 percent. Later updates of this data show that firms have reallocated some of their IT infrastructure spending toward apps, but the differences among industries illustrated by the data holds.

43. Gartner Group. "IT Key Metrics Data 2016: Key Industry Measures" (2016) http://www.gartner.com/doc/3172921/it-key-metrics-data- (accessed June 20, 2016). Consulting firm Gartner updates these figures annually.

44. Weill, P., and S. Aral. "Generating Premium Returns on Your IT Investments." *Sloan Management Review* 47, no. 2 (2006): 39–48.

45. Scherpereel, C. "The Option-Creating Institution: A Real Options Perspective on Economic Organization." *Strategic Management Journal* 29, no. 5 (2008): 455–470.

46. Benaroch, M., S. Shah, and M. Jeffery. "On the Valuation of Multistage Information Technology Investments Embedding Nested Real Options." *Journal of Management Information Systems* 23, no. 1 (2006): 239–261.

47. McGrath, R. G., W. J. Ferrier, and A. L. Mendelow. "Real Options as Engines of Choice and Heterogeneity." *Academy of Management Review* 29, no. 1 (2004): 86–101.

48. Bollen, N. "Real Options and Product Life Cycles." *Management Science* 45, no. 5 (1999): 670–684.

49. Scherpereel. "Option-Creating Institution."

50. Fichman, R., M. Keil, and A. Tiwana. "Beyond Valuation: Real Options Thinking in IT Project Management." *California Management Review* 47, no. 2 (2005): 74–96.

51. Huchzermeier, A., and C. H. Loch. "Project Management under Risk: Using the Real Options Approach to Evaluate Flexibility in R&D." *Management Science* 47, no. 1 (2001): 85–101.

52. Robert Merton and Myron Scholes won the 1997 Nobel prize in economics for their work on options theory, which is the foundation for real options thinking.

53. Schwartz, E., and C. Zozaya-Gorostiza. "Investment under Uncertainty in Information Technology: Acquisition and Development Projects." *Management Science* 49, no. 1 (2003): 57–70.

54. In contrast, such flexibility is of little value when your customers' preferences are predictable and you are reasonably certain that your rivals will retaliate with matching project investments.

55. Tiwana, A. *Platform Ecosystems*. Waltham, MA: Morgan Kaufmann, 2014. Pages 179–190.

56. Fichman, R. "Real Options and IT Platform Adoption: Implications for Theory and Practice." *Information Systems Research* 15, no. 2 (2004): 132–154.

57. Panayi, S., and L. Trigeorgis. "Multi-stage Real Options: The Cases of Information Technology Infrastructure and International Bank Expansion." *Quarterly Review of Economics and Finance* 38, no. 3 (1998): 675–692.

58. Keil, M. "Pulling the Plug: Software Project Management and the Problem of Project Escalation." *MIS Quarterly* 19, no. 4 (1995): 421–447.

59. Fichman, R., and S. Moses. "An Incremental Process for Software Implementation." *Sloan Management Review* 40, no. 2 (1999): 39–52.

60. Fichman, Keil, and Tiwana. "Beyond Valuation."

61. How, R. "At Starbucks, the Future Is in Plastic." *CNN Money* (August 1, 2003) http://www.money.cnn.com/magazines/business2/business2_archive/2003/08/01/346326 (accessed March 6, 2016).

62. Fast Casual. "No Traffic, No Problem." *Fast Casual* (October 31, 2014) http://www.fastcasual.com/news/no-traffic-no-problem-starbucks-plans-to-take-the-coffee-to-the-customer-in-2015/ (accessed March 6, 2016).

63. Wired. "Starbucks's Grande Plan: Selling Coffee Via Apps." *Wired* (November 3, 2015) http://www.wired.com/2015/11/no-one-is-killing-it-with-retail-store-apps-like-starbucks (accessed November 7, 2015).

64. Starbucks. "Starbucks Reports Record Q3 Financial and Operating Results" (2016) http://investor.starbucks.com/phoenix.zhtml?c=99518&p=irol-newsArticle&ID=2187298 (accessed July 30, 2016).

65. Garcia, T. "Starbucks Has More Customer Money on Cards than Many Banks Have in Deposits." *MarketWatch* (June 11, 2016) http://www.marketwatch.com/story/starbucks-has-more-customer-money-on-cards-than-many-banks-have-in-deposits-2016-06-09/print (accessed March 7, 2016).

Chapter 5

1. Brynjolfsson, E., and M. Schrage. "The New, Faster Face of Innovation." *Wall Street Journal* (August 17, 2009).

2. Heller, M. *The CIO Paradox: Battling the Contradictions of IT Leadership*. Brookline, MA: Bibliomotion, 2012. Pages 3, 14, and 33.

3. Weill, P., and J. Ross. *IT Governance: How Top Performers Manage IT Decision Rights for Superior Results*. Boston: Harvard Business School Press, 2004. Pages 4 and 41.

4. Ross, J. "Six IT Decisions Your IT People Shouldn't Make." *Harvard Business Review* November (2002): 84–95.

5. Tiwana, A., and S. Kim. "Discriminating IT Governance." *Information Systems Research* 26, no. 4 (2015): 656–674.

6. Brown, C. V. "Examining the Emergence of Hybrid IS Governance Solutions: Evidence from a Single Case Site." *Information Systems Research* 8, no. 1 (1997): 69–94.

7. Tiwana and Kim. "Discriminating IT Governance." See also Weill and Ross. *IT Governance.* Page 2.

8. Tiwana, A. "Governance-Knowledge Fit in Systems Development Projects." *Information Systems Research* 20, no. 2 (2009): 180–197.

9. Fama, E., and M. Jensen. "Separation of Agency and Control." *Journal of Law & Economics* 26, no. 2 (1983): 301–326.

10. Your IT colleagues charged with implementing IT decisions (the *how* part) must be evaluated as business people using business impact metrics. See Feld, C., and D. Stoddard. "Getting IT Right." *Harvard Business Review* February (2004): 72–81.

11. Weill and Ross. *IT Governance.* Pages 59 and 130.

12. Sambamurthy, V., and R. Zmud. "Arrangements for Technology Governance: A Theory of Multiple Contingencies." *MIS Quarterly* 23, no. 2 (1999): 261–290.

13. For a broader, non-IT analog to this trade-off, see Nickerson, J., and B. Silverman. "Why Firms Want to Organize Efficiently and What Keeps Them from Doing So: Inappropriate Governance, Performance, and Adaptation in a Deregulated Industry." *Administrative Science Quarterly* 48, no. 3 (2003): 433–465.

14. Weill and Ross. *IT Governance.* Page 135.

15. Benaroch, M., Y. Lichtenstein, and L. Fink. "Contract Design Choices and the Balance of Ex Ante and Ex Post Transaction Costs in Software Development Outsourcing." *MIS Quarterly* 40, no. 1 (2016): 57–82.

16. Weill and Ross. *IT Governance.*

17. Responsiveness, unlike reliability, is rarely constrained by how fast your Internet connections are; rather, it's constrained by the architecture of the apps used throughout your firm and the hardware infrastructure on which they run.

18. Agarwal, R., and V. Sambamurthy. "Principles and Models for Organizing the IT Function." *MISQ Executive* 1, no. 1 (2002): 1–16.

19. Charan, R. *What the CEO Wants You to Know: How Your Company Really Works.* New York: Crown Business, 2001. Page 113.

20. Bhatt, G. D., and V. Grover. "Types of Information Technology Capabilities and Their Role in Competitive Advantage: An Empirical Study." *Journal of Management Information Systems* 22, no. 2 (2005): 253–278.

21. Weill and Ross. *IT Governance.* Page 170.

22. Sambamurthy, V., and R. W. Zmud. "The Organizing Logic for an Enterprise's IT Activities in the Digital Era." *Information Systems Research* 11, no. 2 (2000): 105–114.

23. Shpilberg, D., S. Berez, R. Puryear, and S. Shah. "Avoiding the Alignment Trap in IT." *Sloan Management Review* 49, no. 1 (2007): 51–55.

24. Nestlé. "Globe Program Overview" (2005) http://www.nestle.com/asset-library/documents/library/presentations/investors_events/investors_seminar_2005/globe_jun2005_johnson.pdf (accessed July 7, 2016).

25. Tiwana, A., and B. Konsynski. "Complementarities between Organizational IT Architecture and Governance Structure." *Information Systems Research* 21, no. 2 (2010): 288–304.

26. Tanriverdi, H., P. Konana, and L. Ge. "The Choice of Sourcing Mechanisms for Business Processes." *Information Systems Research* 18, no. 3 (2007): 280–299.

27. Sosa, M., S. Eppinger, and C. Rowles. "The Misalignment of Product Architecture and Organizational Structure in Complex Product Development." *Management Science* 50, no. 12 (2004): 1674–1689.

28. Crilly, D., and P. Sloan. "Autonomy or Control? Organizational Architecture and Corporate Attention to Stakeholders." *Organization Science* 25, no. 2 (2014): 339–355.

29. Tiwana, A. "Does Technological Modularity Substitute for Control? A Study of Alliance Performance in Software Outsourcing." *Strategic Management Journal* 29, no. 7 (2008): 769–780.

Chapter 6

1. Data source: Standish. "Standish Group 2015 Chaos Report" (2015) http://www.infoq.com/articles/standish-chaos-2015 (accessed May 23, 2016).

2. Larger projects are defined as more than $10–15 million.

3. Mann, C. "Why Software Is So Bad." *MIT Technology Review* July/August (2002): 33–38.

4. Charette, R. "Why Software Fails." *IEEE Spectrum* 42, no. 9 (2005): 42–49.

5. MIT's annual budget was $3.2 billion in 2015. A 66 percent failure rate in projects totaling $1 trillion equals $660 billion. $660 billion/$3.2 billion = ~200 years.

6. Downes, L. "Man, Plan, Canal." *The Industry Standard* July (2001): 62–65.

7. These are 2016 estimates; the shortcut is the London to Bombay route.

8. The Economist. "What Is This That Roareth Thus?" *The Economist* (September 6, 2007) http://www.economist.com/node/9719105.

9. Sketch based on a July 1907 public domain photograph by an unknown photographer from the archives of London Transport Museum (Image U9207).

10. Jeffery, M., and I. Leliveld. "Best Practices in IT Portfolio Management." *MIT Sloan Management Review* 45, no. 3 (2004): 41–49.

11. Tiwana, A. *Platform Ecosystems*. Waltham, MA: Morgan Kaufmann, 2014. Page 247.

12. Tiwana, A., and M. Keil. "The One-Minute Risk Assessment Tool." *Communications of the ACM* 47, no. 11 (2004): 73–77.

13. Bloch, M., S. Blumberg, and J. Laartz. "Delivering Large-Scale IT Projects on Time, on Budget, and on Value." *McKinsey Quarterly* October (2012): 1–6.

14. Wayne, A. "Obamacare Website Costs Exceed $2 Billion, Study Finds." *BusinessWeek* (September 24, 2014) http://www.bloomberg.com/news/articles/2014-09-24/obamacare-website-costs-exceed-2-billion-study-finds (accessed March 12, 2015).

15. Baker, S. "Obamacare Website Has Cost $840 Million." *The Atlantic* (July 30, 2014) http://www.theatlantic.com/politics/archive/2014/07/obamacare-website-has-cost-840 -million/440478 (accessed August 10, 2014).

16. Ives, B., and M. Olson. "User Involvement and MIS Success: A Review of Research." *Management Science* 30, no. 5 (1984): 586–603; Straub, D. W., and J. K. Trower. "The Importance of User Involvement in Successful Systems: A Meta-Analytical Reappraisal." Minneapolis: MIS Research Center, University of Minnesota, 1988. See also Oreg, S., and J. Goldenberg. *Resistance to Innovation: Its Sources and Manifestations*. Chicago: University of Chicago Press, 2015. Page 76.

17. Norton, M., D. Mochon, and D. Ariely. "The IKEA Effect: When Labor Leads to Love." *Journal of Consumer Psychology* 22, no. 3 (2012): 453–460.

18. Research on technology adoption has consistently shown this. See, for example, Karahanna, E., and D. Straub. "Information Technology Adoption across Time: A Cross-sectional Comparison of Pre-adoption and Post-adoption Beliefs." *MIS Quarterly* 23, no. 2 (1999): 183–213; Xu, X., V. Venkatesh, K. Tam, and S. Hong. "Model of Migration and Use of Platforms: Role of Hierarchy, Current Generation, and Complementarities in Consumer Settings." *Management Science* 56, no. 8 (2010): 1304–1323.

19. For a review of the large body of research on users' resistance to innovation, see Oreg and Goldenberg. *Resistance to Innovation*. Pages 41–49.

20. Ibid. Page 84.

21. Hibbs, C., S. Jewett, and M. Sullivan. *The Art of Lean Software Development*. Sebastopol, CA: O'Reilly, 2009. Page 100.

22. Sussna, J. *Designing Delivery: Rethinking IT in the Digital Service Economy*. Sebastopol, CA: O'Reilly, 2015.

23. Agarwal, R., and A. Tiwana. "Evolvable Systems: Through the Looking Glass of IS." *Information Systems Research* 26, no. 3 (2015): 473–479.

24. Koopman, P. "Better Embedded System Software" (2010) http://www.betterembsw .blogspot.co.uk/2010/10/embedded-software-costs-15-40-per-line.html (accessed March 10, 2016).

25. Data source for figure: Standish. "Standish Group 2015 Chaos Report."

26. Tiwana and Keil. "One-Minute Risk Assessment Tool."

27. Fjeldstad, S., M. Lundqvist, and P. Olesen. "From Waterfall to Agile: How a Public Agency Launched New Digital Services." *McKinsey Quarterly* (March 2016) http://www .mckinsey.com/business-functions/business-technology/our-insights/from-waterfall-to-agile -how-a-public-agency-launched-new-digital-services (accessed April 7, 2016).

28. Simon, H. *The Sciences of the Artificial*. 3rd ed. Cambridge, MA: MIT Press, 1996. Page 29.

29. Hibbs, Jewett, and Sullivan. *Art of Lean Software Development*.

30. This is known as the Brooks law, named after Fred Brooks, who was the lead designer of the seminal IBM 360 mainframe computer in the 1960s.

31. Marchewka, J. *Information Technology Project Management*. 4th ed. New York: Wiley, 2012. Page 44.

32. Feld, C., and D. Stoddard. "Getting IT Right." *Harvard Business Review* February (2004): 72–81.

33. King, R. "Walmart Changes the Way It Prioritizes IT Projects." *Wall Street Journal* (October 21, 2014) http://www.blogs.wsj.com/cio/2014/10/21/wal-mart-changes-the-way-it-prioritizes-it-projects (accessed March 12, 2016).

34. Nash, K. "Walmart Spent $10.5 Billion on Information Technology in 2015." *Wall Street Journal* (April 21, 2016) http://blogs.wsj.com/cio/2016/04/21/wal-mart-spent-10-5-billion-on-information-technology-in-2015/ (accessed July 9, 2016).

35. Oreg and Goldenberg. *Resistance to Innovation*. Page 84.

Chapter 7

1. Such backsourcing transitions can often take a year or two and are plausible only if your firm retained employees with up-to-date technology skills.

2. Whitaker, J., S. Mithas, and M. S. Krishnan. "Organizational Learning and Capabilities for Onshore and Offshore Business Process Outsourcing." *Journal of Management Information Systems* 11–42 (2011); Bardhan, I., J. Whitaker, and S. Mithas. "Information Technology, Production Process Outsourcing, and Manufacturing Plant Performance." *Journal of Management Information Systems* 23, no. 2 (2006): 13–40.

3. Colias, M. "GM Gives Shop-Click-Drive a Big Push." *Automotive News* (November 9, 2015) http://www.autonews.com/article/20151109/RETAIL/311099959/gm-gives-shop-click-drive-a-big-push (accessed Dec 3, 2015).

4. Bennett, J. "Why GM Hired 8,000 Programmers." *Wall Street Journal* (February 17, 2015) http://www.wsj.com/articles/gm-built-internal-skills-to-manage-internet-sales-push-1424200731.

5. The Economist. "Keeping It under Your Hat." *The Economist* (April 13, 2016) http://www.economist.com/news/business-and-finance/21696911-tech-fashion-old-management-idea-back-vogue-vertical-integration-gets-new (accessed April 29, 2016).

6. Lee, J., S. Miranda, and Y. Kim. "IT Outsourcing Strategies: Universalistic, Contingency, and Configurational Explanations of Success." *Information Systems Research* 15, no. 2 (2004): 110–131; Chang, Y., and V. Gurbaxani. "Information Technology Outsourcing, Knowledge Transfer, and Firm Productivity: An Empirical Analysis." *MIS Quarterly* 36, no. 4 (2012): 1043–1063; Pearlson, K., and C. Saunders. *Managing and Using Information Systems (4/E)*. New York: Wiley, 2010.

7. Tiwana, A., and A. Bush. "A Comparison of Transaction Cost, Agency, and Knowledge-Based Predictors of IT Outsourcing Decisions." *Journal of Management Information Systems* 24, no. 1 (2007): 263–305.

8. Levina, N., and J. Ross. "From the Vendor's Perspective: Exploring the Value Proposition in Information Technology Outsourcing." *MIS Quarterly* 27, no. 3 (2003): 331–364.

9. Lee, Miranda, and Kim. "IT Outsourcing Strategies."

10. Smith, R., and S. Eppinger. "Identifying Controlling Features of Engineering Design Iteration." *Management Science* 43, no. 3 (1997): 276–293.

11. Smith, R., and S. Eppinger. "A Predictive Model of Sequential Iteration in Engineering Design." *Management Science* 43, no. 8 (1997): 1104–1120.

12. Monteverde, K. "Technical Dialog as an Incentive for Vertical Integration in the Semiconductor Industry." *Management Science* 41, no. 10 (1995): 1624–1638.

13. Tiwana, A. "Beyond the Black-Box: Knowledge Overlaps in Software Outsourcing." *IEEE Software* 21, no. 5 (2004): 51–58; Overby, S. "GM Bets on Insourcing, Brings Back 10,000 IT Jobs." *CIO* (October 2012) http://www.www.cio.com/article/718053/GM_Bets_on_Insourcing_Brings_Back_10_000_IT_Jobs.

14. Benaroch, M., Q. Dai, and R. Kauffman. "Should We Go Our Own Way? Backsourcing Flexibility in IT Services Contracts." *Journal of Management Information Systems* 26, no. 4 (2010): 317–358.

15. Whitten, D., and D. Leidner. "Bringing IT Back: An Analysis of the Decision to Backsource or Switch Vendors." *Decision Sciences* 37, no. 4 (2006): 605–621.

16. Tiwana, A., and S. Kim. "Concurrent IT Sourcing: Mechanisms and Contingent Advantages." *Journal of Management Information Systems* 33, no. 1 (2016): 101–138.

17. Whitaker, Mithas, and Krishnan. "Organizational Learning and Capabilities."

18. Google's business version of Gmail, Microsoft's Office 365 suite, Dropbox for Business, and Salesforce.com's customer relationship management apps are common examples of cloudsourcing.

19. Bapna, R., A. Barua, D. Mani, and A. Mehra. "Cooperation, Coordination, and Governance in Multisourcing: An Agenda for Analytical and Empirical Research." *Information Systems Research* 21, no. 4 (2010): 785–795.

20. Pearlson and Saunders. *Managing and Using Information Systems*. Page 194.

21. Cohen, L., and A. Young. *Multisourcing: Moving Beyond Outsourcing to Achieve Growth and Agility*. Boston: Harvard Business School Press, 2006. Page 111.

22. Tiwana, A., A. Bush, H. Tsuji, A. Sakurai, and K. Yoshida. "Myths and Paradoxes in Japanese IT Outsourcing." *Communications of the ACM* 51, no. 10 (2008): 141–145.

23. Boudreau, K. "Open Platform Strategies and Innovation: Granting Access vs. Devolving Control." *Management Science* 56, no. 10 (2010): 1849–1872.

24. Sarker, S., S. Sarker, A. Sahaym, and N. Bjorn-Andersen. "Exploring Value Cocreation in Relationships between an ERP Vendor and Its Partners: A Revelatory Case Study." *MIS Quarterly* 36, no. 1 (2012): 317–338.

25. The Economist. "Cookies, Caches and Cows." *The Economist* (September 27, 2014) http://www.economist.com/news/international/21620221-translating-technological-terms-throws-up-some-peculiar-challenges-cookies-caches-and-cows (accessed October 7, 2014).

26. Zirpoli, F., and M. Becker. "What Happens When You Outsource Too Much?" *Sloan Management Review* 52, no. 2 (2011): 59–64.

27. Denning, S., "The Boeing Debacle." *Fortune* (January 21, 2013) http://www.forbes.com/sites/stevedenning/2013/01/21/what-went-wrong-at-boeing.

28. Staples, S. "Outsourcing vs. Insourcing: You Need Both." *InformationWeek* (September 19, 2013) http://www.informationweek.com/it-strategy/outsourcing-vs-insourcing-you-need-both/d/d-id/1111613 (2013).

29. Parmigiani, A. "Why Do Firms Both Make and Buy? An Investigation of Concurrent Sourcing." *Strategic Management Journal* 28 (2007): 285–311.

30. Weigelt, C., and M. Sarkar. "Performance Implications of Outsourcing for Technological Innovations: Managing the Efficiency and Adaptability Trade-Off." *Strategic Management Journal* 33, no. 2 (2012): 189–216; Mani, D., A. Barua, and A. Whinston. "An Empirical Analysis of the Impact of Information Capabilities Design on Business Process Outsourcing Performance." *MIS Quarterly* 34, no. 1 (2010): 39–62.

31. See Banker, R. D., and S. A. Slaughter. "The Moderating Effects of Structure on Volatility and Complexity in Software Enhancement." *Information Systems Research* 11, no. 3 (2000): 219–240; Tiwana and Bush. "A Comparison of Transaction Cost."

32. American business schools train such business analysts in management information systems programs.

33. Weigelt and Sarkar. "Performance Implications of Outsourcing." See also Tiwana, A. "Systems Development Ambidexterity: Explaining the Complementary and Substitutive Roles of Formal and Informal Controls." *Journal of Management Information Systems* 27, no. 2 (2010): 87–126.

34. Gopal, A., K. Sivaramakrishnan, M. Krishnan, and T. Mukhopadhyay. "Contracts in Offshore Software Development: An Empirical Analysis." *Management Science* 49, no. 12 (2003): 1671–1683.

35. Chen, Y., and A. Bharadwaj. "An Empirical Analysis of Contract Structures in IT Outsourcing." *Information Systems Research* 20, no. 4 (2009): 484–506.

36. Benaroch, M., Y. Lichtenstein, and L. Fink. "Contract Design Choices and the Balance of Ex Ante and Ex Post Transaction Costs in Software Development Outsourcing." *MIS Quarterly* 40, no. 1 (2016): 57–82.

37. Overby, S. "Smaller, Shorter-Term Deals Shake up IT Outsourcing Industry." *CIO* (October 2014) http://www.cio.com/article/2448960/outsourcing/smaller--shorter-term -deals-shake-up-it-outsourcing-industry.html (accessed March 14, 2015).

38. Bartel, A., S. Lach, and N. Sicherman. "Technological Change and the Make-or-Buy Decision." *Journal of Law, Economics, & Organization* 30, no. 1 (2014): 165–192.

39. Anderson, S., and H. Dekker. "Management Control for Market Transactions." *Management Science* 51, no. 12 (2005): 1734–1752.

40. Controls have been extensively studied in IT research. See, for example, Rustagi, S., W. King, and L. Kirsch. "Predictors of Formal Control Usage in IT Outsourcing Partnerships." *Information Systems Research* 19, no. 2 (2008): 126–143; Koh, Ang, and Straub. "IT Outsourcing Success"; Tiwana, A., and M. Keil. "Control in Internal and Outsourced Software Projects." *Journal of Management Information Systems* 26, no. 3 (2010): 9–44.

41. Gopal, A., and S. Gosain. "The Role of Organizational Controls and Boundary Spanning in Software Development Outsourcing." *Information Systems Research* 21, no. 4 (2010): 960–982.

42. Kirsch, L., V. Sambamurthy, D. Ko, and R. Purvis. "Controlling Information Systems Development Projects: The View from the Client." *Management Science* 48, no. 4 (2002): 484–498.

43. Benaroch, Lichtenstein, and Fink. "Contract Design Choices."

44. Choudhury, V., and R. Sabherwal. "Portfolios of Control in Outsourced Software Development Projects." *Information Systems Research* 14, no. 3 (2003): 291–314.

45. This nonprofit organization is part of Carnegie Mellon University. Any vendor or even your firm's own IT unit can apply for a CMM rating.

46. Skill sets are measured in terms of individuals with formal IT education, firms' CMM levels, and cultural fit with US workplace norms. Beware that this is a broad generalization to entire nations with millions of programmers that must be taken with a grain of salt. It is entirely from the perspective of meeting the business needs of American firms. The data used to construct the figure are based on Amoribieta, I., K. Bhaumik, K. Kanakamedala, and A. Parkhe. "Programmers Abroad: A Primer on Offshore Software." *McKinsey Quarterly* 2001, no. 2 (2001): 128–139, and Levinson, M. "Indian Programmers vs. American Programmers: Whose Code Is Best?" *CIO* (July 6, 2011) http://www.cio.com/article/2406458/careers-staffing/indian-programmers-vs--american-programmers--whose-code-is-best-.html (accessed February 7, 2016).

Chapter 8

1. Talbot, D. "Cybersecurity: The Age of the Megabreach." *MIT Technology Review* 119, no. 2 (2016): 70–71. The figures are from 2016.

2. The Economist. "Heist Finance." *The Economist* (May 28, 2016). Page 67. The figures are for 2016.

3. The Economist. "Digital Disease Control." *The Economist* (July 12, 2014). Pages 9–10. See also https://hbr.org/2015/03/see-your-company-through-the-eyes-of-a-hacker.

4. Data source: "2015 Cost of Data Breach Study: Global Analysis." *Ponemon Institute Research Report* (2015): 1–31. http://www.nhlearningsolutions.com/Portals/0/Documents/2015-Cost-of-Data-Breach-Study.pdf.

5. Society for Worldwide Interbank Financial Telecommunication.

6. The Economist. "The Internet of Things (to Be Hacked)." *The Economist* (July 12, 2014). Page 13.

7. The Economist. "The Spy in Your Pocket." *The Economist* (February 28, 2015). Page 21.

8. Firms are legally required to reveal any loss of sensitive customer information in many countries.

9. Austin, R., and C. Darby. "The Myth of Secure Computing." *Harvard Business Review* June (2003): 120–126.

10. Social engineering can be through direct interaction with an employee or through phishing (legitimate-looking e-mails that trick them into typing their credentials) or key-logging spyware that captures and stores what a user types for later pickup.

11. Upton, D., and S. Creese. "The Danger from Within." *Harvard Business Review* September (2014): 1–9.

12. Riley, M., B. Elgin, D. Lawrence, and C. Matlack. "Missed Alarms and 40 Million Stolen Credit Card Numbers: How Target Blew It." *BusinessWeek* (March 17, 2014).

13. Winnefeld, J., C. Kirchhoff, and D. Upton. "Cybersecurity's Human Factor: Lessons from the Pentagon." *Harvard Business Review* September (2015): 87–95.

14. Marketwatch. "Annual Financial Reports for Target Corporation." *Marketwatch* (2016) http://www.marketwatch.com/investing/stock/tgt/financials (accessed June 11, 2016).

15. Temizkan, O., R. L. Kumar, S. Park, and C. Subramaniam. "Patch Release Behaviors of Software Vendors in Response to Vulnerabilities: An Empirical Analysis." *Journal of Management Information Systems* 28, no. 4 (2012): 305–338.

16. Spyware is also called malware, an abbreviation for *mal*icious soft*ware*. Other common IT security tools include *antispyware* to seek and destroy malicious software and *firewalls* that separate your firm's networks from the Internet.

17. Chen, Y., K. R. Ramamurthy, and K.-W. Wen. "Organizations' Information Security Policy Compliance: Stick or Carrot Approach?" *Journal of Management Information Systems* 29, no. 3 (2013): 157–188.

18. Some firms hire reformed *white hat* hackers to try breaking into their own systems to expose vulnerabilities.

19. For example, cashiers in a store cannot override the price of a scanned item; only their manager can. Access privileges must cover physical access to systems as well.

20. In the United States, rila.org and the Information Sharing Analysis Center (ISAC) spans retailers, and Financial Services ISAC (fsisac.com) spans finance firms.

21. Ross, J. "Six IT Decisions Your IT People Shouldn't Make." *Harvard Business Review* November (2002): 84–95.

22. The Economist. "The Internet of Things (to Be Hacked)."

23. The Economist. "Joker in the Pack." *The Economist* (July 16, 2016). Pages 8–10.

24. Bailey, T., J. Brandley, and J. Kaplan. "How Good Is Your Cyberincident-Response Plan?" *McKinsey* (2013) http://www.mckinsey.com/business-functions/business-technology/our-insights/how-good-is-your-cyberincident-response-plan.

25. Morisy, M. "How PayPal Boosts Security with Artificial Intelligence." *MIT Technology Review* 119, no. 2 (2016): 73–74. Additional data from PayPal's annual report.

26. The Economist. "All Systems Stop." *The Economist* (August 13, 2016). Page 46.

Chapter 9

1.   Kelly, K. *The Inevitable: Understanding the 12 Technological Forces That Will Shape Our Future*. New York: Viking, 2016. Page 6.

2.   Schoemaker, P., and G. Day. "How to Make Sense of Weak Signals." *Sloan Management Review* 50, no. 9 (2009): 81–89.

3.   Tiwana, A. "Separating Signal from Noise: Evaluating Emerging Technologies." *MIS Quarterly Executive* 13, no. 1 (2014): 45–61.

4.   The hype cycle idea was popularized by the Gartner consulting group; see http://www.wikipedia.org/wiki/Hype_cycle.

5.   In statistics, we call false positives in cell 2 Type I errors and false negatives in cell 4 Type II errors.

6.   Tiwana, A. *Platform Ecosystems*. Waltham, MA: Morgan Kaufmann, 2014. Pages 271–275.

7.   Agarwal, R., and A. Tiwana. "Evolvable Systems: Through the Looking Glass of IS." *Information Systems Research* 26, no. 3 (2015): 473–479.

8.   The Economist. "A Printed Smile." *The Economist* (April 30, 2016). Pages 71–72.

9. The Economist. "The Replicator." *The Economist* (May 28, 2016). Pages 71–72.

10. The Economist. "The Third Industrial Revolution." *The Economist* (April 19, 2012) http://www.economist.com/node/21553017 (accessed July 8, 2012).

11. Knight, W. "The People's Robots." *MIT Technology Review* (2016): 44–53.

12. King, R. "Lawmakers Investigate Impact of Automation and Robotics on U.S. Jobs." *Wall Street Journal* (2016) http://blogs.wsj.com/cio/2016/05/25/lawmakers-investigate -impact-of-automation-and-robotics-on-u-s-jobs (accessed May 8, 2016).

13. Kelly. *The Inevitable*. Page 54.

14. Data estimates for 2016 are based on Knight. "The People's Robots."

15. The Economist. "Made to Measure." *The Economist* (May 30, 2015). Pages 3–4.

16. Immelt, J. "GE's Jeff Immelt on Digitizing in the Industrial Space." *McKinsey Quarterly* (2015) http://www.mckinsey.com/business-functions/organization/our-insights/ges-jeff -immelt-on-digitizing-in-the-industrial-space (accessed June 30, 2016).

17. The Economist. "Smart Farms: Silicon Valley Meets Central Valley." *The Economist* (June 11, 2016). Page 4.

18. Manyika, J., M. Chui, P. Bisson, J. Woetzel, R. Dobbs, J. Bughin, and D. Aharon. "Unlocking the Potential of the Internet of Things." *McKinsey Global Institute Report* (2015) http://www.mckinsey.com/business-functions/business-technology/our-insights/the -internet-of-things-the-value-of-digitizing-the-physical-world.

19. Gustafsson, K. "For a Better Fit Online, Take a Selfie." *BusinessWeek* (September 5, 2014). Pages 22–23.

20. Kelly. *The Inevitable*. Page 37.

21. For example, what happens to click-through rates if you made a round button oval instead.

22. Kelly. *The Inevitable*. Page 55.

23. The Economist. "Of Prediction and Policy." *The Economist* (August 20, 2016). Page 61. This has potentially immediate financial payoffs. For example, better prediction of bail jumpers would reduce the need for policing in the United States by twenty thousand police officers, reducing law enforcement costs by almost $3 billion a year.

24. Kelly. *The Inevitable*. Page 50.

25. Knight, W. "Car-to-Car Communication." *MIT Technology Review* (2015) http://www .technologyreview.com/s/534981/car-to-car-communication (accessed April 18, 2016). The first such car was a 2017 Cadillac. However, until there are more cars to talk to (i.e., network effects are achieved), the value of this technology is limited.

26. The Economist. "The Fantastic Voyage." *The Economist* (May 21, 2016). Page 71.

Index

Tables and figures are indicated by *t* and *f*, respectively.